ESSEX WORTHIES

Robert Rich, 2nd Earl of Warwick, 1587-1658
by Van Dyck
*Reproduced by kind permission of the Metropolitan
Museum of Art, New York (John S. Bache Collection)*

ESSEX WORTHIES

A biographical companion to the County

by

WILLIAM ADDISON

PHILLIMORE

1973
Published by
PHILLIMORE & CO. LTD.
London and Chichester

Head Office: Shopwyke Hall,
Chichester, Sussex, England

© William Addison, 1973

ISBN 0 85033 080 7

Text set by Phillimore
Printed in Great Britain by
Eyre & Spottiswoode Ltd., Her Majesty's Printers,
at Grosvenor Press, Portsmouth

PREFACE

THIS is not so much a collection of mini-biographies as an attempt to show why certain persons and families who have figured in Essex life are remembered, where they lived and what their connections with the county were. I intended to call it *A Biographical Companion to Essex,* but that seemed too cumbersome a title, and why should I want to stray from the path first trodden by my master, Thomas Fuller? What I do want to stress is that each subject has been considered from the county point of view, and biographical material, however important, that has little county relevance has been left out. This means that much less is said about the parts played by major subjects in national history than about their local activities. In short, my object has been to provide a county focus in the form of a 'Who and Where' for those who like to be reminded of persons as well as buildings and topographical features when they travel around Essex.

As most of the notes were originally made for my own interest, the selection may be thought to be weighted in favour of historical associations. I hope, however, that these interests will prove to have been wide enough to reflect the character of the county and provide clues to most of the distinctive features in its social and political life.

The key to most of the sources will be found in the bibliographical volumes of the *Victoria County History of Essex,* the *Transactions* of the Essex Archaeological Society (E.A.T.), the *Essex Review* (E.R.), the *Essex Naturalist* (E. Nat.) and the *Essex Journal.* Sources less familiar are indicated where required.

I have had advice and help from too many friends over the years to do justice to them individually here. I am sure they know how grateful I am; but I must make an exception to acknowledge my great indebtedness to Dr. F.G. Emmison, M.B.E., F.S.A., F.R.Hist.S., whose friendship I enjoyed throughout his 30 years as County Archivist of Essex, and who since his retirement has continued to place his vast knowledge of the county unreservedly at my disposal.

WILLIAM ADDISON

LIST OF ILLUSTRATIONS

Frontispiece
Robert Rich, 2nd Earl of Warwick, by Van Dyck

Grateful acknowledgment is made to the Friends of Historic Essex for a grant towards the printing of the illustrations.

ABDY

Anthony Abdy (d. 1640), whose name is derived from Abdy in Yorkshire, was an alderman of the City of London who settled at Albyns, Stapleford Abbots, and founded a family seated in Essex for over 250 years. All his three sons received baronetcies; his daughter, Alice, married Sir John Bramston of Skreens, Roxwell (q.v.).

The eldest son, Thomas, of Felix Hall, Kelvedon, was created a baronet in 1641. At his death in 1685 he was buried in the parish church of Kelvedon, where the family is commemorated by monuments dating from 1685 to 1710.

Robert, the second son, was created a baronet in 1660. He bought the Albyns estate in 1654, and from that date the manor descended with the baronetcy until the latter became extinct with the death of Sir John, 4th baronet, in 1759. Sir Robert Abdy, 3rd baronet of the Albyns line, was described by Morant as 'a man of deep knowledge in antiquity and natural history, a great connoisseur in medals of which he had a fine collection; and, what is more valuable, a true patriot, and a person of unshaken integrity, and remarkable humanity.' He represented Essex in Parliament from 1727 until his death in 1748. His son, the 4th baronet, died unmarried and was succeeded by the Rev. T. Abdy Rutherford, who assumed the surname and arms of Abdy. His second son, Anthony, left an only son, Thomas, who was created a baronet in 1850. He was Member of Parliament for Lyme Regis, 1847-52; High Sheriff of Essex, 1875. Monuments and mural tablets to the Abdys of Albyns are to be seen in Stapleford Abbots church.

John, third son of the original Anthony Abdy of Albyns, lived at Moores, Salcot Virley. He was created a baronet in 1660. At his death without issue in 1692 this baronetcy became extinct.

Edward S. Abdy (1791-1846), who published a work on the United States of America in 1835, was a son of Anthony Abdy of Albyns.

ABELL

The Abells were wealthy clothiers who flourished at West Bergholt, Fordham, and other villages and small towns in north-east Essex during the 16th and 17th centuries. The most distinguished member of the family, Thomas (d. 1540), entered the priesthood and became chaplain to Catherine of Aragon, who entrusted him with a secret

commission to the Emperor Charles V concerning her divorce from
Henry VIII. In 1530 she presented him to the living of Bradwell-
juxta-Mare. He was committed to the Tower for preaching against
the royal divorce; but after a short term was released with an
injunction not to preach. For disobeying this he was re-arrested,
and after six years in the Tower was martyred on 30th July 1540.
In 1532 he published 'Invicta Veritas: an answer to the determination
of the most famous universities that by no manner of lawe may it be
lawfull for the most noble Kinge of Englande King Henry to be
divorced from the Quene's grace, his lawfull and verie wyfe.'

ADAMS See FLOWER

AIRY

Sir George Biddell Airy (1801-92), Astronomer Royal, was educated
at Colchester Royal Grammar School and at a school in St. Isaac's
Walk. His home at the time was in George Street. After a brilliant
career at Trinity College, Cambridge, he became Plumian Professor
of Astronomy in 1828. In 1836 he was appointed Astronomer Royal at
Greenwich Observatory, which he equipped with instruments designed
by himself. He wrote voluminously on astronomical subjects and in
1896 published his Autobiography.

ALBEMARLE, DUKE OF See MONCK

ALIBON

Sir Richard Alibon (1621-88), judge, is commemorated at Dagenham
by a fine monument ascribed by Mrs. Esdaile to Nost. He was born
at Dagenham and became a judge under James II. If his complaints
after failing to obtain convictions against the Seven Bishops are any
guide to his character, he lacked the first quality to be looked for in
a judge: impartiality. But those were not the days of impartial judges.
Sir Robert Baldock, born at Stanway, who argued that the plea of
the bishops was libellous and a reflection on the justice and honour
of the king, was also an Essex man. Within a week of the trial,
Alibon was promoted to be judge of the King's Bench. He lost office,
however, when the king was obliged to flee.

ALLEN

Benjamin Allen (1663-1738), naturalist, was the close friend of John
Ray (q.v.) and Samuel Dale (q.v.) of Braintree. He was the son of
a London doctor of the same name and appears to have established
his own practice as a physician in Braintree sometime before 1692.
In the same year he attracted Ray's attention by announcing his discovery of winged glow-worms. His home in Braintree was The Great
House, overlooking the Great Square, which was then the best house
in the town.

Allen is remembered chiefly for his work on medicinal waters: The
Natural History of the Chalybeat and Purging Waters of England,
published in 1699 by the printers to the Royal Society and dedicated
to his patron, the 4th Earl of Manchester (afterwards Duke) of Leighs
Priory. It is one of the earliest works on the subject and mentions
eight Essex springs. Unfortunately, it was badly written, so the
re-written second edition is to be preferred.

About 1723 Allen started to compile a Commonplace Book. In it he

recorded some of his remedies, many of which amusingly reflect the
credulity of his age. He claims, for example, that 'Mr. Middleton,
our Minister, was cured of a dropsy of ye cod or scrotum by eating
gentian every morning,' and that in 1708 'the chair-maker of Witham'
was cured of dropsy by drinking beer in which mustard-seed had
been steeped. Even John Ray did not escape. Allen records that Mr.
Ray was cured of jaundice by taking an infusion of the dung of a
stallion in beer. Ray himself was fully convinced of the effectiveness
of the treatment. In January 1797 he wrote to Sir Hans Sloane giving
the complete prescription, which was the dung, as stated, steeped in
ale overnight, with a little saffron added, and in the morning strained
and sweetened with sugar. He says that he drank half-a-pint at a time
and was completely cured by two doses.

For consumption, Allen prescribed sheep's dung in milk.

Other parts of the Commonplace Book are devoted to astronomy,
dreams, and warnings from heaven. His linking of cause with effect
took odd turns. For example, he seems to have believed that the fact
that Queen Anne died on the day that an Act against Dissenters came
into force was not without religious significance. Fortunately, his
finds in natural history were recorded without too much interpret-
ation. He retired from practice about 1727. When he died at the age
of 75 he was buried in Black Notley churchyard.

ALLEN

John Allen (1476-1534), Archbishop of Dublin, was rector of South
Ockendon while acting as Wolsey's agent in suppressing the minor
monasteries, 1524-5. In 1528 he became Archbishop of Dublin and
Chancellor of Ireland. In 1534 he was murdered by followers of
Lord Thomas FitzGerald.

ALLEN

Sir John Allen (or Alleyne), Lord Mayor of London in 1525 and 1535,
was a member of Henry VIII's Privy Council. He lived at Thaxted,
where he was a generous benefactor. Stow describes him as 'a man
of great wisdom, and also of great charity.' At his death, unmarried,
in 1544 his estates were inherited by his brother, in whose family
they continued for many generations.

ALLEN

Matthew Allen (d. 1845), pioneer in the treatment of insanity, who
published his Essay on the Classification of the Insane in 1837, had
a private asylum at High Beach in Epping Forest. His most distinguished patient was John Clare, the poet, who was in his care from
1837 to 1841. Allen was a man of great personal charm whose ideas
attracted much attention in literary as well as medical circles. He
was in the forefront of the humane treatment of mental illnesses.
After five years as physician and superintendent at York Asylum,
Allen chose High Beach for his own home because,
    'here, together with domestic comfort, diversity of
    occupations and amusements suited to their various
    states, the retirement, pure air and sweet scenery
    around, afford ample scope for walks without annoyance,
    and apparently without restraint, which, with judicious
    moral and medical management, combine many acknowledged
    requisites to assist the disturbed and diseased mind to re-
    gain its tranquillity.'

Most of his ideas anticipated modern methods of treatment. His asylum was in three neighbouring houses: Fairmead House (demolished), Lippitt's Hill Lodge and Springfield, one of which was reserved for women under Mrs. Allen's care. Clare improved at High Beach and wrote many descriptive poems there. In 1841, however, he left and walked home to Northamptonshire. Later in the same year he was certified insane and removed from his home at Northborough to the county General Lunatic Asylum.

Soon after Clare left High Beach, Allen formed a company for carving wood by machinery named The Patent Decorative Carving and Sculpture Company. Tennyson, who was living at High Beach at the time, was attracted by the scheme and invested money in it. The enterprise failed and Allen became bankrupt in 1843. The irony of the two ventures was that while the medical enterprise went far towards curing - at least temporarily - one poet, the commercial enterprise nearly drove another insane. There is an echo of Allen's affair in Tennyson's poem Sea Dreams.

ALLEYNE

Edward Alleyne of Hatfield Peverel (d. 1638), landowner, who served as High Sheriff of the county, and was created a baronet in 1629, married Elizabeth, co-heir of George Scot of Little Leighs. The marriage brought him estates at Little Leighs, Stapleford Tawney, and Matching. At his death in 1638 he was succeeded by his grandson, Sir Edmund, 2nd baronet, who married Frances, only daughter and heiress of Thomas Gent (q.v.) of Moyns, Steeple Bumpstead. Their daughter married as her second husband George, third son of Henry, Duke of Norfolk, and inherited the Alleyne estates at her father's death in 1656. The baronetcy reverted to her father's uncle, Sir George, 3rd baronet, who died in 1664. He was succeeded by his son, Sir George, 4th baronet, who married the youngest daughter of John Clopton of Little Waltham. He died in 1702 and was succeeded by Sir Clopton, 5th baronet, at whose death unmarried in 1726 the title devolved upon his brother, Sir George, 6th baronet, who also died unmarried and was succeeded by his nephew, Sir Edmund, 7th baronet, who became the third in succession to die unmarried. At his death in 1729 the baronetcy became extinct and the estates passed to his sister, who bore the family name of Arabella. She was the wife of the Rev. James Chalmers, vicar of Earls Colne and rector of Little Waltham.

ALTHAM

James Altham (d. 1583), landowner, who has a handsome monument on the south side of the sanctuary in Latton church, was a Lancashire man who made a fortune in London and bought three Latton manors between 1562 and 1566. When he died in 1583 he was succeeded by his second son, Edward (d. 1605), who in turn was succeeded by Sir James Altham, who married Elizabeth Barrington of Hatfield Broad Oak. At his death without issue he was succeeded by his brother, Sir Edward, who married as his second wife, Joan Leventhorp of Shingle Hall, Sawbridgeworth (Herts.), and it is her correspondence that is the principal source for our knowledge of a family that continued to flourish in West Essex until the end of the 18th century. Her husband, Sir Edward, had the estate carefully surveyed in 1616, and a map was produced showing every house and building on the estate, even to the butts and whipping-post. The map is enlivened by illustrations of the famous Harlow Bush Fair and the annual Rogation

Procession, with the parson and congregation going round the bounds of the parish singing the Litany.

For a century between 1680 and 1782 the Latton living was held by members of the Altham family. The most distinguished of the many descendants of this long line of country squires and parsons of Mark Hall and Latton was Elizabeth Barrett Browning.

APPLETON

The Appletons acquired the South Benfleet property by the marriage of Thomas Appleton of Suffolk (temp. Henry VIII) with a daughter of Sir Robert Tyrell of Herons (q.v.). Their great-great-grandson, who was created a baronet in 1611, married a daughter of Sir Thomas Mildmay of Moulsham (q.v.). He was one of the local landowners who made an agreement with Joos Croppenburg in 1622 to embank Canvey Island. Sir Henry Appleton, a royalist officer in the siege of Colchester, was taken prisoner by Fairfax.

The baronetcy continued until 1710, when it became extinct on the death of Sir Henry Appleton, 6th baronet. There are monuments in South Benfleet church to Sir William (1705) and Dorothy his wife (1719), with achievement of arms, as well as to other members of the family.

ARCHER

The Archer family of Coopersale in Theydon Garnon claimed descent from Simon de Bois, who attended Henry V at Agincourt and was commanded by the king to change his name to Archer, in recognition of the exceptional skill he displayed in a shooting match at Havering-atte-Bower.

Sir John Archer (1598-1682), the great man of the family, was the son of Henry Archer of Coopersale and Hemnalls in Theydon Garnon (d. 1616), who endowed a local charity. Sir John represented Essex in the parliament of 1656. He was appointed a judge in 1659 and a judge of the Common Pleas in 1663. Roger North has a somewhat cryptic reference to him. He says that he was one of those 'of whose abilities time hath kept no record, unless in a sinister way.' This is probably a reference to Archer's retirement. In 1672 Charles II tried to get him removed from office, but failed because Archer refused to surrender his patent until the proper procedure provided for the removal of a judge from office had been carried out, and this required addresses to both Houses of Parliament. Charles saw dangers in this and simply suspended him from duty. As he continued to enjoy all the emoluments of office under the arrangement, he complied with the royal pleasure and lived comfortably at Coopersale to the age of 84.

Sir John, the judge, married twice. The Sir John who succeeded him set up a memorial to his father in the chancel of Theydon Garnon church; but he failed to provide an heir. At his death without issue in 1707 he left the estate to William Eyre, of Gray's Inn, on condition he took the name of Archer and married Sir John's niece, Eleanor Wrottesley. Unfortunately, Eleanor died without issue, and William Eyre Archer married Susanna, daughter of Sir John Newton, Bart. Their son, another John Archer, succeeded to all the Archer estates, although he had no Archer blood in his veins. He had no male heir. At his death in 1800 the estates were inherited by his daughter,

Susanna, who in 1770 had married Jacob Houblon of Hallingbury
Place (q.v.). At her death the Coopersale estate went to her grand-
son, John Archer-Houblon, and descended with the Hallingbury
Place estate in the Archer-Houblon family.

The last John Archer of Coopersale was a man of wealth who could
afford to indulge in personal idiosyncracies. His own (Eyre) family
estate was at Welford in Berkshire, and when he moved from one
estate to the other the operation assumed the dignity of a royal
progress. The procession was led by a coach with six horses,
driven by a coachman supported by two postilions and three out-
riders. This carried the upper servants. Then came a post-chaise
with four horses, carrying Mrs. Archer and her maids, a phaeton
in which Mr. Archer himself invariably travelled wrapped in a
swan's-down coat. This carriage also had four horses, and was
followed by two grooms. Behind these came a chaise-marine with
four horses, carrying numerous services of family plate, escorted
by the under-butler and three stout fellows armed with blunderbusses.
Next came the hunters, with their cloths of scarlet trimmed with
silver, attended by the stud-groom and huntsman, who had made sure
that each horse had a fox's brush tied to the front of the bridle. The
hounds, with the whipper-in, the hack-horses and the inferior stable-
men, brought up the rear.

See W. G. Benham: E.R. xxx i 160-79

ARDERNE

Sir Peter Arderne, of Mark Hall, Latton,(d. 1467), has a fine altar
tomb in Latton church. He was the son of John Arderne, a baron of
the Exchequer. In 1440 he became deputy-steward of the king in the
Duchy of Lancaster. In 1443 he was admitted Serjeant and shortly
afterwards King's Serjeant-at-Law. Three years later he became
lord of the manor of Latton Merk. In 1448 he became Chief Baron of
the Exchequer and justice of the King's Bench. His wife was
Catherine Bohun, who with her husband founded a chantry in the
church of Netteswell.

ARGALL

Sir Samuel Argall (d. 1626), adventurer and deputy-governor of
Virginia, lived at Walthamstow. He was among the first adventurers
to Virginia, distinguishing himself as a seaman and gaining the confidence of eminent politicians. He is chiefly remembered for his part
in the abduction of Pocahontas, which led to the release of English
captives (see Purchas). On receiving a knighthood from James I in
1622 he was described as being of Walthamstow.

ARKWRIGHT

The Rev. Joseph Arkwright of Mark Hall, near Harlow, was the
grandson of Sir Richard Arkwright, inventor of the spinning frame.
He took up the mastership of the Essex Hounds in 1857 and built the
kennels near Harlow. It was during his mastership that Anthony
Trollope (q.v.) hunted with the Essex hounds and drew on his exper-
iences for many scenes in his novels, notably in Can You Forgive
Her ?, vol. i, Chaps. 16 and 17.

The fact that the second Richard Arkwright was able to buy the
Mark Hall estate in 1819 for his son Joseph for a sum exceeding
100,000 guineas is an indication of the wealth he had been able to

amass in the cotton mills of Lancashire. The patronage of the
Latton living went with the estate, and in 1820 the new owner was
instituted as vicar, although he only appeared in the pulpit once a
year: on Christmas Day when, presumably, the curate in charge of
the parish had a day off. After 30 years as vicar, he was succeeded
by his son, Julius, for whom a new vicarage had been built. Julius
was vicar for 14 years, but only survived his father by one month.

ARMSTRONG-JONES

Sir Robert Armstrong-Jones (1857-1943), F.R.C.S., F.R.C.P.,
medical superintendent of Claybury, Woodford, from 1892 to 1916,
made that hospital renowned for modern methods of treatment for
mental diseases. He was knighted in 1917. His grandson, Anthony
Armstrong-Jones, married Princess Margaret, and was created
Earl of Snowdon.

ASCHAM

Roger Ascham (1515-68), scholar, was a Yorkshireman who entered
the service of Sir Anthony Wingfield as a child and eventually
became one of the greatest classical scholars of the age. He came
to live at Walthamstow on obtaining through the influence of Sir
William Petre a grant from the queen of the lease of Salisbury Hall
Farm. The Scholemaster, which occupied the last five years of his
life, was written there at the invitation of Sir Richard Sackville.

Ascham made few friends at court, but was esteemed by scholars.
Camden says that he was 'too much given to dicing and cock-fighting,'
and consequently lived and died a poor man; but the truth of this has
been disputed in so far as it relates to dicing. He does appear to
have been interested in cock-fighting, an interest acquired, perhaps,
in his Yorkshire childhood. He was a stout advocate of archery in
his Toxophilus, first published in 1545, and doubtless did his stat-
utory shooting practice on the Walthamstow butts. This interest in
sport distinguished him from many of his studious contemporaries,
and it may well have been this interest in the pleasures of ordinary
folk that gave his prose so much natural vigour.

Ascham became interested in the education of the Princess Elizabeth
while she was in the care of Sir Anthony Denny (q.v.), and when her
tutor, William Grindal, died, he was appointed to succeed him. He
remained on good terms with his pupil to the end of his life, and when
he died she is reported as having said,
> 'I would rather have cast £10,000 into the sea
> than have lost my Ascham.'

ASHURST

The Ashurst family of Castle Hedingham was founded by Henry
Ashurst, a London merchant who devoted much of his wealth to the
propagation of the Gospels in America and their translation for the
conversion of the people of India. One of his granddaughters became
the wife of William, Lord Cowper, the first Lord Chancellor of
Great Britain.

Henry, eldest son of the first Henry of Castle Hedingham, was
created a baronet in 1688; William, the second son, was Lord Mayor
of London in 1693 and represented the City in Parliament for many
years. The Castle house at Hedingham, afterwards the home of the
Majendie family, was built in 1719 by Robert Ashurst.

ATKINSON

John Christopher Atkinson (1814-1900), antiquary and local historian,
was born at Goldhanger, where his father was curate. His grandfather was vicar of Wethersfield. J. C. Atkinson became domestic
chaplain to William Henry Dawnay, 7th Viscount Downe, one of whose
sons, Eustace Henry (1850-1928), married Lady Evelyn de Vere
Capel, granddaughter of Arthur Algernon, 6th Earl of Essex.
Viscount Downe owned the advowson of Danby-in-Cleveland, Yorkshire,
and presented Atkinson, who held the living for 53 years until his
death. In 1891 he published one of the classics of local history:
Forty Years in a Moorland Parish, a work that must make Essex
people regret that he was not presented to an Essex living.

AUDLEY

Thomas, Lord Audley of Walden (1488-1544), Lord Chancellor, was
born of obscure parents at Earls Colne and maintained close, if
seldom honourable, connection with Essex throughout his career.
He was Town Clerk of Colchester at 28, returned to Parliament as
one of the burgesses of Colchester at 35. Advancement came quickly
after he had succeeded in attracting the attention of the king by his
conduct as steward to the Duke of Suffolk. By following a policy of
gratifying all the king's wishes the highest offices were opened to
him. In 1529 he became Speaker of the House of Commons, an office
to which he was appointed expressly to preside over the Parliament
that authorized the break with Rome. On Wolsey's fall he was made
Chancellor of the Duchy of Lancaster, and successively King's
Serjeant and Chancellor of the Court of Augmentations. Upon the
resignation of Sir Thomas More in 1532 he was appointed Lord
Keeper of the Great Seal and knighted. In the following January the
title of Lord Keeper of the Great Seal was changed to that of Lord
Chancellor, the office he continued to hold for 12 years, setting the
seal of legal authority on whatever the king desired.

As Lord Chancellor, Audley sanctioned the king's divorce from
Catherine of Aragon, presided at the trial, and was present at the
execution of Anne Boleyn, obtained the dissolution of the marriage
with Anne of Cleves, and passed judgement on Catherine Howard.
In 1535 he stooped to the basest act in his career when he passed
judgement on More and Fisher after trials that had made a mockery
of justice.

A man so assiduous in the king's interest could not be expected to be
tardy in promoting his own. 'Never had chancellor so little to live
by,' he complained as soon as he saw that recompense was available,
adding that his salary could 'scarce suffice for his housekeeping.'
In 1538 he was raised to the peerage as Baron Audley of Walden,
installed a Knight of the Garter, and given what Fuller described as
'the first cut in the feast of abbey lands.' This cut included, in
addition to the abbey of Walden, a grant of the manor of Berechurch
Hall, together with lands in Little Walden, Brook Walden,
Thunderley, Arkesden, Great Chrisall and Elsenham. Other religious
foundations that came to him were the Priory of St. Botolph in
Colchester, with the manors attached to it, the lay rectories and
advowsons of several parishes, with rent-charges out of a dozen or
more benefices. A complete list of the properties that came to him in
Essex at the Dissolution would be too long to reproduce here. It can
be found in Morant. 'In a busy world,' he confessed to the Bishop of

Colchester, 'I sustained damage and infamy, and this shall restore me to honesty and commodity.'

Audley's memory might be universally reviled if it were not for his one great act of charity. In 1542 he re-established and re-endowed Buckingham College, Cambridge, renaming it Magdalene College. Fuller tells us that some would have it that this was done because 'Maudlin', as Magdalene was commonly pronounced, had Audley's surname between the initial and final letters - M-Audley-n. Be that as it may, in re-endowing the college, which was already closely associated with the abbey at Walden, he provided that Magdalene College and his Walden property should be linked in perpetuity. To this day the owners of the estate have the right to appoint the Master of the College. Audley died at his Aldgate house on the 30th April 1544, after resigning the Great Seal on the 21st of the same month. He was buried in Saffron Walden church in a tomb of which Fuller said, 'the marble was not blacker than the soul, nor harder than the heart, of him whose bones were laid beneath it.'

Lord Audley married twice. His first wife was a daughter of Sir Thomas Barnardiston, an East Anglian squire. By his second wife, Lady Mary Grey (q.v.), daughter of Thomas, second Marquis of Dorset, a cousin of the king, he had two daughters, Margaret and Mary, who were aged four and three respectively at the time of his death. Mary died unmarried, Margaret married Henry Dudley, son of the Duke of Northumberland, who was killed at St. Quintin in 1557. She then married, in 1558, Thomas, 4th Duke of Norfolk, a widower of 22 with an only son, and it was the son of Thomas, Duke of Norfolk, and Margaret Audley who built the mansion of Audley End (see Thomas Howard, 1st Earl of Suffolk).

The association of the name of Audley with Essex was continued by the Lord Chancellor's bequest of the manor of Berechurch to his brother, in whose heirs it continued until 1714. The last of the line, Henry, was described by Morant as 'a weak and wicked man,' a slave of his vices. Having gone through his property, he took shelter from his creditors in the Fleet Prison, where he died in 1714. On hearing of his death his widow, from whom he had long been separated, sent money for his body to be buried decently at Berechurch.

See W. Howard-Flanders: Thomas, Lord Audley of Walden
                          E.A.T. n.s. x 289
    A. L. Reade: The Audley Family, Notes and Queries, 1927.

AYLETT

Five branches of this family seated in Essex have their pedigrees recorded in the Herald's Visitation of 1664-8. The most distinguished member was Dr. Robert Aylett (1583-1654), an ecclesiastical lawyer who acted as Laud's agent and judge of the commissary court charged with the responsibility of compelling uniformity and, in particular, with enforcing the railing in of the communion table at the east end of the chancel.

Aylett married Penelope, daughter of William Wiseman of Mayland, and lived for many years at Feeringbury, a country house for centuries of successive bishops of London. He enjoyed a considerable reputation during his lifetime as a writer of religious verse. His letters are preserved in the State Papers. There is a monument to his memory under the west window in Great Braxted church. From this we learn that he died in 1654 in his 73rd year. He had been married three times but died without issue.

See J. H. Round: E.A.T. n.s. x 26
C. F. D. Sperling: E.A.T. n.s. x 266
J. H. Round: Eng. Hist. Rev. xxxviii (1923) 423

AYLOFFE

The Ayloffe family crossed over from Kent during the 15th century and settled at Hornchurch, where an elaborately carved altar tomb commemorates William Ayloffe, 1517, and Audrey his wife. Their descendants were to be influential in the county for 300 years.

William Ayloffe, appointed a judge of the Queen's Bench in 1577, was one of the judges at the trial of Edmund Campion for high treason in 1581, and is remembered chiefly in connection with an invented miracle. The story is told in a book entitled An Epistle of Comfort to the Reverend Priestes, and to the Honorable, Worshipful, and other of the Laye Sort, restrayned in Durance for the Catholicke Fayth. It relates that while the jury were considering their verdict, Judge Ayloffe remained in court when the other judges retired, and as he relaxed he drew off his glove. To his amazement he found that his hand was covered with blood for which he could find no explanation. He wiped it off, but to no avail. The blood continued to reappear, to the wonder of all who were present in court at the time, and bore witness to what was regarded as a miracle.

The judge died in 1585, and by his wife, Jane, daughter of Eustace Sulyard of Fleming in Suffolk, left three sons. The eldest, William, fourth of that name, lived at Great Braxted and was knighted along with other Essex gentlemen on James I's accession to the throne in 1603. In 1612 he was created a baronet. His successor, Sir Benjamin, was a loyal supporter of Charles I who appointed him High Sheriff at the beginning of the Civil War. He served as a Knight of the Shire at the Restoration.

At his death in 1663 he was succeeded by his son, William, who thus became the 3rd baronet. He died without surviving issue and was succeeded by his brother, a second Benjamin, who married a daughter of Sir John Tyrell of Heron Hall (q.v.). At his death in 1722 the baronetcy passed to his nephew, the Rev. John Ayloffe, who died in 1730 and was the last of his line. The baronetcy then passed to a descendant of the issue of the third marriage of the 1st baronet, Sir Joseph Ayloffe, 6th and last baronet (1709-81), a distinguished antiquary who contributed regularly to Archaeologia, the journal of the Society of Antiquaries, of which he was a leading Fellow and Vice-President for many years. He is now remembered for his calendars of ancient charters, published in 1772, a work that had been started by Philip Morant (q.v.). Nor is this his only link with Morant, whose history of Essex was published in 1760-8. In 1764 Ayloffe published a lengthy prospectus for the proposed publication of a 'Topographical and Historical Description of Suffolk', for which he had been collecting material for 15 years. The response was so disappointing that the project had to be abandoned. If it had succeeded, Sir Joseph Ayloffe might have become the 'Philip Morant of Suffolk'. As it is, his name is almost forgotten, and as he died at the age of 73 in 1781, 11 years after Morant, without surviving issue, the baronetcy became extinct.

See S. S. Dutton: E.R. x/v 97
    C. L. Stewart: E.R. /ix 181

BACON

Knightly families of this name held manors in the 13th century in the parishes of Dengie and Mountnessing. The original Bacons of Essex were probably a branch of the Suffolk family.

BADEW

Richard de Badew (fl. 1320-30), founder of University Hall, afterwards Clare College, Cambridge, was born at Great Baddow near Chelmsford and educated at Cambridge, where he became eminent. He was Chancellor of the University in 1326, and in the same year purchased two houses in Milne Street, which he gave to the University for use as a college to be called University Hall. It met with only modest success. Ten years later it was supporting no more than ten scholars. Then in 1338, Elizabeth de Burgh, Countess of Clare and granddaughter of Edward I, refounded it under the name of Clare College, after having had assigned to her by a deed of 1338 by Richard de Badew (described as 'Founder, Patron and Advocate of the House called the Hall of the University of Cambridge') all the rights and titles of the original foundation.

BALDOCK See ALIBON

BALDWIN

A family of this name lived at Felsted from the 12th century. Baldwin of Felsted appears as the king's gold and silver smith in the Pipe Rolls of 1184-5:

> 'to Baldwin of Felsted twelve shillings for
> the care of the boys of the widow of Rochford
> and for the King's work £18.17.7. By order
> of the King.'

Knight's History of England (vol i, p.602) records:

> 'Two candlesticks made of gold and silver
> which Robert, abbot of St. Albans, sent to
> his countryman, Pope Adrian, are stated to
> have excited the warm admiration of the pont-
> iff, who declared that he had never seen more
> beautiful workmanship. A large cup of gold,
> made by order of the same abbot, by a gold-
> smith named Baldwin, is described by Matthew
> Paris as being "adorned with flowers and
> foliages of the most delicate workmanship, and
> set round with precious stones in the most ele-
> gant manner." '

BALL

John Ball (d. 1381) came to Colchester from York to be rector of St. James' and found a ready audience among the villeins of North Essex for his fervent preaching that all men are born equal. From Essex he travelled into Kent, where he was confined three times in the Archbishop's prison at Maidstone for preaching doctrines derived from Wycliffe. At the outbreak of the Peasants' Revolt he was released by the Kentish insurgents, and on Blackheath preached his famous sermon calling upon the people to overthrow the Government and set up a Commonwealth based on social equality and universal brotherhood.

William Morris (q.v.) was an ardent admirer and expressed his sympathy with Ball's basic creed in A Dream of John Ball.

Ball was finally brought before the king at St. Albans and sentenced to be hanged, drawn and quartered as a traitor. The king actually witnessed the hanging at St. Albans on the 15th July 1381.

BANCROFT

Francis Bancroft, founder of Bancroft's School, Woodford, gave his estates in Essex, Suffolk and Middlesex to the Drapers' Company in 1727 to found almshouses and a school for boys. The first school under the endowment was founded in 1737 at Mile End. It was moved to Woodford in 1889, after a brief stay at Tottenham.

BANYARD

James Banyard, a shoemaker of Rochford, came under the influence of two visiting preachers, Robert Aitkin and William Bridges, and was so impressed by their insistence on the simplicity of true doctrine that he founded the Peculiar People to give expression to his own belief in two basic tenets: assurance of holiness and assurance of salvation. Their first chapel was opened at Rochford in 1838.

To the original tenets was added one of belief in healing by the laying on of hands and anointing with oil in the name of the Lord. It was this third tenet that attracted most attention. To the general public the distinctive characteristic of the Peculiar People was their rejection of medical aid. With the introduction of the Welfare State, insistence on medical certificates of fitness in terms of employment and general acceptance of clinical and hospital services, the Peculiar People gradually adapted themselves to new conditions and modified their rule, insisting only that medical aid should be accompanied by prayer.

The movement never spread to other parts of the county.

BARCLAY

The Barclays were one of several Quaker banking families who settled in Essex during the 18th century. Among others that became prominent were the Hanburys, Gurneys, Tukes, Gibsons, and Trittons. Most of them intermarried and are well documented in published diaries and reminiscences. The Barclays came from Scotland. David Barclay (1682-1769), their common ancestor, son of Robert Barclay the Quaker apologist, set up in business in Cheapside as a merchant draper at the beginning of the century. He married as his second wife the daughter and heiress of John Freame, the Quaker goldsmith and banker.

The story is told of the first Barclay banker, that one day when the king and queen were driving down Cheapside, the horses in their carriage took fright and bolted, whereupon David Barclay ran out and stopped them, and on recognising the king and queen said: 'Friend George, wilt thou not bring they wife Charlotte into my house to recover from her alarm ? '

David Barclay of Walthamstow (1728-1809) was the son of David of Cheapside. In addition to being a partner in the banking business, he owned the brewery that later became 'Barclay Perkins', as well as large plantations in Jamaica, which he bought for the express purpose of liberating the slaves who worked them. These were sent in a specially chartered vessel to Philadelphia, where they were put out by Quaker friends as apprentices. In his work for the emancipation of the slaves he was associated with several of his Quaker kinsfolk and with Thomas Fowell Buxton (q.v.), who although not himself a Quaker was closely connected with them through birth, marriage and sympathy. David Barclay was fortunate enough to live to see the law passed for the suppression of the slave trade.

Another of his philanthropic enterprises was the setting up of a 'Home of Industry' near his home at Walthamstow. Trees were yet another interest. In 1796 he wrote a memorandum for the Board of Agriculture pleading that some of the waste land being enclosed should be planted with timber and that trees should not be planted in hedgerows.

He distributed much of his fortune before his death, not as now to avoid death duties, but to give himself the pleasure of seeing his relatives well established during his lifetime. His principal heir was his grandson, Hudson Gurney, who became the millionaire banker, traveller, archaeologist and scholar. Hudson Gurney died at the age of 98 in 1864.
See an article on David Barclay in
 Chambers' Edinburgh Journal 1849; S.
 Fothergill: Memoir &c., and E.R.xlix 173
 C. W. and H. F. Barclay and A. W. Fox; History of the Barclay
 Family (3 vols. 1924-34)

BARING-GOULD

The Rev. Sabine Baring-Gould (1834-1924), author of 130 volumes on an astonishing variety of subjects, father of 15 children, spent ten of his 90 years as rector of East Mersea and produced Mehala, a weird, grim tale of the marshes, described by Swinburne (mistakenly) as a novel 'as good as Wuthering Heights.' In 1881 he presented himself to the family living of Lew Trenchard in Devon, where his family had been seated for nearly 300 years.

BARNARDO

Dr. Thomas John Barnardo (1845-1905), philanthropist, was converted in 1862 and began his evangelical mission in the Dublin slums. He entered London Hospital as a missionary medical student in 1866, and became a Fellow of the Royal College of Surgeons in 1879. In 1867 he founded the East End Mission for Destitute Children, which was followed in 1870 by the opening of the Boys' Home at Stepney, which in turn developed into Dr. Barnardo's Homes. Three years later Sir John Sands, chairman of the London Stock Exchange, gave him Mossford Lodge, Barkingside, as a wedding present, and the rear portion of the house was quickly adapted as a home for 60 girls. From this beginning grew the village of cottage homes, of which by 1879 there were 24 in grounds extending over 30 acres. When the founder died in 1905 the number of cottages had increased to 64, providing homes for 1,300 girls. Boys were admitted shortly before the outbreak of war in 1939 so that families would no longer need to be split. The original house at Stepney continued in use as headquarters until 1969, when the administration was moved to a site at Barkingside. At the time of his death, it was estimated that Dr. Barnardo had helped a quarter of a million children.

BARRETT-LENNARD

The descendants of John Barrett of Hawkhurst in Kent, who settled
in Essex on marrying Alicia de Belhus in 1400, were landowners at
Aveley for more than 500 years. Thomas, the son and heir of John
and Alicia, married a daughter of John Pointz of North Ockendon;
another son, John, was a generous benefactor of the abbey at
Stratford Langthorne. The family home of Belhus was rebuilt by
John Barrett, great-grandson of the original John, who married
four times and had 13 children. At his death in 1526 he was succeeded by his grandson, Edward (1521-85), then aged five. His son
and heir, Charles, married a daughter of Sir Walter Mildmay (q.v.),
but died while his father was still alive. He is commemorated by a
brass in Aveley Church. His son, Edward (1581-1644), who like his
grandfather succeeded as an infant, was one of the most distinguished
of the long line of Barretts and Barrett-Lennards. He was knighted
in 1608, and in 1618 received a licence to enclose a deer park around
Belhus. In 1627 he was raised to the peerage as Baron Barrett of
Newburgh, County Fife. The following year, as Lord Newburgh, he
was appointed Chancellor of the Exchequer and continued in public
life until, as a royalist, he was obliged to retire when the conflict
came between king and Parliament. At his death without issue in
1644 he was found to have bequeathed Belhus to his cousin, Richard
Lennard, on condition he took the name of Barrett.

The first appearance of the Lennard family in Essex was in 1565,
when John Lennard negotiated for the marriage of his son, Samson,
with Margaret, sister of Gregory Fynes, Lord Dacre, who purchased the manor of Romford in 1573. On his death, Margaret Lennard
inherited the Dacre title, which continued in the Lennard family for
nearly 200 years.

In 1674 Thomas, Baron Dacre, married Lady Ann Fitroy, a natural
daughter of Charles II, and a few months later was created Earl of
Sussex.

The Richard Lennard who took the name of Barrett on inheriting
Belhus was the grandson of the sister of Lord Dacre who had married into the Lennard family. He served the county well as High
Sheriff and M.P., and when he died in 1696 he was succeeded by
his eldest son, Dacre Barrett-Lennard.

Dacre Barrett-Lennard's grandson, Thomas (1717-86), succeeded
to the Dacre barony in 1755. He was eminent as an antiquary and
enjoyed the friendship of Philip Morant, Dr. Johnson and Horace
Walpole. He had no legitimate children, but two natural children who
became his heirs. These children were brought up at Belhus and
treated in all respects as if they had been legitimate. The story of
their 'adoption' by Lady Dacre is that one morning Thomas was
brought into her room at Belhus and immediately exclaimed: 'Oh,
what a pretty lady !' This so pleased Lady Dacre that she said
excitedly: 'Come to me, you dear little boy, and I will be a second
mother to you.' When a sister was born to Thomas, she was baptised
Barbara, the name of the child Lady Dacre had lost, and she also
was brought up as a child of the family. 60 or 70 years later, the
'adopted' Thomas was described as,
> 'a handsome old gentleman of the courtly old
> school, somewhat short in stature, but with

the gracious dignity of one with royal blood
in his veins; the proverbial Stuart beauty had
descended to him in its fullness.'

He married at Bobbingworth church, Dorothy St. Aubyns, whose
mother was living at Blake Hall in that parish at the time. For three-
quarters of a century, until his death in 1857 at the age of 95, he
was in every respect an outstanding figure in the public life of Essex.

His eldest son (1788-1856) was elected M.P. for Ipswich in 1820,
and for Maldon six times from 1826 to 1847; but he died a year before
his father, who was succeeded by his grandson, following a pattern
that had persisted throughout the history of the family. This grandson was the Sir Thomas Barrett-Lennard (b. 1826) who published
for private circulation in 1908 An Account of the Families of
Lennard and Barrett, in which he draws attention to the remarkable
fact that there had been only two owners of Belhus between Dacre
Barrett and himself, namely Lord Dacre and his illegitimate son,
Sir Thomas Barrett-Lennard.

Among the delightful family stories told by Sir Thomas about his
ancestors is one that relates how, while Lord Dacre and his brother-
in-law, Lord Chancellor Camden, were strolling near the village
stocks at Aveley, Lord Camden decided that it might be a good idea
to see for himself what it felt like to be confined in them. Lord
Dacre readily gratified his curiosity by sentencing him. But they
found that getting out of the stocks was much more difficult than
getting into them, and the Lord Chancellor had to remain in the un-
dignified situation while help was called. Some time later, when
punishment in the stocks was referred to in court in a tone less
serious than Lord Camden, who was presiding, thought proper, he
interrupted with the remark: 'I have tried them brother, and they
are not pleasant ! '

The glories of Belhus have now departed. The house was demolished
in the late 1950's. An estate had been built close to the park by the
London County Council.

BARRINGTON

The Barringtons of Hatfield Broad Oak were referred to by Camden
as 'that eminent family'. Since then much has been written about the
part they played in Essex history, yet few memorials of their former
greatness remain. A brass at Hatfield Broad Oak commemorates
Thomas, who died in 1472; a marble monument with two cupids weep-
ing over an urn commemorates Sir John, who died in 1691; floor
slabs remind us of other members of the family, including Sir Charles,
who died in 1715, and with whose death the baronetcy ceased to be
connected with Hatfield Broad Oak and became linked with an estate
in the Isle of Wight.

The common ancestor of the Essex Barringtons was Eustace, forester, or woodward, of Hatfield Forest under the Gernon (q.v.), or
Mountfitchet, family. His offspring lived at Barrington Hall and
flourished throughout the Middle Ages in a steady sort of way,
quietly acquiring land in Hatfield Peverel, Stansted Mountfitchet,
Takeley, Little Clacton, Writtle, Havering, Barking, Chigwell,
Ramsden, Birchanger and elsewhere. When the Mountfitchet family
became extinct in the reign of Henry III, the Barringtons succeeded

them both in royal service and as landowners, so that Camden was
able to write: 'The Barrington family are greatly enriched by the
estates of the Mountfitchets which fell to them.' Proud of their hereditary connection with the Essex forest, they jealously guarded
their rights in it. On the attainter of Edward Stafford, Duke of
Buckingham, the manor and forest of Hatfield fell to the Crown, and
Henry VIII granted the woodwardship, with a fee of fourpence a day,
to Nicholas Clark, one of the forest walkers who had been appointed
by the Duke of Buckingham. This provoked Thomas Bonham, guardian
to John Barrington, to present a petition to Wolsey, informing him
that the woodwardship of Hatfield Forest had been held for centuries
by the Barrington family under a grant made by Henry I, which had
been confirmed by several succeeding sovereigns, and praying that
Clark be removed forthwith and John Barrington appointed. The
petition was successful and the request granted.

This John Barrington married a granddaughter of Henry, Lord
Marney of Marney (q.v.). Their son, Thomas, married first, Alice,
daughter of Henry Parker, Lord Morley (q.v.), and secondly,
Winifred, daughter and co-heiress of Henry Pole, Lord Montagu,
granddaughter of Sir Richard Pole by Margaret Plantagenet, Countess of Salisbury, which gave the Barringtons alliance with the royal
blood. In consequence of this marriage, Thomas Barrington was entitled to quarter the royal arms of England.

This second Lady Barrington brought to the family the manors of
Clavering and Bushey, and as co-heir of her father, large estates
in Yorkshire, Lincolnshire, Essex and the Isle of Wight, all of
which descended to her son, Sir Francis. In the meantime Sir Thomas
had purchased the dissolved Priory of Hatfield Broad Oak and taken
up residence there.

Sir Francis Barrington (1550-1628) represented Essex in several
parliaments in Elizabeth's reign, in all the parliaments of James I,
and in the first three of Charles I. He was created a baronet in 1611.
His wife, Joan, was the daughter of Sir Henry Cromwell of
Hinchingbrook and aunt of the Protector.

At his death in 1628, Sir Francis was succeeded by Sir Thomas,
2nd baronet, who was followed by the 3rd,4th, and 5th baronets, all
of whom continued the family record of service and figure prominently
in county histories. At the death without issue of Sir Charles, the
5th baronet, in 1715, the Hatfield property went to the son of his
sister, Anne, who married Charles Shales; the baronetcy and other
properties went to his cousin as heir male. There were five more
baronets in the line before the title became extinct with the death of
the 10th baronet in 1833. The Irish baronetcy of the same name was
created in 1831, but the family who held it do not claim any connection
with the Essex line.

A son of Anne Barrington and Charles Shales took the name of John
Shales Barrington, and built himself a new house at Hatfield, but
never lived in it. His residence was at Waltham Cross in Hertfordshire; but when he died in 1788 he was buried with great pomp at
Hatfield Broad Oak. As he died unmarried the estates passed into
the possession of the 8th baronet. Sir John Barrington, 9th baronet,
began to show interest in Hatfield. He actually made alterations to
the hall; but he also died unmarried, and the line finally became

extinct with the death without male issue of Sir Fitzwilliam, the 10th
and last baronet.

In addition to well known sources, See:
W. Clayton and G. A. Lowndes, E.A.T. n.s. i. 251; ii. 3
J. H. Round: E.R.xxx1.1

BARRINGTON

John Barrington (d. 1416) and his wife (d. 1420) are commemorated
in the stone and fragment of brass at the west end of the nave of
Rayleigh church. John Barrington of Rayleigh was keeper of the
King's Park, a large tract of forest land and a portion of Royal
Forest. The north chapel is believed to have been built by him as
a chantry chapel.

See A. G. Fryer: Rayleigh in Past Days

BASTWICK

John Bastwick (1593-1654), writer of scurrilous tracts directed
mainly against bishops (who are depicted in a series of anecdotes
as gluttonous, lecherous, brutal and arrogant), was born at
Writtle. He served in the Dutch Army, took a doctorate of medicine
at Padua, and practised - when the Law allowed it - at Colchester.
For a tirade against the Roman Catholic Church, printed in Holland
about 1633, he was fined £1,000, excommunicated, prohibited from
practising physic, and ordered to remain in prison until he recanted.
His response was to write a criticism of the court that convicted him,
taxing the English bishops with favouring popery. For an outburst in
1637 he was brought before the Star Chamber, fined £5,000, ordered
to be pilloried, to have his ears cut off, and to endure perpetual
imprisonment. The Long Parliament of 1640 quashed the conviction
and made him a reparation of £5,000, which he never received. Four
years later his wife was granted an allowance for the maintenance of
herself and her husband; but by 1648 he was again publishing tracts,
at this stage directed against the Independents.

BATE-DUDLEY

Sir Henry Bate-Dudley (1745-1824) was one of the most colourful
characters in the Essex of his day. He was parson, sportsman,
magistrate, and for a time editor of the 'Morning Post'. Garrick,
Hogarth, Gainsborough, and Mrs. Siddons were personal friends,
and he moved easily in both town and country society. One thing he
did not enjoy. Essex roads were notoriously bad in his day, and he
lost no opportunity of complaining about them. Fortunately, he did
more than complain. He showed what could be done by improving the
roads in his own parish of Bradwell-juxta-Mare, where he also
spent over £28,000 in draining the marshes and generally improving
the land, notably by mole-draining. In all, he reclaimed 250 acres of
marshland round Bradwell.

While combining the roles of rector and squire he was Master of an
Essex pack of foxhounds. His most famous run ended on the roof of
Cricksea church. The fox in desperation scrambled up an ivy covered
buttress, followed by Sir Henry and three couples of hounds, and
was actually killed on the leads of the chancel. An elegant extension
to Sir Henry Bate-Dudley's home at Bradwell, later called Bradwell
Lodge, was designed by John Johnson (q.v.).

BATTEN

Sir William Batten (d. 1667), admiral, lived at Walthamstow with
his charming wife and his black servant, Mingo. Pepys tells us that
he lived like a prince himself, but made little provision for his
family. Pepys, however, may not have been entirely fair in what he
had to say about Batten, who in 1642 was appointed second in command
of the fleet under the Earl of Warwick, and continued in this command
until 1647. The reason for the suspicions of Batten's integrity found
in Pepys and other chroniclers are not difficult to explain. He changed sides more than once, so neither Parliament nor the king was ever
sure of him.

While on the side of Parliament, Batten went so far as to bombard
Bridlington while the queen was staying there. It was said that the
cannon balls fell so close that she was obliged to take refuge in a
ditch in her night attire. After a dispute with his superiors he deserted, took possession of the Constant Warwick, one of the best
ships afloat, and sailed across to Holland with several other ships
to form the nucleus of the fleet subsequently commanded by Prince
Rupert. He was knighted for the service; but Bridlington was never
forgiven.

At the Restoration he was reinstated in his office of surveyor of the
Navy, which he continued to hold to the end of his life. Of the Prince
Rupert episode, Pepys has a story under the date 4th June 1664:
'Mr. Coventry discoursing this noon about Sir W.
Batten (what a sad fellow he is !) told me how the
King told him the other day how Sir W. Batten,
being in the ship with him and Prince Rupert when
they expected to fight with Warwicke, did walk up
and down sweating with a napkin under his throat
to dry up his sweat: and that Prince Rupert being
a most jealous man, and particularly of Batten, do
walk up and down swearing bloodily to the King,
that Batten had a mind to betray them to-day and
that the napkin was a signal: "but, by God," says
he, "if things go ill, the first thing I will do is
shoot him." '

There are many references to Sir William Batten in Pepys. In July
1662 he and Sir W. Warren discussed the vice-admiral's iniquities
for four solid hours, forgetting even to eat and drink; but in
February 1665, when Sir William was taken ill, Pepys wrote:
'I am at a loss whether it will be better for me to
have him die, because he is a bad man, or live,
for fear a worse should come.'
He did live that time; but a later illness carried him off and Pepys
was able to record the splendour of his funeral. Batten was M.P.
for Rochester from 1661 and master of Trinity House from 1663.

BAYNARD

Ralph Baynard, (fl. 1086), whose capital mansion was Baynard's
Castle in London, was rewarded by William the Conqueror with 25
lordships in Essex. These were forfeited by his grandson, William,
who joined a conspiracy against Henry I. Henry III restored to Hugh
Baynard all the land his ancestors had held in the villages of Messing,
Birch, Baddow, and other places, with the privilege and liberty of
hunting in all the forests of England.

In 1104 Juga Baynard, lady of Little Dunmow, gave lands to the recently dedicated church at Little Dunmow. The barony held by the Baynards eventually passed to the FitzWalters (q.v.), who held Dunmow Priory until the Dissolution.

The Messing estate came into the possession of the Clibborne family about 1600. Christopher Clibborne (b. 1606) possessed Baynards and Harburghs at Messing.

See K. Fry: E.A.T., v 265

BAYNING

Paul, Viscount Bayning (d. 1629), High Sheriff of Essex in 1617, was raised to the peerage as Baron Bayning of Horkesley in 1627 and created viscount later in the same year. He came of a family that moved to Dedham from Nayland in Suffolk towards the end of the 15th century and became so wealthy that Viscount Bayning died worth £153,000. Chamberlain (Letters) tells us that he obtained a divorce from his wife in 1600, and that it was said in the City that he retired from the office of alderman to spite her when he found that she aspired to be Lady Mayoress.

His son, also Paul, lived at Little Bentley Hall, a splendid house that stood for less than 50 years. He has a memorial in Little Bentley church. One of the 1st Viscount's daughters married the 20th and last Earl of Oxford (q.v.) and with her wealth revived for a short time the dissipated fortunes of the de Veres; but the 20th Earl and his countess died without issue.

The countess's sister, Penelope, married Philip Herbert, youngest son of Philip, Earl of Pembroke and Montgomery, and after his death, John Wentworth. She also left no surviving issue. But through his granddaughter, the Duchess of Cleveland, Viscount Bayning became the ancestor of more than one ducal house.

See H. G. Gillespie: Gent. Mag. ix (1940-6), 429

BEAUCOCK

The virtues of Sir Edward Beaucock (1617-1665), courtier, of Bradwell-juxta-Coggeshall are so engagingly set out on his black marble memorial stone in the floor of the church chancel, that all that is needed here is a translation of the inscription into English. It runs:

'Here lies Edward Beaucock, Doctor of Medicine, Knight of the Robe, one of the Gentlemen of the King's Privy Chamber, Master Extraordinary in Chancery, a most active Justice of the Peace. Born in Oxfordshire, died in this County of Essex. A man very easy of access, he seemed born to give good counsel to the human race. Affable to all, he was nevertheless sparing of his friendship; but he made up for the small number of those with whom he was intimate by the firmness of his attachment to them. The one man whose friendship was worth cultivating to the fullest extent. Prematurely snatched away by a pestilential fever he showed that not even the integrity of the most distinguished can secure immunity from an untimely fate. Though recently settled in a strange neighbourhood, he lived without exciting ill-will, and died mourned by those whom he knew, and regretted even by those unknown to him, 15th Sept. 1665.'

Sir Edward was born at Dorchester-on-Thames. From the
Establishment Books of the Royal Household, belonging to the
Lord Chamberlain's department, now deposited at the Public Record
Office, we know that he was appointed a gentleman of His Majesty's
Privy Chamber in Extraordinary in 1661, and knighted in 1665, the
year of his death.

See H. L. Elliot: E.A.T. n.s. x 43

BEAUFORT

Margaret Beaufort, Countess of Richmond and Derby (1443-1509),
mother of Henry VII, held a number of estates in Essex, including
Wakes Hall, Wakes Colne, the manors of Lamarsh, Ridgewell, and
Thorington, and probably that of Salisbury Hall, Walthamstow.
According to Morant her statue stood on the east side of the battle-
ments of Dedham Church. When she founded St. John's College,
Cambridge, she directed that the revenues of Ridgewell and
Thorington should be used.

BEAUMONT

The fine brasses at Wivenhoe are to: William, Viscount Beaumont
and Lord Bardolfe, 1507, and Elizabeth, his widow, who became
the wife of John, Earl of Oxford, 1537.

BEAUMONT

Sir George Howland Beaumont (1753-1827), art patron and landscape
painter, lived at the Clock House, Great Dunmow. The family is
chiefly associated with Leicestershire, where they were seated for
more than 900 years. When Sir George rebuilt Coleorton Hall in
1804-7, the gardens were planned by Wordsworth.

As far as can be traced, the association of the Beaumonts with
Essex began about 1670 when William Beaumont, younger son of
Sir Thomas of Stoughton, Leicestershire, settled at Dunmow, of
which in 1678 his brother became vicar. In 1726 George Beaumont,
William's grandson, was born at the Clock House. He strengthened
the local link by marrying in 1751 Rachel, daughter of Michael
Howland of Stonehall, Dunmow. This was the George who succeeded
to the baronetcy and family estates in Leicestershire. At his death
in 1762, his son of the same name succeeded as 7th baronet at the
age of eight and eventually became one of the most distinguished art
patrons of his day, counting Johnson, Reynolds, Constable, Scott,
Byron and Coleridge, as well as Wordsworth, among his friends and
played a major part in the foundation of the National Gallery, to
which he presented several valuable pictures.

Sir George was brought up at the Clock House, and continued to
live there until he had completed the rebuilding of the older family
home at Coleorton. The Clock House then became the dower house
of the Beaumonts, and was for a long time the home of the 6th
baronet's widow. When she died at the age of 98 in 1814 she was
buried with her husband in the chancel of Dunmow church.

Coleridge visited Dunmow in 1804 to discuss Christabel with Sir
George and Lady Beaumont, who was a granddaughter of Lord Chief
Justice Willes. Wordsworth was at Dunmow in 1809, and both poets
were delighted with the place, which Coleridge described as

'another Grasmere'. Wordsworth, in the first collected edition of
his poems, paid tribute to Sir George and the happiness he had
found in his friendship. On hearing of Sir George's death in 1827
Sir Walter Scott wrote in his diary: 'Sir George Beaumont's dead;
by far the most sensible and pleasing man I ever knew; kind, too,
in his nature and generous.'

See J. V. Mackenzie: E.R. xxviii 152

BECHE

Of Thomas Beche, last abbot of St. John's Colchester, who was
condemned to death and hanged on refusing to acknowledge the
supremacy of Henry VIII, the story is told that the bailiff invited
him to a feast, and under cover of this pretence of goodwill and
friendship presented him with a warrant and hurried him off to
execution.

BEDELL

William Bedell (1571-1642), Bishop of Kilmore and Ardagh, was
born at Black Notley. In 1604 he became chaplain to Sir Henry
Wotton and accompanied him on his embassy to Venice. There he
became friendly with Antonio de Dominis, Archbishop of Spalatro,
with whom he was joint-author of De Republica Ecclesiastica. In
1627 he became Provost of Trinity College, Dublin, and in 1629
Bishop of Kilmore and Ardagh, one see of which he resigned on
grounds of scruple. When rebellion broke out in 1642 he believed
himself safe because of the veneration in which he was held. His
was the only house in the county of Cavan not violated; but in
December of that year he was ordered to evict the people who had
taken shelter under his roof. On refusing to comply he was cast into
prison at the castle of Cloughboughter together with his family.
After about three weeks confinement he and his children were exchanged for some of the principal rebels; but he died on 9th
February 1642, as the result of hardships endured in prison.

See E.R. xxxix 10, A. Hills: E.R. xliv 94

BENDISH

Monuments at Steeple Bumpstead commemorate members of the
Bendish family, of whom the most distinguished was Sir Thomas,
who in 1647 was sent as ambassador extraordinary to the Ottoman
Porte. The first Bendish of Steeple Bumpstead was Thomas, who
purchased land there and married Alice, daughter of William Helion
of the adjoining parish. His grandson, Edmund (d. 1392), accompanied Edward III to the Siege of Calais, 1347-8. Edmund's descendant, Thomas Bendish, who married Dorothy, daughter of Richard
Cutts (q.v.) of Arkesden, was created a baronet in 1611.

Sir Thomas Bendish, 2nd baronet, said by Morant to be 'a man of
great sense and resolution, and steadfastly loyal to his Prince,
Charles I', took a leading part in 1642 in drawing up proposals for
peace between king and parliament. For this he was imprisoned in
the Tower for 22 months and his estate sequestered. In 1647 he
entered upon his 14 years as ambassador at the Turkish court, where
he displayed great courage and endured many insults. Several amus-
ing anecdotes have come down from his stay at Constantinople. On
one occasion the Grand Vizier had a chair removed from the room

before an audience in order to ensure that Sir Thomas would have
to remain standing; but Sir Thomas was equal to the situation. He
simply made one of his gentlemen kneel down and lean on his hands
to provide a seat for him. In 1653 he was even bold enough to stand
up to Cromwell, who had sent out Sir Richard Lawrence to replace
him. Sir Thomas refused to leave. He stayed until recalled by
Charles II. On his return he lived at Bower Hall (demolished in
1926) until his death in 1672.

The Bendish baronetcy became extinct at the death of his grandson,
Sir Henry Bendish, 4th baronet, in 1717.

BENDLOWES (or BENLOWES)

William Bendlowes (1516-84), son of Christopher Bendlowes of
Great Bardfield, was a bencher of Lincoln's Inn and a governor
for several years from 1576. He was greatly esteemed for his skill
in drawing up reports of legal proceedings. Some of his collections
of these were published during his lifetime, others are in the Harleian Collection of MSS. at the British Museum. Bendlowes founded
the free school at Bardfield in 1550, according to Morant; but more
probably by his will in 1584. This was later merged into a National
School.

His son of the same name followed his father in the Law and died in
1613. Another son of William (1), Andrew, was the grandfather of
Edward Benlowes, the poet.

The Benlowes family were of Yorkshire stock. William (I) purchased
land in Great Bardfield, Bocking, Halstead, Sible Hedingham, and
other Essex parishes. His home was Place Farm, where his initials
and the date, 1564, are carved on a corner bracket of the house. A
brass in the church shows how proud he was of having been for 73
days sole Serjeant-at-Law. He was a generous local benefactor who
endowed charities for the benefit of the poor in several Essex parishes,
together with a chantry in Great Bardfield church, where he was
buried.

Edward Benlowes (1602-76), after matriculating at St.John's,
Cambridge, in 1620, travelled the Continent with a tutor, visiting
seven courts of princes. He was the friend and patron of Francis
Quarles (q.v.), Sir William Davenant, Phineas Fletcher and other
poets. After being a Roman Catholic in youth be became a fanatical
Protestant, and as such appears in Pope's Dunciad (1712). At the
end of his travels, Benlowes settled at Brent Hall, Finchingfield,
to the life of a cultured gentleman and virtuoso, gathering about him
books, pictures, engravings, music and curios to engage the interest
of the many friends who visited him. Anagrams, epigrams, mottoes,
and similiar verbal conceits, together with a long succession of
complimentary addresses and poems flowed from his pen; but he put
too much faith in mountebanks, and at the age of 60 was confined in
the debtor's prison in Oxford Castle. His friends obtained his release, and his remaining years were passed as a poor scholar, spending much of his time in the Bodleian. There are two portraits of him
at St. John's, Cambridge, of which he had been a benefactor in his
days of affluence.

See E.R. xxvii 113

BENHAM

William Gurney Benham (1859-1944), High Steward of Colchester, compiler of Benham's Book of Quotations and author of many books and articles on Essex history, was a member of Colchester borough council for over 50 years and did more than anyone else during his lifetime to preserve the character and status of the borough. He was mayor, 1892-3, 1908-9, 1933-4, and in 1933 became an honorary freeman and High Steward. From 1934 to 1944 he edited the Essex Review. He was also an amateur artist of considerable skill and for many years drew humorous toast-cards for Colchester Oyster Feast. He was knighted in 1935. His brother, Charles, was associated with him in many literary enterprises, and was himself an Essex author of repute.

BENSTEDE

Sir John de Benstede (d. 1323 ?), Chancellor of the Exchequer under Edward I, judge and Keeper of the Great Seal, founded a family that continued in Essex until the reign of Henry VII. He was one of the commissioners appointed to treat for peace with Robert the Bruce. He gave his name to Higham Bensted in Walthamstow.

BENSUSAN

Samuel Levy Bensusan (1872-1958) was born into a strict Jewish family at Dulwich. As a journalist he edited Jewish World, and was music critic to the Illustrated London News, the Sketch, and Vanity Fair. His early books were accounts of his travels in countries at that time unfamiliar to tourists. From these studies of far-away places he turned in 1908 to the most homely scenes still unchronicled in England, aspiring to do for the Essex marshes something of what Hardy did for Dorset. His first marshland home was at Asheldham. From there he removed to Mote Cottage, between St. Lawrence and Bradwell-juxta-Mare. Later he lived at both Dunmow and Epping, where he sat on the local bench. In 1932 he removed to his best-known home, Godfreys, a gamekeeper's cottage at Langham, near Colchester, where he remained until shortly before his death in 1958, sitting as a J.P. on the Lexden and Winstree bench until disqualified by age.

Bensusan's chronicles of rural life, which centre in the imaginary Maychester, can never be surpassed as portrayals of the traditional Essex character, now disappearing for ever. Such works as Marshland Voices, Annals of Maychester, and Marshland Calling should remain county classics.

BENTON

Gerald Montagu Benton (1881-1959), antiquary, was a leading authority on the county's antiquities for nearly half a century. He published an account of the monumental brasses of Cambridgeshire in 1902, and from 1911, when he became curate to Canon Steele at Saffron Walden, his studies of Essex antiquities were continuous until his death 58 years later. His standards for recording were high and he demanded similarly meticulous accuracy from everyone who aspired to work in the same fields.

Benton became vicar of Fingringhoe in 1922. He held the living for 37 years. His life's work was dedicated to the interests of the Essex

Archaeological Society, of which he was Hon. Sec. from 1924 to
1950, President from 1950 to 1955, and Hon. Editor from 1929 to
his death.

BENTON

Philip Benton (1815-1898), historian of the Rochford Hundred,
lived as a gentleman-farmer at 'Beauchamps', Shopland, and Little
Wakering Hall. The first part of his history (16 pages) was published in 1867, the last to be published in his lifetime (No. 58) in 1888.
He had by that time retired from farming and taken up residence in
Southend, intending to devote himself to the completion of the work;
but he was struck down with paralysis before he had completed the
final sections, which were to include Southchurch, Sutton, Great
and Little Wakering, etc., the parishes in which he had lived much
of his life and knew well.

BERIFFE

Seven brasses at Brightlingsea commemorate members of the
Beriffe family, of 'Jacobs', and range from 1496 to 1578. The family
built a great part of the church, which has their merchant mark
displayed on it. John Beriffe, of Brightlingsea, who died in 1496,
had three wives and 19 children - 13 sons and six daughters.

BERNERS

Juliana Berners, who wrote a treatise on hunting, hawking, and
heraldry, which was among the first books to be printed in the
English language, belonged to the Berners Roding family. She was
the daughter of Sir James Berners of Berners Roding, who was executed in 1388 for his loyalty to Richard II. Her writing was done
while prioress of Sopwell Nunnery, St. Albans. The first edition
of her treatise was printed in 1481. She is thought to have spent her
youth at court and to have shared in the woodland sports then in
vogue.

John Berners, who died in 1525, was Gentleman Usher to Princess
Elizabeth, daughter of Edward IV, and afterwards Steward to
Edward V. His son, John, was Receiver of Estates in Essex and
Suffolk to Queen Catherine Parr.

BERRINGHAM

Benjamin Shepherd Berringham, autobiographer, was the author of
Exciting Leaves (1891), in which he describes his ordination and
curacies in Essex.

BESSE

Joseph Besse (1683?-1757), Quaker writer, known for his Collection
of Sufferings of the People Called Quakers, was a writing master at
Colchester.

BIGG

William Redman Bigg (1755-1828), painter, had associations with
Colchester. He was elected a Royal Academician in 1814. Most of
his subjects had a strong domestic appeal. Among the best known
were 'Shipwrecked Sailor Boy', 'Boys relieving a Blind Man', and
'Black Monday'.

BINGHAM

Edward Bingham (1829-1901) of Castle Hedingham, potter, was the
son of another potter of the same name who moved into Castle
Hedingham from Gestingthorpe in 1837. By the time he was ten, the
younger Edward was already assisting his father by modelling leaves,
flowers, snakes, and other natural objects for decoration. After ex-
perimenting unsuccessfully with various forms of ornamental pottery
he hit on the trellis design, formed with plaited clay, which in the
50's and 60's became popular in Victorian drawing rooms and conserv-
atories, and was known as Hedingham ware. It was not until after he
read a life of Josiah Wedgwood in 1874 that he became proficient
with glazed ware, which opened up new possibilities. One of the
most popular productions of the period was the Essex jug, with
medallions illustrating the history of the county. In 1894 specimens
of his work were exhibited at the Home Arts and Industries Exhibition at the Albert Hall. His mark was a raised impression of the
Castle Keep.

The Hedingham Pottery was entirely carried on by members of the
Bingham family who dug the clay, mixed the colours, designed and
made the ware, and finally fired the kilns.

In 1899, Bingham's elder son took over the business and sold it two
years later to Messrs Hexter, Humpherson, & Co., of Newton Abbot,
Devon. The firm then became the Essex Art Pottery Co. In 1905 it
was closed, and Hedingham ware is now collected. One of Bingham's
showpieces was a model of Hedingham Castle.

BLACKMORE

Sir Richard Blackmore (d. 1729), physician-in-ordinary to William
III and Queen Anne, has a monument with a Latin inscription in
Boxted church. He wrote extensively on medical, religious, and
literary subjects. His poem Creation was highly praised by Dr.
Johnson.

BLEWIT

Martha Blewit (d. 1681) of the Swan Inn, Birdbrook, has a gravestone recording that she married nine husbands. The same stone
records that Robert Hogan of the same village had seven wives.

BLOMFIELD

Sir Arthur Blomfield (1829-99), architect, was the fourth son of
Charles James Blomfield, Bishop of London (q.v.), and brother of
Alfred Blomfield, suffragan Bishop of Colchester. Among his works
in Essex were Bancroft School, Woodford, and churches at
Colchester, High Beach, Leytonstone, along with much restoration
work, notably at Alphamstone, Birchanger, Colchester, Great
Holland, Kelvedon, Matching, Pitsea, etc. He died and was buried
at Broadway, Worcs., where he had a country home.

BLOMFIELD

Charles James Blomfield (1786-1857), Bishop of London, held the
livings of Great and Little Chesterford and the archdeaconry of
Colchester before becoming Bishop of Chester in 1824, from which
he was translated to London in 1828. In his Letter on the Present
Neglect of the Lord's Day, published in 1830, he describes the

lawlessness to be found in the Saffron Walden district at the time
of the Newmarket Races. It was the custom for horses to be changed
at the Crown inn, near the church at Great Chesterford, and
Blomfield relates how 'More than forty pairs of horses have sometimes been changed there on Easter Day, a great proportion of them
while I was celebrating Divine Service.' With Lord Braybrooke's
support he got the first day of the races changed from Monday to
Tuesday.

BLOUNT, Elizabeth See FITZROY

BOADICEA (or BOUDICCA)

The British warrior queen was strongly supported by the men of
Essex in her rebellion, A.D. 61, when Colchester was attacked
fiercely and much of the Roman colony destroyed. She marched
across Essex to take London and St. Albans, putting to death,
according to Tacitus, 70,000 Romans during the absence of Suetonius
Paulinus, the Roman governor of Britain, who was in Anglesea when
she attacked London. On his return with overwhelming forces she
suffered final defeat, and to avoid falling into the conqueror's hands
took poison. Tradition has it that her last stand was made at
Ambresbury Banks in Epping Forest, but there is no reliable evidence for this.

BOHUN

Humphrey de Bohun, 1st Earl of Essex of the Bohun line (d. 1275),
High Constable of England, was the son of the Humphrey de Bohun
who married Maud, heiress of the de Mandeville earls of Essex
(q.v.). He fought against de Montfort in 1263 and was one of the 12
arbitrators of the Statute of Marlborough, by which the disinherited
rebels were permitted to negotiate for pardon.

He was succeeded by his grandson, Humphrey, 2nd Earl of Essex
(d. 1298), also High Constable, who joined Roger Bigod, Earl of
Norfolk, in opposing Edward I's reforms and was deprived of his
hereditary office in 1297.

Humphrey, 3rd Earl of Essex (1276-1322), married a daughter of
Edward I and had the office of High Constable restored to him. He
fought against Robert Bruce, and after being taken prisoner at
Bannockburn was exchanged for Bruce's wife. He was killed at the
Battle of Boroughbridge, fighting on the side of the barons, and left
five sons and two daughters.

John, eldest son of Humphrey the 3rd Earl, succeeded to the earldom
of Hereford as well as that of Essex. At his death without issue in
1335 he was buried in the abbey of Stratford Langthorne.

John, 4th Earl of Essex, was succeeded by his brother, Humphrey,
5th Earl, who achieved fame for his valiant part in the Hundred
Years' War. He died without heir and was succeeded by his nephew,
Humphrey, 6th Earl, the son of his younger brother, William. With
the death of this last Humphrey in 1373 the male line of the Bohuns
came to an end and the many family titles became extinct. But the
vast Bohun estates were divided between the last earl's two daughters,
Eleanor and Mary. Eleanor married Thomas of Woodstock (son of
Edward III), Duke of Gloucester and Earl of Buckingham. The earldom of Essex was later added to these titles.

This was the Duke of Gloucester of whom the story is told of the surprise visit to Pleshey of Richard II with a company of nobles and trained bands, who had marched through the night from London to arrest Gloucester, the king's own uncle. Gloucester came out to meet the king at the head of a procession of clergy and proceeded into the chapel for mass. There he was seized and carried off to Calais, where he was done to death. His body was subsequently brought to England and buried in Westminster Abbey. His widow, who brought him the Essex lands, retired to Barking Abbey, where she died in 1399. By the time of her death she had recovered most of the lands confiscated by Richard, together with the hereditary right to the title of High Constable of England.

There was only one son of the Gloucester marriage. He died young without issue, and the family estates passed to a daughter, Anne, who married William Bourchier. After lying dormant for a time the earldom of Essex was revived in 1461 in the person of their son, Henry Bourchier (q.v.).

BOOTHBY and BOOTHBY-HEATHCOTE

Thomas Boothby, a London merchant who died in 1622, bought the manor of Chingford and established his family there. His son, Thomas, was created a baronet in 1660. At the death of the last male heir of the Boothby family of Chingford, in 1774, the estate passed to his half-sister, Lydia, daughter and co-heiress of Benjamin Moyer of Low Leyton, who in 1764 married John Heathcote.

BOSANQUET

The Bosanquet family came to Leytonstone in 1743, when Samuel Bosanquet bought Forest House at the end of James Lane. They were London merchants of Huguenot extraction. Samuel Bosanquet, who died in 1765, was Governor of the Bank of England and chairman of Essex Quarter Sessions.

Mary Bosanquet (1739-1815) was the daughter of Samuel. Like many other young ladies of her class, she was given to good works, particularly after her conversion to Methodism. She founded an orphanage for destitute girls in Leytonstone, with a young woman named Ann Tripp as governess. Their object was to take girls off the streets and train them for situations in domestic service. In 1768 the school was moved to Morley in Yorkshire, and Mary continued to direct it there until she met the Rev. John Fletcher of Madeley, Shropshire, who was designated by John Wesley as his successor in the leadership of the Methodist Church. On marrying him in 1781 she transferred the school to Shropshire.

Fifty years after Mary Fletcher's death, one of her relatives gave land at Leyton for a chapel to be built in her memory. The Mary Fletcher Memorial Chapel, built in 1877, was closed in 1969.

Charles Bosanquet, second son of Samuel and brother of Mary, was Governor of the South Sea Company. He moved from Leytonstone to Northumberland, where he died at Rock in 1850.

Forest House (formerly Goring House) stood in the grounds of Whipps Cross Hospital until 1964, when it was demolished.
See HOUBLON.

BOURCHIER

The first of the family in Essex was John de Bourchier (d. 1328),
who acquired one half of the manor of Stanstead Hall, Halstead,
by marrying the only daughter of Walter de Colchester. He became
a judge of the King's Bench in 1321. At his death he was buried in
Halstead church. In 1330 his eldest son, Robert, 1st Lord Bourchier
(d. 1349), was granted by Edward III free warren of all his demesne
lands in Halstead, Stanstead, Markshall, Stisted, Coggeshall, and
17 other lordships in Essex. Six years later he had licence to impark woods in Stanstead, and in 1341 permission to convert his
house into a fortified castle. After representing Essex in Parliament
in 1330, 1332, 1338 and 1339 he was appointed Lord Chancellor in
1340. In 1346 he fought at the side of the Black Prince at Crecy.
Three years afterwards he died of the Black Death, leaving two sons,
John and William. The younger son, William, was the ancestor of the
Bourchiers of Little Easton.

John, 2nd Lord Bourchier, K.G. (1329-1400), who served as Governor of Flanders, has a fine tomb in Halstead church. His only son,
Bartholomew, 3rd Lord Bourchier (1374-1409), the last of the
Bourchier barons to be buried at Halstead, is commemorated by a
fine brass in the south aisle.

The barony passed at his death to Henry (d. 1483), great-grandson
of the 1st Lord Bourchier and grandson of William, his second son.
He married Isabel of York, daughter of Richard Plantagenet, Earl
of Cambridge, and aunt of Edward IV. Shortly after his nephew's
accession to the throne, Henry, Lord Bourchier, was confirmed in
the earldom of Essex in right of his grandmother, Eleanor de Bohun,
wife of Thomas of Woodstock and elder daughter of Humphrey de
Bohun, 6th Earl of Essex. At his death in 1483, five days before the
king's death, he and his countess were buried at Beeleigh, near
Maldon. The monument to their memory was moved to Little Easton
when Beeleigh Abbey was dissolved in 1536. It is now in the Bourchier
(or Maynard) chapel.

Henry, 1st Earl of Essex of the Bourchier line, was succeeded by
his grandson, Henry, 2nd Earl (d. 1540), son of the eldest of his
seven sons by Isabel of York. The 2nd Earl was a member of Henry
VII's Privy Council and Captain of the Bodyguard to Henry VIII,
whom he escorted to the Field of the Cloth of Gold as Earl Marshal.
He was the last of the Bourchier earls. His grandson, Walter
Devereux (1541?-76) (q.v.) was created Viscount Hereford in 1550
by Edward VI and Earl of Essex in 1572. His first wife was Mary,
daughter of Thomas Grey (q.v.), Marquis of Dorset.

BOURCHIER

The Bourchiers of Little Stambridge did not claim connection with
the family of the earls of Essex. Thomas Bowcher (as he signed his
name) purchased the manor of Little Stambridge about 1587, but he
does not appear to have resided there. His son, Sir James Bourchier
was the first of the family to live at Little Stambridge, but he cannot
have done so before 1621. He died in 1635 aged 63. His daughter,
Elizabeth, married Oliver Cromwell.

BRAMSTON

The earliest member of the family to settle in Essex was the son of
Roger Bramston of Whitechapel who married Priscilla, daughter of
Francis Clovile of West Hanningfield Hall. Their son, Sir John
Bramston the elder (1577-1654), carried the family to eminence.
He was born at Maldon and received his early education at Maldon
Grammar School before passing on to Cambridge and the Middle
Temple. After building up a large practice at the Bar he was appointed Queen's Serjeant in 1632, King's Serjeant in 1634, and Lord
Chief Justice in 1635. In the same year he bought Skreens, Roxwell,
where his family lived for more than 200 years. In 1640, along with
five other judges, he was impeached by the Long Parliament for sub-
scribing opinion on ship-money, and required to give surety of
£10,000 to stand his trial. The feeling of Parliament does not appear
to have been very strong against him. In 1647 the Commons nominated
him one of the lords commissioners of the Great Seal; but he persuaded them to pass him over. Similarly, when Cromwell in 1654
urged him to take office again as Lord Chief Justice he pleaded age
and begged to be excused. He died at Skreens the same year and
was buried in Roxwell church. Clarendon called him 'a man of great
learning and integrity', and Fuller described him as being 'accomplished with all qualities requisite for a person of his place and
profession ... deep learning, solid judgment, integrity of life, and
gravity of behaviour,' adding that 'he deserved to live in better times.'

His son, Sir John Bramston the younger (1611-1700), followed his
father in the practice of law and politics. He represented both
Maldon and Chelmsford in Parliament, and frequently acted as chairman of committees of the whole House of Commons. His Autobiography,
published in 1845, described vividly the changing fortunes of his life
and times.

Francis Bramston, third surviving son of Sir John Bramston the
elder, was called to the Bar in 1642; but according to his brother
the troubled times drove him out of his profession, 'the drumming
trumpets blowing his gown over his ears.' At the Restoration he was
made steward of the king's courts in Essex and of the Liberty of
Havering. He was appointed a Baron of the Exchequer in 1678; but
within a year he retired with a pension, and died unmarried in 1683.

BRANDENHAM

Lionel de Brandenham, a powerful landowner in the reign of Edward
III, lord of the manor of Langenhoe, challenged the exclusive right
of Colchester to fishery of the Colne by enclosing part of the river.
Commissioners appointed to enquire into the affair ordered the enclosures to be removed. Enraged by this judgment, Brandenham
laid siege to the town for three months, with the intention of burning
it down.

BRAYBROOKE, BARONS See GRIFFIN and NEVILLE

BROWN

John Brown (1715-66), rector of Great Horkesley, 1756-61, published
tragedies, epics, odes, sermons and essays. He committed suicide
on being forbidden by his doctors to go to St. Petersburg to take up
an educational appointment.

BROWN

John Brown (1780-1859), geologist, was born at Braintree and apprenticed to a stonemason there. Stone fascinated him. Before long
he was devoting all his leisure hours to its study. At about 25 he
set up as a master mason at premises on East Hill, Colchester, and
remained there until at the age of 50 he decided to retire and devote
himself entirely to the study of geology. The remaining 29 years of
his life were spent at Stanway, where he concentrated on the Pleist-
ocene deposits near his home and collected a remarkable series of
specimens of extinct mammalia. For many years he generously supplied fossils and shells to many museums. Smiles, in Self Help, referred to John Brown as a self-educated stonemason who became
eminent in the scientific field of geology. During his last years he
did valuable work on Foraminifera in chalk.

See E. Nat. iv 158: x 288; xix 130

BROWNE

Sir Anthony Browne (1510-67), the Chief Justice of Common Pleas
who founded Brentwood Grammar School in 1557, was the son of
Sir Wistan Browne of Abbess Roding. As a devout Roman Catholic
he was active under Mary I in persecuting Protestants. Among those
who were brought before him was William Hunter, the Brentwood
martyr, a 19 year old apprentice who, according to his brother,
was 'persecuted to death by Justice Browne for the Gospel's sake.'
In August 1557 Browne received a special letter of commendation
from the Privy Council thanking him for his diligent proceeding
against George 'Trudge-over-the-World' Eagles, whom he had taken
and condemned to be executed at Chelmsford.

Sir Anthony Browne was knighted in 1556. He became Chief Justice
in 1558, but was removed from office by Elizabeth, although he
continued to perform his duties as a judge till his death. Sir Anthony
bought Weald Hall about 1550 and lived there for the last 17 years of
his life. He died in 1567 without issue, and his estate passed to his
great-nephew, Wistan Browne, a grandson of his brother John.

BROWNE

Humphrey Browne, of Ridley Hall, Terling, was a younger brother
of Wistan Browne and uncle of Anthony of South Weald. He was
King's Serjeant, 1536; Judge of the Common Pleas, 1542, and retained the office through four reigns. Plowden relates that in Hilary
Term, 1559, he 'did not argue at all, because he was so old that his
senses were decayed and his voice could not be heard.' Although he
was clearly too old to be competent he continued to adjudicate for
nearly four years more, and until within a few days of his death.

BRYAN

Sir Francis Bryan (d. 1550), poet, translator, soldier, and diplomat, was one of the most brilliant figures at the court of Henry
VIII. He was the son of Lady Margaret Bryan, who lived at Leyton
and was governess to the princesses Mary and Elizabeth and prince
Edward, Sir Francis was first cousin of Anne Boleyn, and was sent
to the Pope to try to persuade him to dissolve Henry's marriage
with Catherine of Aragon. Later he turned against Anne when it
was no longer diplomatic to support her. He had two other ill-
fated relations: he was a nephew of the 3rd Duke of Norfolk and

an intimate friend of his cousin, the Duke's son, the poet Earl of
Surrey, who was condemned and executed on the frivolous charges
of treasonably quartering royal arms and advising his sister to
become the king's mistress.

Sir Francis Bryan came into possession of Faulkbourne Hall by
marrying Philippa, heiress of the Montgomery owners of the estate.
In 1548 he went to Ireland as Lord Marshal, and died two years
later.

BUCKINGHAM, Dukes of, See STAFFORD

BUCKINGHAM, Marquis of, See GRENVILLE

BULL

John Bull and Richard Farnham, two Colchester weavers, about 1640
claimed to be the two prophets mentioned by the prophet Zachariah,
and the two witnesses referred to in Revelations, xi 3. They declared
that they had power to shut off the rain from heaven and to smite the
earth with plagues. They prophecied that three and a half days after
they died they would rise from the dead and Richard Farnham would
be king on David's throne and John Bull priest in Aaron's seat, and
that they would reign for ever. Both died of plague; but their converts declared that they had gone away in vessels of bulrushes and
would return to rule over the kingdom with a rod of iron.

BUNYAN

John Bunyan is said to have stayed frequently with the English and
Tabor families at Bocking and to have preached in the square out-
side the 'White Hart' as well as in the barn at Bocking End. The
first part of Pilgrim's Progress was written in the County Gaol at
Bedford. On his release from prison in 1676 Bunyan visited the
English family at Bocking End, and there worked on either Pilgrim's
Progress or The Life and Death of Mr. Badman, both of which owed
much to his reading of The Plaine Man's Path-way to Heaven, by
Arthur Dent (q.v.).

BURGH

Hubert de Burgh (d. 1243), Chief Judiciar of England and builder of
Hadleigh Castle, figures in Shakespeare's King John, act iv, on the
strength of a story derived from Ralph de Coggeshall. He first appears as judiciar in June 1215, the month in which Magna Carta was
signed at Runnymede, and there is evidence that de Burgh played an
influential part in obtaining it. His name occurs in the list of the
barons who upheld the 25 conservators of the charter. In 1216 he
vigorously defended Dover Castle against the French, but was obliged to make a truce with Louis. De Burgh continued to hold office
under Henry III, and in 1217 commanded the first English fleet to
win a great naval victory by destroying the French fleet off North
Foreland.

On the death of the regent in 1219, de Burgh assumed great power,
fighting valiantly to uphold the right of Englishmen to all offices in
their own administrative system. His strong line inevitably earned
him many enemies, and in 1231, the year in which he completed the
building of Hadleigh Castle, these gained the upper hand. Various

charges were brought against him, most of which were based on a
superstitious belief that he had gained the king's favour by sorcery.
His property and offices were taken from him and he fled for sanctuary to Merton Priory. From there he went to Brentwood, where
his nephew, the Bishop of Norwich, owned a property. When his
pursuers caught up with him at Brentwood he took refuge in the
bishop's chapel; but he was dragged out and a smith was hastily
summoned to make fetters for him. It is of this occasion that the
famous story is told of how the smith recognised the captive, and
throwing down his tools declared:
> 'As the Lord liveth, I will never make iron shackles for
> him; but will rather die the worst death there is. God be
> judge between him and you for using him so unjustly and
> inhumanly.'

Hubert de Burgh married five times. His third wife was Isabella,
daughter and heiress of William, 2nd Earl of Gloucester, and widow
of Geoffrey de Mandeville, 5th Earl of Essex (q.v.). His chief association with Essex is with Hadleigh and Leigh. In addition to the
grant of a right to build a castle at Hadleigh, de Burgh was granted
by Henry III fishing rights in Hadleigh Ray, and although we know
that there were fishermen at Leigh at Domesday, this grant by
Henry III in 1220 is the first recorded fact in the history of the
Leigh fishing industry.

When the smith refused to make chains for him, de Burgh was bound
with cords and carried to London. But the Bishop of London inter-
vened, threatening to excommunicate all concerned in the breach of
the peace of Holy Church if Hubert were not returned. The threat
succeeded. He was sent back to Brentwood, with orders that he
should remain in the chapel and there be watched over by the Sheriff.
Many other tribulations followed before his tempestuous career ended
with his death 'full of days' at Banstead in 1243.

BURGOYNE

Montagu Burgoyne (1750-1836), country gentleman, married Mary,
daughter of Eliab Harvey of Claybury Hall, Woodford, in 1780, and
purchased the Mark Hall estate at Latton, Near Harlow. For the
next 40 years he was a prominent and provocative figure in the public life of the county. Perhaps the least controversial of the many
parts he played was that of verderer of Epping Forest from 1798 to
1819. Burgoyne had an overdeveloped capacity for making enemies
and frequently found himself at loggerheads with Authority. This
foible lost him the nomination for the parliamentary candidature of
Essex when John Bullock died in 1809. One of the county's most
colourful elections followed. When John Archer-Houblon (Tory) was
chosen, Burgoyne stood as 'an unofficial and radical Whig,' stating
that he stood for complete reform of the House of Commons and re-
organisation of the resources of the Empire for defence. He announced that he would not buy any votes, and would not be answerable
for one shilling expended in his name. He even went so far as to
refuse to provide transport to carry his supporters to the poll. The
result was that, as the Chelmsford Chronicle put it, 'Burgoyne did
all the talking in the election and Archer-Houblon got nearly all the
votes.'

Burgoyne sold his Latton estate for 100,000 guineas, plus £10,000
for the timber, to Richard Arkwright (q.v.) in 1819, and left the
county.

BUXTON

Members of the East Anglian Radical family of Buxton were associated with Coggeshall as owners of property in the town from 1537, if
not earlier. They were connected by marriage with the Paycockes
(q.v.). Emma, daughter of Robert Paycocke married Robert Buxton
early in the 16th century. Other Buxton marriages recorded in the
Coggeshall registers start with William (1561), Thomas (1562) and
Robert (1601). The earliest Buxton burial at Coggeshall was that of
John (1568).

The most eminent branch of the family begins with the Thomas Fowell
Buxton who in 1782 married Anna, daughter of Osgood Hanbury of
Truman Hanbury & Co., brewers. He was of Earls Colne. Their son,
Thomas Fowell Buxton (1786-1845), philanthropist, joined the brewery partnership in 1808 and became wealthy; but the poverty and
ignorance of the people of East London, many of whom were his own
workpeople, shocked him. His charitable work started with a simple
scheme for educating the children of his firm's employees; but this
quickly led to a vigorous drive to improve social conditions generally.
At one memorable Mansion House meeting he appealed so eloquently
for funds to relieve the starving weavers of Spitalfields that he
raised £43,000 on the spot. From 1816 onwards he spent much time
in helping his sister-in-law, Elizabeth Fry (q.v.), in prison reform.
In 1818 he entered parliament as member for Weymouth, joining
Wilberforce in agitating for the abolition of the slave trade, and
eventually becoming leader of the movement. In 1840 he was created
a baronet. At his death in 1845 he was given a monument in
Westminster Abbey.

Edward North Buxton, 2nd baronet (1812-58), married his cousin,
Catherine Gurney, by whom he had twelve children.

Thomas Fowell Buxton, 3rd baronet (1837-1916), was only 21 when
he succeeded his father as head of a family that had assumed great
social as well as business interests. Although a Low Churchman, he
had been imbued by the Gurneys with the Quaker concern of his many
cousins and aunts for good works. He married Lady Victoria Noel,
daughter of the 1st Earl of Gainsborough, and made his home at
Warlies, near Epping, the social centre of West Essex. His nine
children were all drawn into his schemes for local improvements,
particularly in safeguarding open spaces against the encroachment
of London. They were greatly influenced by his two favourite mottoes:
'A man can do an immense amount of good if he doesn't care who gets
the credit.' and 'When in doubt, do the enterprising thing.' He was
chairman of the Epping Bench for 40 years and verderer of Epping
Forest from 1880-1908. He was also M.P. for King's Lynn, 1865-8,
and governor of South Australia, 1895-9.

With his brother, Edward North Buxton, he played a dominant part
in fighting the cause of the commoners in Epping Forest (with the
munificent backing of the City of London Corporation), which led to
the passing of the Epping Forest Act, 1878. Some idea of the part
played in West Essex by the single-minded Buxton family will be
appreciated from the fact that when Sir Thomas Fowell Buxton's
mother died at the age of 97 she left 128 descendants, most of whom
were prominent in social work.

Edward North Buxton (1840-1924), of Knighton, third son of the 2nd
baronet, was a verderer of Epping Forest from 1880 to his death 44
years later. His contribution to its conservation remains unsurpassed,

and his small guide to the Forest will remain a local classic. Under
his guidance, a system of management was established that has been
followed continuously since his time. He was succeeded as a verderer
by his son, Gerald, his grandson, Edward North, and his great-
grandson, Mark. The last of his many generous gifts of open spaces
was that of Hatfield Forest, which he bought and presented to the
National Trust in 1924.

See C. L. Buxton: The Buxtons of Coggeshall (1910)
    J. E. Ritchie: The Essex Buxtons, E.R. iv 157
    Sir Thomas Fowell Buxton (1786-1845): Memoirs

BYRD

William Byrd (1543?-1623), composer, lived for 30 years at
Stondon Massey, first as tenant and later as owner of Stondon
Place. His place of birth is unknown. It was probably in Lincolnshire, where he was organist of the cathedral from 1563 to 1572.
He says that he was 'bred up to music under Thomas Tallis', who
had been organist at Waltham Abbey and with whom he shared duties
as organist at the Chapel Royal. Byrd and Tallis had a special patent
for selling music and music paper, and when Tallis died in 1585 this
became Byrd's monopoly.

In 1593 Byrd purchased from the Crown the lease of Stondon Place,
a farmhouse that had been confiscated by the Crown from the owner,
William Shelley, 'a papistical plotter'. As Byrd was a Roman
Catholic it must have gone against the grain with the Shelley family
to see a member of the same faith living in their house unmolested.
Why he should have enjoyed such favour is not known; but his
friendship with the Petre family may have helped. However that
may be, he further strengthened his position by gaining from the
queen in 1595 a grant of adjoining property, together with Stondon
Place, for the lives of his three children, Christopher, Elizabeth
and Rachel, the property being leased to him as 'part of her Majestie's inheritance, part and parcel of the possessions of William
Shelley, attainted and convicted of high treason.' Byrd and his family were, however, presented regularly as 'papistical recusants'.

When John Shelley died in 1597 his widow pleaded for the right to
the rents of the property for her son, John, and this appears to have
been allowed. James I renounced his rights to the estate on payment
of a fine by the Shelleys of £10,000, but he would do nothing to assist Mrs. Shelley in her efforts to get William Byrd and his family
out of Stondon Place. In 1610 Byrd purchased the property outright,
and in 1623, when an old man of 80, he made his will and left it to
his daughter-in-law, Catherine Byrd, the wife of his eldest son,
Christopher. Byrd's house was rebuilt by Richard How in 1700.
In 1877 this second house was destroyed by fire (except for the coach
house, recently restored by Mrs. Borland), but was reconstructed
as far as possible on the old foundations.

Byrd was involved in a series of legal actions while at Stondon Place.
The first was - not surprisingly - with Mrs. Shelley, widow of the
owner. In 1596 he was indicted for stopping up a footpath; but the
charge against him was dismissed: largely, it was said, through the
influence of local landowners, who wanted the right of way closed.
Happily, these old quarrels are all forgotten, and at the tercentenary
celebration a mural tablet was placed to Byrd's memory in Stondon
church.

The Byrd pedigree is recorded in the Herald's Visitation of Essex,
1634, but it begins only with the composer himself.

See E. H. Fellowes: William Byrd (2nd edn. 1928) E.R. xxxii 159,
E.R. xliii 31.
Victoria County History, Essex iv

CALAMY

Four members of the Puritan family of Calamy bore the name Edmund.
The first, Edmund Calamy the elder (1600-66), was lecturer at
Rochford and one of the authors of Smectymnuus, a reply to Bishop
Hall's claim of divine right for episcopacy. He was a member of the
Westminster Assembly 1643, opposed Charles I's trial and execution,
and later advocated the Restoration. It was said that his wife influenced him in refusing the sees of Lichfield and Coventry. He was a
member of the Savoy Conference 1661. In 1662 he was ejected from
his ministry and the following year imprisoned for unlicensed preaching, although he had taken no part in politics during the Commonwealth. His death in 1666 was said to have been hastened by his
distress at the devastation caused by the Great Fire of London. After
driving through the ruins in a coach he retired to his house and never
left it afterwards.

Edmund Calamy the younger (1635-85), eldest son of Edmund Calamy
the elder, was intruded rector of Moreton, 1659-62. After 1662 he
withdrew to London and preached mainly in private houses.

The third Edmund Calamy (1671-1732), nonconformist biographer,
was the only son of Edmund Calamy the younger. Among his works
were an Account of the Ministers ejected by the Act of Uniformity,
1702, a continuation of the Account, 1727, and an autobiography
published in 1829. His son, Edmund Calamy the fourth (1697-1755),
continued the Presbyterian record of the family until the middle of
the 18th century.

CANFIELD

Benet Canfield (1563-1611), mystic, began life as William Fitch, son
of a father of that name who is commemorated by a brass in Little
Canfield church, on which he is described as 'late lorde of this
towne.' William Fitch, the elder, died in 1578, aged 82. William
Fitch, the younger, took the vows of a Franciscan novice at Douai
in 1586, as Brother Benedict of Canfield, a Capuchin friar. He
returned to England with a companion in 1589. The two were arrested as priests, examined by Sir Francis Walsingham and imprisoned in the Tower, from which Canfield was later transferred to
Wisbech Castle. He was released by the queen's order at the request
of Henry IV of France in 1592 and returned to the Continent to become
Master of Novices and Guardian of the Convent at Rouen, where he
died in 1611, aged 48.

Interest in Benet Canfield was unexpectedly revived by the publication
of Grey Eminence, by Aldous Huxley, in which Canfield's method of
prayer, first set out in The Rule of Perfection, is described.

CANHAM

Catherine (Kitty) Canham (1720-1752), daughter of Robert Canham,
a prosperous farmer of Beaumont Hall, married the Rev. Alexander
Gough, vicar of Thorpe-le-Soken, as many a prosperous farmer's

daughter had married the local vicar before her; but unlike most
such marriages, Kitty's was not a happy one, and one day she disappeared, leaving no hint of where she was going or whether she
intended to return. It was not surprising that her distressed husband
should have found difficulty in tracing her, because when she did
turn up it was as a 'viscountess'.

After leaving Essex she met John, Lord Dalmeny, son of the 2nd Earl
of Rosebery. The couple fell in love and 'married', apparently without Kitty giving away her secret. They spent four years travelling
the Continent, until, in 1752, Kitty was taken seriously ill at Verona
and died. Just before her death she asked for pencil and paper and
managed to write:
> 'I am the wife of the Reverend Alexander Gough, Vicar of
> Thorpe-le-Soken, in Essex. My maiden name was Catherine
> Canham. My last request is to be buried at Thorpe.'
Such a request was not as easily gratified in 1752 as it would be
today, but Lord Dalmeny communicated the request to the husband
and arrangements for the burial were made. Meanwhile Kitty's
embalmed body was packed in a case and carried to the coast, where
Lord Dalmeny, describing himself as Mr. Williams, a merchant of
Hamburg, chartered a ship for England. He intended to land at
Harwich, but the ship was driven off course by storm and boarded
by Custom House officers, who expected to find contraband. When
the chest was opened and the body exposed, Lord Dalmeny had to
reveal his identity as son of the Earl of Rosebery.

Eventually Kitty was brought home to Thorpe-le-Soken, and at the
interment the two 'husbands' stood together in deep mourning, the
two faithful spouses of an erring wife.

CANT

Benjamin R. Cant (1830-1900), rose-grower, whose grandfather
established a nursery-garden business at Colchester in 1766, became a distinguished rosarian. He won four silver cups at the first
exhibition of the National Rose Society in 1858 and from that time to
the present day Cants of Colchester have been among the foremost
rose-growers of the world. They have won thousands of cups. In
1875, Frank Cant, nephew of Benjamin R. Cant, established a rose
farm and extended the family's influence as rose-growers.

CAPEL

The Capel family in Essex trace their descent from John Capel of
Stoke-by-Nayland in Suffolk, who died in 1449. William, a younger
son of John of Stoke, prospered as a London merchant, and in 1486
bought the manor of Little Rayne, which remained the principal seat
of the family for more than a century. He served as Lord Mayor in
1503. Stow records of him that he 'caused a cage in every ward to
be set for the punishing of vagabonds.' About this time he built the
brick tower of Rayne church, one of the finest in the county. By the
time he died in 1515 he had considerably extended his estate in Essex,
which he bequeathed with Rayne Hall to his son Giles.

Sir Giles Capel (1485-1556), who took part in the Coronation Tourn-
ament in 1509, was closely associated with Rayne throughout his life.
He continued to extend the Capel properties in the County, and when
he died in 1556 his will gave further evidence of his pride in.Rayne
and his affection for the church in which he had worshipped. In leaving

his estate to his son, Henry, he made it a condition that he should
find,
> 'five tapers of good and clean wax to be burned every
> Easter about my sepulchre yearly during the time that
> the sepulchre is upp.'

He further directed that his best helmet should 'be set over my
funeralls.' The Capel helmet remained over Sir Giles's tomb until
the old church (apart from the tower) was demolished in 1840. It
then disappeared, but turned up some years later in a builder's
yard and was restored to the church. Subsequently it was sold to
the New York Metropolitan Museum and replaced by a replica.

Sir Henry survived his father by one year only, and was succeeded
by his younger brother, Edward, who held the estate for 20 years
but did not live at Rayne. He was followed by another Sir Henry
(1537-1588), who had 11 children, one of whom was Gamaliel and is
commemorated by a tablet of alabaster and marble, with kneeling
figures of man and wife at a prayer desk (1613) in Abbess Roding
church.

Sir Henry, with his 11 children, was succeeded by his eldest surviving son, Arthur (1557-1632), who lived at Rayne from 1577 to
1588. As he had 20 children the succession became too complicated
to trace here. The point to note is that sometime between 1572 and
1577 Sir Henry Capel left Rayne Hall and went to live at Little
Hadham Hall in Hertfordshire, which became the chief seat of the
family, with Rayne Hall retained as either the residence of the heir
or a dower house. Fifteen of Arthur Capel's 20 children were baptised at Hadham.

Sir Henry Capel, the next in the line, had nine children; but although
he lived much of his life at Hadham and died there, he was brought to
Rayne for burial in 1622, as also was the next Henry, who died in
1633. With his burial the family connection with Rayne ended; but
not with the county of Essex. Arthur, 1st Baron Capel of Hadham
(1610-49), the royalist leader, son of Sir Henry of Rayne, took part
in the defence of Colchester. His literary remains were published in
1654, with the title Daily Observations or Meditations. His eldest
son was created Earl of Essex in 1661.

CAPEL CURE

Robert Capel Cure, who bought the Blake Hall estate at Bobbingworth
from Sir Narborough D'Aeth in 1789, died in 1816. His wife was
Margaret, daughter of Sir Thomas Burch Western (q.v.), which
gives the later Capel Cures descent from Anne Plantagenet, granddaughter of Edward III. His son, who added the Bobbingworth Hall
estate in 1834, kept a notebook recording his own farming activities
along with those of his tenant farmers.

Among the tablets to the family in Bobbingworth church is a fine 15th
century bas-relief, believed to be by Pietro Lombardo and to have
come from the palace at Mantua. It was taken from the Shropshire
home of the family, Badger Hall, when that house was pulled down
about 1953 and erected in the church by Nigel Capel Cure as a memorial to his parents.

CARLISLE, Earl of, See HAY

CASTELL

Edmund Castell (1606-85), Semitic scholar, was rector of Woodham
Walter and Hatfield Peverel. In 1660 he published verses congrat-
ulating Charles II on his restoration, and six years later was appointed a royal chaplain. He assisted Brian Walton in producing the
Polyglot Bible, and himself produced a Lexicon in seven languages,
a life work on which he expended a considerable fortune. At his
death he bequeathed his oriental manuscripts to Cambridge University.

CAVENDISH

John de Cavendish, whose family name was Gernon, acquired the
Pentlow estate in 1369. His son of the same name became Chief
Justice of the King's Bench in 1373 and so incensed the rebels during
the Peasants' Revolt that he was carried to Bury St. Edmunds and
beheaded.

Sir Thomas Cavendish, the second Englishman to sail round the
world, was of this family. The founder of the ducal families of
Devonshire and Newcastle was Sir William Cavendish, one of the
commissioners for taking the survey of religious houses at the
Dissolution.

CAVENDISH

Margaret, Duchess of Newcastle (1625-1674), writer, was the youngest daughter of Thomas Lucas of St. John's, Colchester. She accompanied Queen Henrietta Maria to Paris as one of her maids of honour
in 1645, and in the same year married, as his second wife, William
Cavendish, Marquis (afterwards Duke) of Newcastle. After living at
Paris, Antwerp and Rotterdam in financial distress, she came to
England to plead for an allowance out of her husband's confiscated
estates. At the Restoration she became a figure of ridicule. Her
brother, Sir Charles Lucas (q.v.), was executed after the Siege of
Colchester.

Most of our knowledge of the Duchess is derived from her Memoirs,
in which she owns to being one who 'took delight in a singularity,
even in accoutrements of habits.' She claims that she wrote for her
own pleasure and did not care whether she was read or not. It is
however, plain that she hoped for lasting fame for her plays and
philosophical writings. 'It pleased God,' she remarks, 'to command
his servant Nature to indue me with a poetical and philosophical
genius.' For a contemporary estimate of her plays we turn to Pepys
and Evelyn, who knew her well. In 1667 Pepys wrote:
  'To see the silly play of the Duchess of Newcastle, The
  Humourous Lovers, the most silly thing that ever came
  upon a stage. I was sick to see it; but yet, would not
  but have seen it, that I might the better understand her.'
On another occasion he wrote:
  'Thence home, and then, in favour to my eyes, staid at
  home reading the ridiculous history of my Lord Newcastle,
  made by his wife, which shows her to be a mad, conceited,
  ridiculous woman, and he an ass to suffer her write what
  she wrote to him and of him.'
But in a kinder vein he wrote:
  'Met my Lady Newcastle going with her coaches and foot-
  men all in velvet; herself, whom I never saw before, as
  I have often heard her described, for all the town talk is

now a days of her extravagancies, with her velvet cap,
her hair about her ears; many black patches because
of pimples about her mouth, naked-necked, without
anything about it, and a black just-au-corps. She
seemed to me a very comely woman, but I hope to see
more of her on May Day.'

Charles Lamb was the first to write appreciatively of her work.
Her plays are never likely to be revived, and her philosophical
writings can never again be taken seriously; but her Social Letters
have been reprinted in Everyman's Library, and her virtues as a
wife are set out for posterity in the epitaph over the tomb of the
Duke and Duchess in Westminster Abbey.

CEDD

St. Cedd (d. 664) was recalled by King Oswy in 653 from his mission
to the Middle Angles and commissioned to convert the East Saxons.
In the following year he was consecrated Bishop of the East Saxons,
administering his diocese from two centres: Ythancestir at Bradwell-
juxta-Mare, which was the site of the Roman fortress of Othona,
and Tilbury on the Thames. He died of yellow plague at his monastery
at Lastingham in Yorkshire in 664. As 30 of his followers died of the
plague soon afterwards, the East Saxons believed that the old gods
had been offended and were taking their revenge. In consequence
many of Cedd's converts reverted to paganism.

CELY

The Cely family of Aveley were merchants of the Staple, 1475-88.
Many of their family and business papers are in the Public Record
Office and throw light on the problems of the mediaeval wood trade
during this period.

See H. E. Maldon: The Cely Papers, Camdon Soc. 3rd series 1
                                (1900)

CHALLIS

James Challis (1803-82), astronomer, was the fourth son of John
Challis of Braintree. His wife was the widow of Daniel Copsey of
the same town. In 1836 he succeeded Sir George Biddell Airy (q.v.)
as Plumian professor of astronomy and experimental philosophy in
the University of Cambridge. At the same time he was appointed
director of the Cambridge Observatory, an office he held for 25
years. Between 1832 and 1864 he published 12 volumes of
Astronomical Observations. He is now chiefly remembered in
connection with the discovery of Neptune. Like so many of his period,
he wrote widely on theological subjects as well as on mathematics
and physics.

CHAMBERLEN

Peter Chamberlen (1601-83), surgeon, of Woodham Mortimer Hall,
moved into Essex soon after the death of Charles I to escape from
criticism of his use of forceps in operative midwifery. His family
had been Huguenot refugees, and his grandfather had introduced the
use of forceps, which remained a family secret through four generations. He was physician to Charles II. In 1685 his son, Hugo, was
entrusted with the bringing into the world of an heir to King James II;
but he arrived one hour late. In 1692 he officiated at the birth of a

son to the Princess Anne, but the child died immediately after birth. The Chamberlens were pioneers in more respects than one. Peter (1601-83) advocated the incorporation of London midwives in 1634, and the provision of public baths in 1648. Hugo, the son, court physician and F.R.S., published in 1694 details of a scheme for a State Medical Service, supported out of taxation. Ill luck appears to have dogged him in England, so towards the end of his life he settled in Amsterdam. His tomb is in Woodham Mortimer churchyard.

Edmund Chapman, a surgeon who practised at Halstead, published an account of the Chamberlen forceps in his Essay on Midwifery in 1733. Two other Essex surgeons, William Giffard of Brentwood and Benjamin Pugh of Chelmsford, also wrote descriptions of them. The full story is told in The Secret Instrument, by Walter Radcliffe (1948).

CHANCELLOR

Frederic Chancellor (1825-1918), Diocesan Surveyor to the St. Albans diocese, which then included Essex, designed many Essex churches, and in 1890 published The Ancient Sepulchral Monuments of Essex. He was one of the founders of the Essex Archaeological Society and contributed to both the Transactions of the Society and the Essex Review. Throughout his long life of 92 years he was active in many spheres. He was seven times mayor of Chelmsford, a freeman of the borough, and a member of the County Council. He designed the Chelmsford Corn Exchange, demolished in 1969, and the present (third building) Felsted School. There is a fine collection of his plans and drawings in the Essex Record Office.

CHANCELLOR

Frederick Wykeham Chancellor (1865-1945), ecclesiastical architect, was born at Chelmsford, the son of Frederic Chancellor (q.v.). He was diocesan surveyor of St. Albans from 1902 to 1914, and subsequently of Chelmsford. Chancellor was responsible for the restoration of St. Peter-on-the-Wall, Bradwell, of Layer Marney Towers, Leez Priory, and many parish churches. From 1938 to 1944 he was President of the Essex Archaeological Society. He left an important collection of drawings of Essex churches, recording many features before restoration.

CHARRINGTON

Frederick Nicholas Charrington (1850-1936), temperance reformer, joined the family firm of brewers, but after a short time sold his interest in the brewery for a figure in excess of £1,000,000 and spent the money campaigning for temperance. He founded his Tower Hamlets Mission in 1870, when only 20 years of age. His 'conversion' came on seeing a brutal drunkard strike down his wife, who was pleading for money to buy bread for their children outside one of his own public-houses. The blow, he said, 'knocked her into the gutter and me out of the brewery.'

In his philanthropic work he became associated with Lord Shaftesbury, chiefly in the West End. In Essex he established 'a home for gentlemen suffering from the baneful and insidious effects of alcohol' at Osea Island in the Blackwater in 1903. The advantage of the location was thought to be that there were no public-houses there; but Maldon fishermen, with traditions of smuggling in their blood, were soon running a lucrative line in the illicit supply of liquor.

CHEKE

Sir Thomas Cheke of Pyrgo, Havering-atte-Bower, married as his second wife, Essex, daughter of Robert, Earl of Warwick. He represented Essex in several parliaments and shortly before his death in 1659 claimed the FitzWalter barony on the death of the 6th and last Earl of Sussex. The claim was renewed by his heir, Robert, at the Restoration; but in 1669 the Privy Council decided in favour of the rival claimant, Benjamin Mildmay (q.v.), who was descended from a daughter of the 2nd earl and clearly had the better claim. The basis of the Cheke claim was a contention that once the barony had been absorbed in the earldom it must descend with it.

Sir Thomas Cheke, the younger, inherited the family property on the death of his brother Robert. He married, first, Dorothy Sidney, daughter of Philip Viscount Lisle, afterwards Earl of Leicester; secondly, Laetitia Russell, niece of William Earl of Bedford. In 1671 he was appointed Steward of the Manor of Havering; in 1679, Lieutenant of the Tower. In 1687 he was one of those who were removed from office by James II on the ground that they could not be relied upon to support his policy. He died in 1688, and was buried in his chapel at Pyrgo. Later he was re-interred with other members of his family in the parish church of Havering-atte-Bower.

CHILD

Sir Josiah Child (1630-99) of Wanstead, autocratic governor of the East India Company, was the second son of a London merchant. When he purchased the Wanstead estate in 1667 he was already a rich man, and his wealth increased rapidly as the result of his East India enterprises, which included the systematic use of bribery. His chief work, A New Discourse of Trade, first published in 1668, went through four editions during his lifetime, and continued to be reissued until 1775. He was created a baronet in 1683.

On 16th March, 1683, Evelyn wrote in his Diary:
'I went to see Sir Josiah Child's prodigious cost in planting walnut trees about his seate, and making fish-ponds, many miles in circuit, in Epping Forest, in a barren spot, as often these suddainly monied men for the most part seate themselves. He from a merchant's apprentice, and management of the East India Company's stock, being arriv'd at an estate ('tis said) of £200,000; and lately married his daughter to the eldest sonn of the Duke of Beaufort, late Marquis of Worcester, with £50,000 portional present and various expectations.'

Sir Josiah was High Sheriff of Essex in 1689. At his death in 1699 he was buried in Wanstead Old Church, but when the new church was built his monument was given an imposing place on the south side of the chancel.

Sir Josiah married three times. Only two of his sons, Josiah and Richard, survived him. Of these, Josiah died without issue in 1704, and Richard was left sole heir.

Sir Richard Child continued his father's work in forming lakes and planting trees. The largest of the four lakes was formed by diverting the River Roding and widening its original bed to form the beautiful ornamental water that is now the principal feature of Wanstead Park. In 1715 he pulled down the old manor house of Wanstead, which had

been associated with Mary 1, who went from there to be crowned
queen, with Elizabeth 1, who visited it in 1561 and 1578, James 1,
who visited it three times, and James II, while Duke of York, as
well as many eminent subjects. Colen Campbell was commissioned
to prepare plans for a new house on the site of such magnificence
that it would be to the East of London what Hampton Court was to
the West. The result was so palatial that it was considered 'one
of the noblest houses, not only in England, but in Europe.' It was
built of Portland stone with a frontage 260 feet long and a portico
supported by six Corinthian columns.

Soon after the great house was completed the 'South Sea Bubble'
burst. Sir Richard suffered severe losses, but came out better
than some. He was M.P. for Maldon, a Knight of the Shire for
Essex, 1710-1722, and 1727-1734. His wife was Dorothy, daughter
of John Glynne. Her mother had been a Tylney of Tylney Hall, near
Basingstoke. This estate came to the Childs, so when, in 1732, Sir
Richard was created an earl, he took the title of Earl Tylney. He
had already been ennobled in 1718 as Baron Child of Newton and
Viscount Castlemaine. In March 1734 an Act of Parliament enabled
his eldest son and his heirs to assume the surname of Tylney.

The 1st Earl Tylney died in 1750 and was succeeded by his grandson
the 2nd Earl, who spent most of his time in Italy collecting works of
art. It was he who built the grotto at the southern end of the lake
which was demolished by fire in November, 1884, but part of the
facade of which remained as an ornamental feature until damaged
beyond repair by vandals in 1969. The total cost of the completed
grotto was said to be £40,000. The interior was lavishly decorated
with shells, pebbles, mirrors, stalactites and curiously designed
ornaments. The floor was embedded with pebbles and the bones of
deer. At one end there was a large coloured glass window commanding a view of the lake. The roof was domed.

With the death of the 2nd Earl in 1784 the title of Earl Tylney became
extinct and Wanstead passed to a nephew, Sir James Long, Bart.,
of Draycot, Wiltshire, who assumed the name of Tylney-Long. He
died in 1794, leaving one son and one daughter. The son did not long
survive, and at his death while still a minor, the property passed to
the daughter, Catherine Tylney-Long, during whose minority the
house was let to the Prince of Condé and other Bourbon exiles. For
the tragic marriage of Catherine Tylney-Long with the Hon. William
Pole Wellesley, eldest son of Lord Maryborough, afterwards Earl
of Mornington, see Wellesley.

CHINNERY

William Chinnery of Gilwell, near Chingford, married the daughter
of a Mr. Tresillian, a Cornishman who bought Gilwell about 1790
and restored the old house, introducing chimney pots of a style new
to Essex but then in vogue in Cornwall. Chinnery and his wife moved
into Gilwell from their London home at the end of 1798 and lived there
until 1812, when he fled to the Continent on being charged with app-
ropriating Treasury funds to his own use. The Crown seized Gilwell
and retained the property until 1882. Mrs. Chinnery died at a great
age at Chatillon. There are no surviving members of the family.

CHRISTY

Miller Christy (1861-1928), Essex historian and naturalist, acquired his great love for natural history while a pupil at the Quaker School at Epping. From there he went to Bootham, where he continued his studies in natural history. Before he was 20 he was already a regular contributor of notes to learned journals. In 1880 he was fortunate in being able to visit Canada as a member of the Tuke Emigration Commission, established to settle Irish peasants in Manitoba. This led to a study of natural history, Manitoba Described, published in 1885. A further study, undertaken in collaboration with his life-long friend, Ernest Thomas Seton, the naturalist, led to his editing in 1894 the voyages of Foxe and James for the Hakluyt Society. A long succession of books and contributions to learned journals followed: Trade Signs of Essex, 1887, and in the same year, A Handbook of Essex, in which every parish is described; Birdnesting and Birdskinning, 1888; Birds of Essex, 1890; A History of the Mineral Waters and Medicinal Springs of Essex (with Miss Thresh), 1910. He contributed many articles to the Transactions of the Essex Archaeological Society and the Essex Naturalist, the journal of the Essex Field Club, of which he was one of the founders. His history of Essex Trades and Industries appears in the second volume of the Victoria History of Essex. He was the writer of several lives in the Dictionary of National Biography.

CLARK

Charles Clark (1806-80), of Great Totham, printer, was a tenant farmer who between 1830 and 1862 produced a long series of pamphlets, verses and satires, including an edition of Tusser's (q.v.) A Hundreth Good Poyntes of Good Husbandrie, at a private press, first at Great Totham Hall and later at Heybridge. He was born at Heybridge and started composing verses at an early age. Before 1831 he was helping his neighbour, George W. Johnson, to compile a history of Great Totham, published that year by Clark 'entirely at his own cost'.

His fanatical advocacy of Malthusian principles, coupled with his personal oddities, made him a noted eccentric whose works came to be collected as curiosities. One of his foibles was the launching of balloons with his own compositions attached to them. Not even the queen was spared from his agitation for birth-control, which as a bachelor he was in a privileged position in advocating. In 1843 he produced a new version of the National Anthem beginning 'God stop Quick Vic, our Queen'. He was much addicted to puns and verses in the form of acrostics. In 1844 he claimed to have advanced the art of versification by producing verses that rhymed at the beginning as well as the end of the lines.

From about 1860 Clark lived in retirement at Heybridge, to which he had removed about 1853. His works of local interest are likely to survive as curiosities and reflections of contemporary manners. The most notable is John Noakes and Mary Styles; or An Essex Calf's Visit to Tiptree Races, published by John Russell Smith, of Soho, in 1839.

See E.R. 1xiii 137

COLE

William Cole (1844-1922), naturalist, was the founder of the Essex Field Club and its principal honorary secretary for 42 years. He was born at Islington and educated in north London to the age of 17, when he entered a shipbroker's office in Mark Lane. In 1877 the family moved to Laurel Cottage, Buckhurst Hill, and three years later (in 1880) the Essex Field Club was founded. Cole did not marry, and as several of his brothers and sisters also remained unmarried and shared his interests, their home became a centre for like-minded enthusiasts.

In 1910 Cole had a nervous breakdown from which he never wholly recovered. In 1919 he was granted a small Civil List pension, which enabled him to spend his last years in retirement at St. Osyth in a Martello Tower on the shore. He died in 1922 at the age of 78.

COLLER

Duffield William Coller (1805-1884), historian of Essex, was born at Ingatestone, where his boyhood was influenced by his godmother, Sister Duffield, a Roman Catholic refugee nun who lived at Ingatestone Hall. Her intention was that he should be trained for the priesthood; but at Sister Duffield's death the plan was altered and Coller was apprenticed to a local tailor. He ran away from home in 1821, and on being found and brought back he was apprenticed to a shoemaker at Rayleigh. Again he left home but by this time his literary bent was firmly established. He began contributing verses to periodicals and in 1827 he was apprenticed to George Meggy and Thomas Chalk, printers, of Chelmsford. At last he was able to settle. He went through the full course of seven years apprenticeship, and at the same time developed his gifts as a writer. His association with the Chelmsford Chronicle continued for more than 40 years, and for approximately half that time he served as editor, leaving to become editor of the Essex Weekly News. He also edited the Essex Literary Journal, much of which he wrote, and the Essex Magazine. He will continue to be remembered as author of The People's History of Essex, published in 39 monthly parts from February, 1858 to March 1861. Coller was twice married and had a large family.

COLT

Nether Hall, Roydon, came into the possession of the Colt family about 1450, when Thomas Colt of Carlisle bought the manor and built a fortified manor house, now a ruin. This Thomas was administrator of the estates of Richard, Duke of York, father of Edward IV. In 1459 he was attainted with other Yorkist leaders and all his estates were declared forfeit. The following year brought the Yorkists back into the ascendant, and under Edward IV his estates were restored to him. His loyalty was further rewarded by appointment to several lucrative offices, including that of Keeper of the Rolls of Chancery in Ireland. Edward IV extended his Essex possessions by a grant of the manor of Chingford. Thomas Colt of Nether Hall was closely associated with Sir Peter Arderne (q.v.) of Mark Hall, Latton, as an Essex justice of the peace from 1461 to 1465. On his brass in Roydon church he is depicted in the armour of the period, wearing a collar of honour.

At his death in 1471 he was succeeded by his son John, who was a minor at the time, and was placed by the king under the guardianship of Sir John Elrington, Treasurer of the Household, whose daughter, Elizabeth, he married. At Elizabeth's death he married Mary, daughter of Sir John de Lisle. Both wives are commemorated in brasses at Roydon. John's second son, Thomas, has a brass in Waltham Abbey. One of his daughters, Jane, married Sir Thomas More.

During John Colt's lifetime the manor of Little Parndon was added to the family estates, which passed down in the family until in 1635 they came into the possession of Sir Henry Colt, who wasted his inheritance and at his death left nothing in West Essex except a newly built house in Little Parndon. By this time the family had come to be more closely associated with West Suffolk, and in particular with Colt Hall, Cavendish; but Sir Henry's son, George, found little to inherit in either county.

COLVIN

Brigadier-General Sir Richard Beale Colvin (1856-1936), Lord Lieutenant of Essex, 1929-36, lived at Monkhams, Waltham Abbey. He married in 1895 Lady Gwendoline Audrey Adeline Brudenell, youngest daughter of the 2nd Earl of Stradbroke. In 1885 he became Master of the East Essex Foxhounds, and from 1890 was Master of the Essex and Suffolk. In 1901 he raised the Essex Yeomanry under the Earl of Warwick, and commanded it until 1910. In 1917 he was elected M.P. for West Essex on Lord Lambourne's elevation to the peerage, and retained the seat until he retired from parliament in 1923.

Sir Richard succeeded Lord Lambourne as Lord Lieutenant. He was himself succeeded by Sir Francis Whitmore (q.v.). He will be remembered for his work, The Lieutenants and Keepers of the Rolls of the County of Essex, published in 1934.

COMYNS

Sir John Comyns (1667-1740), judge, was the son of William Comyns of Lincoln's Inn, a descendant of the Comyns family of Dagenham. His mother was Elizabeth, daughter of Matthew Rudd of Little Baddow. He was a Member of Parliament for Maldon 1701,1708,1710 to 1715, and 1722 to 1726. In 1728 he was sworn a Baron of the Exchequer, and transferred in 1736 to the Common Pleas. Two years later he was appointed Lord Chief Baron of the Exchequer. Although Sir John Comyns married three times he died without issue. His home was Hylands, Writtle, where he is commemorated in the parish church by a magnificent monument surmounted by a bust. His fame rests on two works, published posthumously: his Reports in 1744, and his Digest of the Laws of England in 1762.

CONSTABLE

John Constable (1776-1837) was born at East Bergholt on the Suffolk side of the Stour, but he was educated at Dedham Grammar School and found as much inspiration on the Essex bank of his beloved river as he did on the Suffolk bank. So Essex has an equal claim with Suffolk to the best interpreter of the landscape they share, now known as the Constable Country. It was his 'Dedham Vale' that established him as a great artist. 'I love every stile and stump, and every lane in the village, so deep rooted are early impressions,' he wrote. Most of his friends, as well as most of his subjects, were drawn from humble life, although his father was a prosperous miller who intended his son for the Church. He stood, in fact, in the same relationship to painting as Wordsworth's to poetry. ' A gentleman's park, ' he once said, 'is my aversion.' But he had one friend in influential art circles, a friend he also shared with Wordsworth: Sir George Beaumont of the Clock House, Dunmow (q.v.). Another Essex man with whom he was closely linked was Luke Howard (q.v.), who gave him a better understanding of the cloud forms that he had studied for very different reasons while a boy in his father's mill at Flatford.

CONYERS

The Conyers family moved from Walthamstow to Epping in 1739 when Edward Conyers purchased the Copt Hall estate. Soon after coming into possession of the great house built by Sir Thomas Heneage (q.v.) he erected in the chapel a window of Flemish glass, which he bought from John Olmius of New Hall, Boreham. This window, which is now at St. Margaret's, Westminster, had been intended for Westminster Abbey in commemoration of Prince Arthur's marriage with Catherine of Aragon.

John Conyers I succeeded to the Copt Hall estate in 1742, and commissioned John Sanderson to prepare plans for rebuilding the house, then in an advanced state of decay. By 1751 the third Copt Hall was being built on an eminence near the site of the two former Copt Halls, but in Epping instead of Waltham parish. The new Copt Hall was ready for occupation in 1758.

John Conyers II employed James Wyatt to redecorate the principal rooms in 1775-7.

The most colourful member of the Conyers family was Henry John Conyers (1782-1853), the great-grandson of the first Conyers of Copt Hall. A character of the Old School, he was master of the Essex Hounds, 1805-8, 1813-53. Both on and off the hunting field he was much given to uninhibited expression of his feelings. According to R. F. Ball, who contributed the article on Foxhunting to Victoria. County History, he was far from being an ideal Master of Hounds:
  'Though making a boast of his large expenditure on hunting,
  he was content with a roughish pack of hounds and damp
  kennels; and his treatment of foxes on his own property,
  where the Duke of Richmond used to shoot with him, was
  as indefensible as his language in the hunting field.'
But he always claimed 'that he loved best those whom he damned most.'

As a candidate for parliament and a verderer of Epping Forest, many lively stories were told of him. He lived in an age when such wealthy landowners as he were a law to themselves, and he may be accepted as representative of the more bucolic of his kind in every county in late 18th century England. At his death in 1853 he left no son to succeed him.

COOKE

The Cookes of Gidea Hall, Romford, were descended from Thomas Cooke, a Lavenham man who prospered in London and in 1439 was one of the four wardens of the Drapers' Company when it received its charter of incorporation from Henry VI. He was Lord Mayor in 1462-3, and in the same year created a Knight of the Bath. He bought the Essex estate in 1453. Twelve years later he was granted a royal licence to impark 200 acres of land and to build himself a castle of stone and chalk, turreted, moated, embanked, machicolated and battlemented. The building of this fortified manor house was begun in 1467, but was interrupted when Sir Thomas was impeached of high treason for having Lancastrian sympathies. After a period in the Tower, during which his wife was committed to the custody of the Lord Mayor, he was released on payment of £8,000 to the king and £800 to the queen.

Between Sir Thomas and Sir Anthony Cooke (1504-76), the great man of the family, came Philip, knighted in 1497, and John, who died in 1516.

Sir Anthony Cooke (1504-76) completed the building of Gidea Hall (begun by his great-grandfather 100 years earlier) during the reign of Edward VI, to whom he was tutor; but he was obliged to live in exile during Mary's reign. When not occupied with the education of Edward VI, by whom he was created a Knight of the Bath, he spent much time on the education of his own daughters. They were frequently joined in their studies by Lady Jane Grey, who may be said to have received most of her education at Gidea Hall. This led to his being charged with favouring Lady Jane's claim to the throne and to a short term in the Tower. On his release in May 1554 he fled with his neighbour, Sir John Cheke (q.v.), to Strasbourg, where he attended the lectures of Peter Martyr, who had been Professor of Divinity at Oxford.

On Elizabeth's accession he lost no time in returning. In 1558 he was appointed High Steward of the Liberty of Havering-atte-Bower and elected a Member of Parliament for Essex.

Sir Anthony Cooke married Anne, daughter of Sir William FitzWilliam I (q.v.) of Gaynes Park, Epping, by whom he had four brilliant daughters. She died, aged 63 in 1589 and was buried in Westminster Abbey. Mildred, the eldest daughter, married as his second wife, William Cecil, Lord Burleigh. Anne, the second daughter, became the second wife of Sir Nicholas Bacon, Lord Keeper of the Great Seal, and the mother of Francis Bacon. Elizabeth, the third daughter married as her second husband, Lord John Russell, heir of Francis, 2nd Earl of Bedford and became a litigious and quarrelsome court busybody. Katherine, the fourth daughter, married as her second husband, Sir Henry Killigrew. None of Sir Anthony's sons distinguished themselves in any way. There is an alabaster monument to Sir Anthony himself in the parish church of Romford.

The Gidea Hall completed during Edward VI's reign was a curious building, mainly due ot its having been started in feudal times, when defence was so important a consideration. It was pulled down in 1720 and replaced by a mansion built by Sir John Eyles.

See E.R. xx 201, xxi 1

CORNWELL

Jack Cornwell (1900-16), V.C., was born at Manor Park. He attended Walton Road School, now the Cornwell Secondary Modern School, for boys. Before joining the Navy he worked for a short time as a van boy. He was awarded the Victoria Cross for bravery at the battle of Jutland. At his death he was buried in Manor Park Cemetery, where a stone was erected from money collected by East Ham schoolchildren.

CORSELLIS

The Layer Marney estate was bought in the 17th century by Nicholas
Corsellis (1604-74), a London merchant whose family was of Dutch
extraction. His epitaph, which appears to claim that he taught the
English the art of printing, has been misinterpreted. Printing had
been established in the 15th century in England, and could not be
introduced by a 17th century merchant. The explanation of the reference is that it was not to the individual commemorated but to the
name he bore. The Corsellis tradition is that in the 15th century
Archbishop Bourchier persuaded Henry VI to send an emissary to
Haarlem, where a printing press had been set up, in order to learn
the craft. This agent, a man named Robert Turnour, persuaded a
Dutch compositor named Frederick Corsellis to carry off a set of
letters and accompany him back to England, where he started printing at a press at Oxford before one was started at Westminster.
Frederick Corsellis may well have been a member of the Layer
Marney family.

In 1674, a second Nicholas Corsellis inherited the Layer Marney
estate from his father, after having inherited Wivenhoe from his
uncle James.

COTTON

The Cotton family of Leytonstone, associated with Walwood House,
built by William Cotton, Governor of the Bank of England, produced
several public-spirited citizens during the 19th century. This William
Cotton was born at Leyton in 1786, educated at Chigwell, and in 1812
married Sarah Lane, who claimed descent from the father of the lady
who aided Charles II to escape by carrying him to the coast on her
pillion disguised as a serving man. While Governor of the Bank of
England, William Cotton invented the automatic machine used in the
Bank for weighing gold. He was a generous benefactor, contributing
large sums towards the building of churches in the rapidly developing districts of East London and south-west Essex. Bishop Blomfield
called him his 'Lay Archdeacon'. His son, Sir Henry Cotton, became a judge and member of the Judicial Committee of the Privy
Council. Agnes Cotton, youngest daughter of William Cotton, opened
a Home for Friendless Girls at Forest Glade, Whipps Cross Road,
in 1865. In 1879 she built the 'Home of the Good Shepherd' for young
girls, which she assigned to the community of the 'Clewer Sisters'
before her death in 1899.

See W. G. Hammock: Leytonstone and its History (1904)

COURTAULD

The first member of the Courtauld family to settle in England came
as a Huguenot refugee soon after the revocation of the Edict of Nantes
in 1685, bringing with him an infant son, Augustine, who served
seven years apprenticeship as a goldsmith from 1701 to 1708. He was
admitted a freeman of the Goldsmiths' Company in 1712, becoming both
a fine craftsman in silver and a well-to-do London citizen. At his
death in 1751 he was succeeded by his son, Samuel (1720-65), who
had been apprenticed to his father, and continued to follow his craft
at premises in Cornhill to the end of his short life. His widow, who
was the daughter of a Huguenot silk weaver, named Ogier, sold the
business in 1780 to a distinguished goldsmith called John Henderson.
The Essex Courtaulds are descended from George, Samuel Courtauld's
second son.

George Courtauld (1761-1823), great-grandson of the original Courtauld to settle in England, forsook the family craft for his maternal grandfather's business of silk-throwing, and in 1798 set up in business with a partner at a mill at Pebmarsh, which was pulled down in 1902. After a few years the firm removed to a larger mill at Bocking.

George Courtauld was a restless, enterprising character, temperamentally unsuited to working in partnership. At the age of 59 he emigrated to the State of Ohio, where he bought large tracts of land, on which he settled his family the following year, inspiring all, apparently, except his son, Samuel, with a vision of founding a new order of society in Ohio. Although a man of indomitable spirit, who displayed great courage and surmounted many trials, the hardships of a pioneering life proved too much for him and he died in 1823.

Samuel Courtauld (1793-1881), the son who stayed behind, prospered at the Bocking factory, and when his father died he was able to bring the family back to Essex. He was a man of immense drive and energy, and under his vigorous leadership the firm was carried to pre-eminence. In 1846, 1,600 workpeople were entertained to a dinner in a field opposite his residence at High Garrett, between Halstead and Bocking. About 1854 the firm was renamed Samuel Courtauld & Co., and about the same time the Gosfield Hall estate was purchased. In 1861 there were between 2,000 and 3,000 workpeople employed by Courtaulds. From that time onwards the growth was continuous, and after the acquisition in the early years of the 20th century of the British right to manufacture rayon yarn by the viscose process, Courtaulds became an international concern.

Later members of the family have distinguished themselves both locally and nationally as enlightened benefactors. Sir William Courtauld (1870-1940) built and furnished a new Town Hall at Braintree in 1938. Samuel Courtauld (1876-1947) became a distinguished art patron. He acquired great wealth by his skilful direction of the firm while chairman of the Board of Directors; but was a man with wider horizons who had a profound belief in the importance of spiritual values in human relations and a conviction that art was 'religion's next of kin'. In 1923 he gave £50,000 for the purchase of paintings by a select number of French artists for the Tate Gallery, and on his wife's death in 1931 founded the Courtauld Institute of Art. For many years he was chairman of the National Gallery's Board of Trustees; he was also a trustee of the Tate Gallery. His only daughter married R. A. Butler, later Lord Butler of Saffron Walden. She died in 1954. Lord Butler married as his second wife the widow of Augustine Courtauld (1904-57), the arctic explorer, who published an autobiography in 1957 under the title Man the Ropes.

COWDRAY, Viscount See PEARSON

COYS

William Coys (1560-1627), botanist, lived at Stubbers, North Ockendon. His wife was a daughter of Giles Allen of Haseleigh Hall, and by her had a family of 14 children. John Goodyer, a Hampshire botanist, visited Coys in 1618, and took away with him a list of plants grown at Stubbers. This is the earliest known MS. list of an English garden in which the plants are properly distinguished by their scientific names. The garden had already been known to Gerard in 1597. Stubbers was acquired by the Essex County Council in 1947.

CRACHEROOD

This family held the manor of Cust Hall and the estate known as
Cracherood's in Toppesfield for over 300 years. The first of the
line was John, who died in 1534, leaving four sons and four daughters. His great-great-grandson is represented in a brass in
Toppesfield church. The estate was sold in 1780.

CRANFIELD

Lionel Cranfield, Earl of Middlesex (1575-1645), Stuart financier
and Minister of State, lived at Copt Hall, Epping. After a successful business career, in which he amassed a fortune exporting fine
woollen cloth to the Netherlands and dabbling in such varied commodities as pepper, dyewood, grain, and guns, he was appointed
Surveyor General of the Customs in 1613, and within two years
increased the royal income by £30,000 a year. In 1619 he was appointed Master of the Court of Wards, and after six years in that
office had increased the income by one-quarter. In 1621 he became
Lord Treasurer; the following year he was created Earl of Middlesex.

As Lord Treasurer he advocated a policy of strict economy, which
made him unpopular at court when it was discovered that his cuts
were to be applied to the incomes of court favourites. He immediately
fell foul of Buckingham, the king's favourite. In 1624 he was impeached and found guilty of 'bribery, extortion, oppression, wrong and
deceit'. He was fined £50,000 and imprisoned in the Tower for a
short time. After his release he lived quietly at Copt Hall, Epping,
and became interested in encroachments on the royal forests.

Cranfield's career and policy have continued to interest historians
because of his application of business methods to State finance. He
owed his rise to Villiers, who no doubt thought he would be successful in raising revenues for the king, but did not foresee that in the
reorganising of court administration he himself would be affected.
Cranfield's achievements in reorganising the administration of the
Customs, curtailing the expenses of the Household and the Wardrobe,
cleaning up the administration of wardships, and bringing about econ-
omies in the Navy, were all impressive. He fell because his policies
brought him into conflict with court favourites who in Cranfield's
eyes failed to earn their keep. Seen from the modern point of view,
he failed through excess of zeal.

Cranfield was the uncle of Sir John Suckling, the poet. Frances, the
fourth child of Cranfield's second marriage, claimed that she was on
familiar terms with her romantic cousin. This is supported by Pope,
who believed she was the mistress and goddess of the poems. If this
is true, the romance must have started early in her life, because she
was only 16 in 1641 when Suckling fled to France.

On the death of the 3rd Earl of Middlesex, Copt Hall passed to Frances's
son, Charles Sackville. A portrait of Frances Cranfield by Van Dyck
may be seen at Knole.

See R. H. Tawney: Business and Politics under James I
                   Victoria County History, Essex v

CREFFIELD

The Creffield family of Colchester is believed to be descended from Flemish immigrants. The first reliable reference to them is in the court rolls of the manor of Crepping Hall, Wakes Colne, where Thomas Creffield appears as a tenant in 1348. The name continued in the district for 400 years and from there spread to Fordham, Pebmarsh and Colchester.

Ralph Creffield became a free burgess of Colchester in 1656 and was evidently a man of substance. He was an alderman of the borough and mayor in 1668, 1673, 1677 and 1680. He died at the age of 77 about 1703. His grandson, also Ralph, lived at Holly Trees, Colchester, and was both an alderman and a freeman of the borough. He died at the age of 36 in 1723. Of his sons, only Peter survived. He died in 1748, leaving only one daughter, Thamar, wife of James Round of Birch Hall (q.v.).

After the death of her husband, Mrs. Ralph Creffield of Holly Trees married Charles Gray, M.P. for Colchester in five parliaments, 1747-80, and owner of Colchester Castle, who bequeathed the castle to his 'dear friends and relations, James Round, Esquire, and Thamar, his wife, late Thamar Creffield, spinster, from whose good family a great deal of my substance has been derived'.

See East Ang. Mag; n.s. iii 226; E.A.T. n.s. viii 226; E.R. liii 159

CRIPPS

Arthur Shearley Cripps (1869-1952), poet and missionary, is commorated in the church of Ford End (a parish carved out of Great Waltham), of which he was twice vicar. His first ministry was from 1895 to 1900, his second from 1927 to 1930. Between the two was his first long period of missionary service in Southern Rhodesia, to which he returned in 1930, although as a champion of native rights he would never use the name if he could avoid it. It is a fitting tribute to his great work for Africa that the memorial at Ford End, which was the gift of the diocese of Mashonaland, depicts the Crucifixion, with all three figures personified as native Africans. In old age this saintly man became blind and impoverished, but he continued to hold the devotion of the people he served and among whom he died.

CRISP

Stephen Crisp (1628-92), Quaker, was born at Colchester, the son of a prosperous bay-maker. In 1655 he was converted to Quakerism by the preaching of James Parnell (q.v.), the first Quaker martyr. From 1660 to the end of his life he was a Quaker missionary, preaching and writing books. He bequeathed an interesting collection of papers and letters to the Colchester Meeting. These were summarised for publication in 1892 by Charlotte Fell Smith (q.v.).

CRITTALL

Francis Henry Crittall (1860-1935), industrialist and benefactor, was born at Braintree, where his father was an ironmonger. In his Fifty Years of Work and Play (1934) he states that his grandfather and great-grandfather both kept the 'Swan' at West Wickham in Suffolk. In 1883 Francis Crittall took over the family business. Two or three years later he and his brother started the manufacture of metal window

frames. The business prospered, and in 1889 the Crittall Manufacturing Company was established. Francis's son, Valentine George
Crittall (1884-1861), succeeded him as head of the firm. He represented Maldon, 1923-4, as Labour member. He was knighted in 1930,
and raised to the peerage as Baron Braintree in 1948. At his death
in 1961 the barony became extinct. Francis Crittall's dream of creating a town in which his workpeople could live in a healthy and pleasant environment was realised in the building of Silver End, started
in 1926 in conjunction with a subsidiary factory for disabled men.

CROMPTON

Rookes Evelyn Bell Crompton (1845-1940), pioneer of commercial
electric power, was the founder of the Chelmsford firm of Crompton
Parkinson. He was a Yorkshireman, born at Thirsk, the son of a
local landowner, and he maintained his interest in Yorkshire throughout his life. His mother was descended from John Evelyn, the diarist.
Crompton came to Essex in 1871 as partner in the steam-valve manufacturing company of T. H. P. Dennis & Co. His first great contribution to industry was his introduction of the manufacture of gener-
ators, by means of which he was instrumental in supplying electric
light and power to Buckingham Palace, King's Cross Station, the
Mansion House, and the Law Courts.

The first private house in Europe to have electric light was Berechurch
Hall, Colchester, the home of Mr. Coope, the brewer. As a result
of having the firm in Chelmsford, the county town was the first town
in England to have electric street lights.

In 1885 Crompton made a double-check electric tram-car. In 1890 the
first London underground train on the City and South London tube was
powered by a Crompton engine.

In 1907 Rookes Crompton was elected first president of the Institute
of Automobile Engineers. In 1927, Crompton and Co., of Chelmsford
was merged with F. & A. Parkinson Ltd., of Guiseley, Yorkshire,
to form Crompton Parkinson Ltd. Crompton remained a director of
the firm until his death at the age of 94 in 1940. He published his
reminiscences in 1928. In 1968 the firm was taken over by the
Hawker Siddley Company.

CROMWELL

Oliver Cromwell (1599-1658), Lord Protector, married in 1620,
Elizabeth, daughter of Sir James Bourchier (q.v.), a London mer-
chant who lived at Grandcourts, Felsted, and Little Stambridge.
His four sons, Robert, Oliver, Richard, and Henry, attended
Felsted School. One of the four, Robert, died in 1639, aged 18.
His daughter, Frances, married Robert Rich, who was considered
by Cromwell to be 'a vicious man, given to play and such-like things'.
Rich died within four months of the ceremony.

Cromwell bought New Hall, Boreham (the Duke of Buckingham's place),
from the commissioners appointed to sell traitors' estates, for the
derisory sum of five shillings; but he spent little time there and in
1653 exchanged it for Hampton Court. In a letter to his son, Richard,
he wrote:
    'You know that there is often a desire to sell Newhall,
    because in these four years last past it hath yielded very
    little or no profit at all.'

In 1659 Richard Cromwell referred to New Hall as intended as 'a portion for my sister, Frances'.

Cromwell was related to the Mashams of Otes, High Laver (q.v.), and visited them there. His cousin, Jane, daughter of Sir Oliver Cromwell of Hinchingbrooke, is buried in the chancel of Chipping Ongar church.

CROMWELL

Thomas Cromwell (1485?-1540), Earl of Essex, entered the service of Wolsey on returning from service overseas under the Duke of Bourbon. He was Wolsey's agent at the dissolution of the smaller monasteries, and as such was active in Essex. About the time of his appointment as Chancellor of the Exchequer (1533), Sir Thomas More said:

> 'Mark, Cromwell, you are now entered into the service of a most noble, wise, and liberal prince; if you will follow my poor advice, you shall, in your council-giving to his Grace, ever tell him what he ought to do, but never what he is able to do ... for if a lion knew his own strength, hard were it for any man to rule him.'

He did not heed the advice.

In his conduct as Visitor-General of the Monasteries, Cromwell sowed the seeds of his own dissolution. In 1536 he was raised to the peerage as Baron Cromwell of Oakham in Rutland. He filled in succession the posts of Master of the Jewel Office, Principal Secretary, Master of the Rolls, and Lord Privy Seal. In 1540 he was created Earl of Essex and invested Lord High Chamberlain. His fall came after the king's marriage with Anne of Cleves, which he had negotiated. He was accused of treason by the Duke of Norfolk and executed.

CUTTS, or CUTTE

According to Leland, the present Horham Hall, on the border of Thaxted and Broxted, was built by Sir John Cutts (d. 1520), Treasurer of the Household to Henry VIII, who purchased the estate in 1502. In 1514 Queen Catherine of Aragon granted him a lease during her lifetime of the manor of Thaxted. He died in 1520, leaving two sons, John and Henry, of whom the elder died in 1528, leaving an only son, John, aged three, who died in 1555, leaving one son, aged ten. This was the Sir John who lived in such extravagant style that in 1599 he was obliged to alienate the manor and borough of Thaxted to Thomas Kemp. At his death in 1615, Horham also passed from the family.

Another branch of the family was seated at Arkesden. Peter Cutts of Woodhall, Arkesden (d. 1547), left a son, Richard (d. 1592), who married Mary, daughter of Edward Elrington of Theydon Bois. He and his wife have a large Elizabethan monument at Arkesden. Their eldest son, Richard (d. 1607), succeeded to the second moiety of family estates in Cambridgeshire on the death of his cousin, Sir Henry Cutts of Childerley.

Richard Cutts of Arkesden was followed by his brother, Sir William (d. 1609), and in turn by his son, Richard, then 11 years old. This Richard died in 1626, leaving a son, John, who was then only six years of age, thus continuing the family tradition of inheriting large estates during infancy. He became the ward of Charles I and married a daughter of Sir Richard Everard of Langleys, Great Waltham (q.v.). Later in life he lived at Childerley. His son, John, Baron Cutts, who

was born at Arkesden, became the gallant soldier who served under
Marlborough and figures in Macaulay's History. He was described
by Swift as being 'as brave and brainless as the sword he wears'.
To Steele however, he was 'Honest Cynthio'. He was handsome and
witty, an accomplished writer of verse, and so reckless a soldier
that he was nicknamed 'Salamander' for his daring under fire. After
showing conspicuous bravery in fighting against the Turks in 1686
at the siege of Buda he returned to England with William of Orange's
invading army in 1688. For his services at the Boyne he was given
an Irish peerage. He again showed outstanding courage under
Marlborough at the siege of Venloo in 1702. The following winter
he was in command of the English forces in Holland and held high
command at Blenheim. From that time onwards his health deteriorated
as the accumulated result of the many wounds he had suffered in a
long succession of arduous campaigns. He died suddenly in Ireland
in 1707, and with his death the barony became extinct. He had already
sold Woodhall, Arkesden, to Thomas Maynard of Bury St. Edmunds.

DALE

Samuel Dale (1659?-1738), botanist, was the son of North Dale, a
silk-throwster of Whitechapel; but he is believed to have been born
at Braintree, where he became the friend of John Ray (q.v.) and
Benjamin Allen (q.v.). He corresponded with Hans Sloane and several eminent botanists of the period. His Pharmacologia (1693), which
was dedicated to the Royal College of Physicians, was the earliest
comprehensive treatise on the subject. He was also interested in
local history, and assisted his neighbour, William Holman (q.v.),
with his work, while at the same time collecting material for his own
History of Harwich and Dovercourt (1730). In 1737 he wrote a sketch
of John Ray which remained unpublished until 1917 (E.R. xv). Like
his friend, Benjamin Allen, Dale was a physician with a large practice in mid-Essex and a prominent nonconformist.

DARCY

The Darcy family claimed descent from one of the Norman knights
who came over at the Conquest. By the 16th century there were four
main branches in the county, seated respectively at Danbury, Maldon,
Tolleshunt D'Arcy, and St. Osyth, the last branch becoming the dominant one.

The foundation of the fortune of the recorded branches of the family
were laid by Robert Darcy, a lawyer's clerk who married the widow
of John Ingoe, a rich merchant of Maldon. He left two sons, Sir
Robert Darcy of Danbury and John Darcy of Tolleshunt.

Sir Robert Darcy of Maldon and Danbury, High Sheriff of Essex and
Hertfordshire in 1420, married a daughter of Sir Thomas Tyrell of
Heron in East Horndon (q.v.). His great-grandson, Sir Thomas
Darcy (1506-58), married Elizabeth, daughter of John de Vere, 15th
Earl of Oxford (q.v.), and it was probably the de Vere connection
that gained him employment at Court, where he became Vice-Chamber-
lain of the King's Household and Knight of the Garter under Edward
VI, and in 1551 was raised to the peerage as Baron Darcy of Chich.
St. Osyth's Priory was granted to him in 1553, and he immediately
set about converting the monastic buildings into a country house for
himself. He died at Wivenhoe in 1558.

John, 2nd Lord Darcy (d. 1581), married a daughter of Lord Chancellor Rich (q.v.). He was Lord Lieutenant of Essex, 1569-81, and

entertained Elizabeth I at St. Osyth in 1561 and 1578. He accompanied the Earl of Essex to Ireland. By his will he directed that monuments should be erected in the church at St. Osyth to his father and
mother, and also to himself and his wife, 'meet for their estates and
degrees'.

Thomas, 3rd Lord Darcy, who erected these monuments has no monument to himself. He was born about 1565, and married Mary, daughter and co-heiress of Sir Thomas Kitson, of Hengrave Hall, Suffolk.
There were five children of the marriage. One son, who died before
his father, and four daughters. The son, Thomas Darcy (d. 1613),
was buried at Hengrave, where his grandmother, Lady Kitson, erected a fine monument to him, bearing a quaint inscription.

The 3rd Lord Darcy's marriage was not a happy one. After about 11
years together he and his wife parted by mutual consent and lived
apart for 40 years. He was said to be weak and perverse, she to be
proud and obstinate. But whatever his faults, Lord Darcy found favour at Court. He was created Viscount Colchester in 1621, Earl
Rivers in 1626, both titles with remainder to his son-in-law, Sir
Thomas Savage. At his death in 1639 the barony of Darcy of Chich
became extinct.

Sir Thomas Savage, on whom the viscountcy and earldom had been
entailed, predeceased him, but his own widow (d. 1644) took the
title of Countess Rivers, and her son succeeded as 2nd Earl Rivers.
His descendant, who died in 1712, left no legitimate issue and gave
his estates to his natural daughter, Bessy, who married the Right
Hon. Frederick Zuleistern de Nassau, Earl of Rochford (q.v.).

DARCY of Tolleshunt and Tiptree

John Darcy, brother of Sir Robert of Maldon and Danbury (see above)
acquired Tolleshunt by his second marriage with a member of the
Bois family. His eldest surviving son by his first wife was Thomas
(b. 1511), who purchased the estate of Tiptree Priory.

DAY

Daniel Day (1683-1767), pump and engine maker of Wapping, owned
a small estate near Fairlop, where he became interested in a fine
old oak, said to have had a girth of 36 feet and a spread of 17 branches.
On the first Friday of July each year Daniel Day entertained his friends
under the tree with a feast of beans and bacon. This annual beano
gradually developed into a fair, until by 1725 the oak was surrounded
by ginger-bread stalls, puppet-shows, wild-beast menageries and
every conceivable adjunct to cockney jollification.

Day and his friends made the journey into Essex in a model boat
mounted on wheels. As a rhymed celebration of the custom had it:

> O'er land our vessel bent its course,
> Guarded by troops of foot and horse;
> Our anchors they were all a-peak,
> Our crew were baling from each leak,
> On Stratford Bridge it made me quiver,
> Lest they should spill us in the river.

Day was a bachelor. When a limb fell from the oak he believed it to be
an omen of his approaching death and had a coffin made for himself
from the timber. When he examined it he expressed a doubt as to
whether it would be long enough. He said he had a feeling that people
stretched a bit after death. Climbing into the coffin to try the fit, he

said he still thought it would prove too short;'but,' said he, 'never
mind about that. Just ask my executors to cut off my head and tuck
it between my legs.'

DAY

Susanna Day (1747-1826) of Saffron Walden, Quakeress, in 1774
married Thomas Day, grocer, linen-draper, and chandler, of
Stansted Mountfitchet and later of Saffron Walden. Both husband
and wife were ministers in the Society of Friends. Among the assistants in her husband's business, who lived in, were Robert Lloyd,
the poet friend of Charles Lamb, who visited him at Saffron Walden,
and Thomas Rickman, the architect, who was responsible for the
spire of Saffron Walden church. Susanna Day was an admirable
letter writer and diarist. She was also clever at cutting out silhou-
ettes from life. She kept a diary from 1797 to 1805.

DEANE

Anthony Deane of Harwich (c. 1625-1721), shipbuilder, has been
badly treated by biographers. Morant, the D.N.B. and Bloom's
Harwich are all unreliable. He was born c.1625, the son of Anthony
Deane of London, and not of the Harwich family of Deane. He owed
much of his advancement to the friendship of Pepys, who found him
'a pretty able man and able to do the king service'. In 1664 the interest of Pepys secured him the appointment of Master Shipwright at
Harwich, where he built eight men-of-war. In 1668 he was appointed
to Portsmouth, where he rose to be Commissioner of the Navy in
1672 and Comptroller of the Victualling in 1675.

In May 1679 Pepys and Sir Anthony Deane were committed to the
Tower to await trial on a charge of transmitting information concerning the English Navy to the French government. These charges were
trumped up by a scoundrel who owed Pepys a grudge and the case
was abandoned on further enquiries being made.

In the year of their imprisonment Pepys and Deane were the two
Members for Harwich. Both appear to have retired from public office
about the same time. Deane described his retirement as 'a little space
between business and the grave'. It extended in his case to more than
30 years. There is a portrait of him in the Pepysian Library at
Cambridge.

DEANE

William Deane, who in 1575 purchased Dynes Hall, Great Maplestead,
and rebuilt the house, was a son of John Deane of the Blackburn district of Lancashire and a daughter of Roger Nowell of Read Hall,
Lancashire. He came to Essex as steward to Anne, Lady Mautravers,
daughter of Sir John Wentworth, and became wealthy as the result of
this marriage. It has often been referred to as one of mistress marrying a servant of low degree, which is quite wrong. The Deanes were
a family of substance, and the Nowells of Read Hall an important
county family. It was quite common for a younger son of good family
to take an appointment as steward, which is what happened here.

After the death of Lady Mautravers, Deane married a second wife,
by whom he had three children. His son, John, succeeded in 1585.
In 1603 he was knighted and later became Lord Lieutenant.

John Deane was brought up under the guardianship of his great-uncle (his father's uncle) Alexander Nowell, Dean of St. Pauls, who spent much time at Dynes Hall. John Deane was M.P. for Essex, 1620-23. He died in 1625 and was buried in Great Maplestead church, where his handsome monument stands. His widow, a daughter of Sir Drue Drury of Riddlesworth, has a beautiful monument at Great Maplestead, in which she is represented standing erect while two angelic figures hold a crown of glory over her head. At her feet is the recumbent figure of her son, Sir Drue Deane.

After four generations of the Deane family had lived there, Dynes Hall was sold in 1653 by an Anthony Deane, but not, as has sometimes been stated, the Anthony of Harwich. Anthony Deane had succeeded his father, Sir Drue Deane of Great Maplestead, in 1651.

DEE

Dr. John Dee (1527-1608), astrologer, was educated at Chelmsford Grammar School. At 15 he left Chelmsford to enter St. John's College, Cambridge.

DEFOE

The Foe family lived at Chadwell, near Tilbury, in the 15th century. In 1694, Daniel Defoe (1661-1731) established a pantile works there. He had a fine house near the river and lived in style with his coach and pleasure boat; but he neglected his business and got into trouble with such publications as The Shortest Way with Dissenters. In 1703 he became involved in a lawsuit about the payment of beer supplied to his workpeople. His relations with them do not appear to have been happy. He was obliged to employ any beggars or casual labourers who happened to be in the district. He himself states:
'I affirm of my own knowledge, when I have wanted a man for labouring work, and offered nine shillings a week to strolling fellows at my door, they have frequently told me to my face that they could get more a-begging; and I once set a lusty fellow in the stocks for making the experiment.'
Defoe's tiles were reputed to be too porous to keep houses weatherproof. Dutch competition put him out of business. He is said to have lost £3,000 in the enterprise.

The early scenes of Moll Flanders (1722) are laid in Colchester, where Defoe had a friend in the Rev. William Smithies, rector of St. Michael's, Mile End. In 1722 Mr. Smithies negotiated a lease for Defoe of an estate called Kingswood Heath, or Severalls, near Colchester, for the use of his daughter, Hannah, who 'lived upon her income in respectable gentility until her death in 1759'.

Defoe's most important work from the county point of view is the Eastern Counties section of his Tour through Great Britain, published in 1724. Parts of it, however, are to be taken with a pinch of salt. It is in this work that he tells the well-known tall story to illustrate the unwholesomeness of the marshes,
'insomuch that all along this country it was very frequent to meet with men that had from five or six to 14 or 15 wives; nay, and some more. And I was informed that in the marshes on the other side of the river, over against Candy, there was a farmer who was then living with his five and twentieth wife, and that his son, who was but about thirty-five years old, had already had about 14.'

The alleged explanation was that the farmers themselves were born
and bred on the marshes, but went inland for their wives, who quickly succumbed and died when exposed to the damp air of the marshes.
Defoe admitted later that it had come to his knowledge that one of his
informers had 'fibbed a little'.

See Margaret Tabor, Essex Journal vol. IV no. iv

DENNY

The Denny family of Waltham Abbey claimed descent from a John
Denny who served in France under Henry V. An Edmund Denny of
Cheshunt, Hertfordshire (d. 1520), was appointed one of the barons
of the Exchequer in 1514. His son, Sir Anthony Denny (1500-49),
married a Champernoun of Devon who was the aunt of Sir Walter
Raleigh and Sir Humphry Gilbert. He was Chief Gentleman of the
Privy Chamber and Groom of the Stole to Henry VIII, who appointed
him one of the guardians of Edward VI. The Abbey lands at Waltham
were granted to him in reward for his services.

Sir Anthony's eldest son, Henry, died in 1574. As his eldest son,
Robert, was then only nine and died two years later, the estates
passed to the second son, Edward (1569-1637), who was knighted
in 1589. He was High Sheriff in 1603 when James I passed through
Waltham to take his place on the English throne, and Stow states
that Sir Edward rode out to receive him attended by 140 men in blue
liveries and white doublets, mounted on horses with red saddles.

Sir Edward was elected M.P. for Essex in 1604. In the same year
he was raised to the peerage as Baron Denny of Waltham. In 1626
he was created Earl of Norwich. At his death in 1637 he left a grandson, the only son of his daughter, Honora, who in 1604 had married
James Hay, 1st Earl of Carlisle (q.v.). The original Denny titles are
now extinct, but the family is represented by a baronetcy, created in
1762.

DENT

Arthur Dent (1553-1608), Puritan divine, was rector of South
Shoebury from 1580 to his death 28 years later. He was one of the
signatories of a petition from many Essex non-conformists who refused to recognise the scriptural validity of the Prayer Book. In 1601
he published The Plaine Man's Path-way to Heaven, a best-seller,
of which by 1637 24 editions had been issued. As her entire marriage
portion, John Bunyan's wife brought with her two books, one of which
was Dent's Plaine Man's Path-way. It proved to be of more value to
her husband than she can have foreseen. It was written in the form of
a conversation between four persons on their journey from this world
to the next and Bunyan used it as a model for his own works.

DERHAM

William Derham (1657-1735), rector of Upminster from 1689, was an
ardent student of natural history who wrote voluminously on religious
and scientific subjects. He was elected a Fellow of the Royal Society
in 1702, was Boyle lecturer in 1711 and 12, and counted Newton,
Wren, Ray, and Hans Sloane among his friends. He corresponded
with Dacre Barrett of Belhus on subjects ranging from experiments
in acoustics to observations on sun spots and the flight of ants. His
writings included Physico-Theology, Astro-Theology, and a life of

John Ray of Black Notley (q.v.). He was one of the first to discover
the velocity of sound, which he did by having guns fired in different
parts of Essex and calculating the distances by counting the vibrat-
ions of a half-second pendulum. One of his experiments was conducted at Foulness, which was chosen because it provided a large plain
for the accurate measurement of distances. Dr. Derham measured
out six miles in a straight line, and caused a gun to be fired at the
end of each mile. He found that the sound passed the first mile post
in $9\frac{3}{4}$ half-seconds, the second in $18\frac{1}{2}$, the third in $27\frac{1}{4}$, and so on
consistently throughout the measured length.

DEVEREUX

The Devereux family claimed descent from the younger of the two
brothers d'Evereux who came over with the Conqueror. Their association with the Essex earldom began with the marriage of John
Devereux, 2nd Lord Ferrers, with Cecily, heiress of the houses
of Bohun and Bourchier.

Walter Devereux, 1st Earl of Essex (1541?-76), succeeded his
grandfather in the viscountcy of Hereford and the baronies of Ferrers,
Bourchier, and Louvaine in 1558. In 1569 he was sent by Elizabeth I
to suppress the northern rising under the Earls of Northumberland
and Westmorland. He was created Earl of Essex in 1572 in consideration of his descent from the Bohun and Bourchier earls (q.v.). The
following year he undertook to conquer Ulster, and in return the queen
granted him the moiety of the county of Antrim. But there was a condition that he was to maintain an army equal to that maintained by the
queen herself. As Fuller said:
> 'To maintain an army, though a very little one, is a
> Sovereign's and no subject's work, too heavy for the
> support of any private man's estate; which cost this
> Earl first the mortgaging, then the selling outright,
> his fair inheritance in Essex.'

To enable him to fulfil this obligation the queen actually lent him
£10,000 at 10% interest, with forfeiture for non-payment - the instrument stating:
> 'The Earl of Essex hath assured, by bargain and sale,
> and with fine, to the Lord Treasurer, Sir Walter Mildmay,
> the Attorney and Solicitor Generals, to the use of our
> Sovereign Lady the Queen, manors, lands, and tenements,
> to the yearly value of £500, in pawn for £10,000, that her
> Majesty lent him for three years', etc.

The Essex lands mortgaged to the queen were the manors of Tolleshunt
Bourchier, Potting and Rushley, Old Hall and Bourchier Hall in
Tollesbury, Tollesbury Wood, Hallingbury Bourchier, Swaynes in
Wivenhoe, Bakers in Goldhanger.

Sir Walter Mildmay, the Lord Treasurer, was not the only Essex
landowner interested in the earl's adventure. Sir William FitzWilliam
of Gaynes Park, Epping (q.v.), Lord Deputy of Ireland, supported by
the Earl of Leicester, protested against the proposal that Essex
should hold the title of Captain General of Ulster, and was successful in persuading the queen to stipulate that he should hold his commission as Governor of Ulster from Sir William as Lord Deputy and
not from the Crown. FitzWilliam's immediate neighbour in Essex, Sir
Thomas Smith of Hill Hall, Theydon Mount, also suffered greatly as
the result of an agreement to colonise part of Northern Ireland, by
which he was granted land in the Ardes, where his only son was

murdered when the Irish took advantage of the queen's withdrawal of
her own troops to revolt.

Two Essex peers, Lords Rich (son of Lord Chancellor Rich) and
Lord Darcy (q.v.), accompanied the earl to Ireland and were involved
in the many problems that attended the venture. Essex's undertaking
would have been difficult enough on any terms. It was made infinitely
more arduous through the understandable jealousy of Sir William
FitzWilliam, who sent home highly critical reports. In this attitude
Sir William had powerful supporters headed by Leicester. Nor could
Sir William be blamed entirely. It was obviously a grave affront to
him as Lord Deputy to have so high ranking a nobleman holding so
important a command in Ireland, even although Essex had agreed,
under pressure, to serve under the Lord Deputy.

This adventure in Ireland cost the earl (in addition to the £10,000
borrowed from the queen) not less than £25,000, yet on Sir William
FitzWilliam's retirement, notwithstanding his belief that Sir William
had been the cause of his misfortunes, he wrote a dignified letter to
Burghley in which he used these words:
> 'I wish that your Lordship will still so use your favour,
> as he seems not to have made shipwreck of a service that
> hath been tied to so many cares and troubles.'

In 1575 Essex was appointed Earl Marshal of Ireland. He died there
the following year. After his death an unfounded rumour alleged that
he had been poisoned at the instigation of Leicester, who married
his widow, the beautiful daughter of Sir Francis Knollys. She was
first cousin of Ann Boleyn.

Robert, 2nd Earl of Essex (1566-1601), eldest son of the 1st Earl,
favourite of Elizabeth I, K.G., Master of the Horse, Earl Marshal
of England, Lord Deputy of Ireland, etc., married Frances, daughter of Sir Francis Walsingham and widow of Sir Philip Sidney. His
crowded career belongs to national rather than local history and
need not be recounted here. He was attainted of high treason and
beheaded in the Tower in 1601.

Robert, 3rd Earl of Essex (1591-1646), parliamentary general, was
restored in blood and honour by James I in 1604. In 1606 he married
the wicked Lady Frances Howard, daughter of Thomas Howard, 1st
Earl of Suffolk (q.v.), of Audley End. The marriage was dissolved
in 1613 and she married Robert Carr, Earl of Somerset, favourite
of James I. The earl then married, in 1630, Elizabeth, daughter of
Sir William Paulet of Edington, Wilts. The 3rd earl served as Lord
Chamberlain to Charles I. He became Commander-in-Chief of the
Parliamentary Army in 1642. At his death in 1646 he was buried in
Westminster Abbey. His only son had died in infancy, so in 1646 the
earldom of Essex again became extinct.

Penelope Devereux (d. 1607), daughter of the 1st Earl of Essex and
sister of Elizabeth's favourite, was engaged to marry Sir Philip
Sidney, but the marriage did not take place and she was married
against her will to the Lord Rich who in 1618 was created Earl of
Warwick (q.v.). She was the Stella of Sidney's sonnets. She deserted her husband for Charles Blount, Lord Mountjoy, afterwards Earl
of Devonshire, whom she had taken as her lover after Sidney's death.
At the accession of James I, Lady Rich was granted 'the place and
rank of the ancientest Earl of Essex, called Bourchier', to whom her
father was heir. Previously she had been ranked according to her
husband's barony. By James I's grant she took precedence at court

of all the baronnesses in the kingdom, and of all earl's daughters, except Arundel, Oxford, Northumberland, and Shrewsbury.

Charles, Earl of Devonshire, and Penelope, Lady Rich, were married at Wanstead in 1605; but in the opinion of the king, who considered himself an authority on such matters, the marriage was illegal, and the arguments on its legality had not been concluded when the earl died in 1606.

See W. B. Devereux: Lives and Deaths of the Devereux Earls of
                     Essex, 1540-1646 (2 vols. 1853)
     M. S. Rawson: Penelope Rich and her Circle (1911)

D'EWES

One of the romantic love stories of Essex is that of Sir Simon D'Ewes, the diarist, who in 1622, at the age of 20, fell in love with Jemima, younger daughter of Edward Waldegrave of Lawford Hall. The account of the courtship (retold in Blackwood's Magazine, vol. 68 p.141) presents a charming portrait of Stuart life. Sir Edward, the father, was won over without much difficulty, but Dame Sarah, the mother, had loftier ambitions for her daughter. In his Life, written by himself (Harleian MSS. 646.27), he says of the notorious Frances Howard (q.v.), Countess of Essex, that she captivated the Prince of Wales, who first enjoyed her.

DUDLEY

Robert Dudley, Earl of Leicester, K.G. (1533-88), Elizabeth I's favourite, son of the Duke of Northumberland who schemed to place his daughter-in-law, Lady Jane Grey, on the throne, was Lord Lieutenant of Essex, 1581-8. He purchased Wanstead from the son of Lord Chancellor Rich (q.v.). In 1578, Elizabeth I paid a five-day visit to Leicester at Wanstead, when Philip Sidney's play The Lady of May was performed in her honour. Later that same year, after the death in mysterious circumstances of his first wife, Amy Robsart (see Sir Walter Scott's Kenilworth), Leicester married Lettice Knowles, widow of Walter Devereux, 1st Earl of Essex (q.v.) at Wanstead, a previous marriage having been performed privately at Kenilworth.

When the Armada was expected to land in 1588, Leicester called up the trained bands and established a camp at Tilbury for the defence of London. It was at this camp that Elizabeth made her famous speech, with Leicester holding her bridle rein. Within a month of the Tilbury review Leicester died on his way to Kenilworth, probably from fever caught on the Essex marshes. He was deeply in debt at the time, but despite this the bill for his funeral amounted to £4,000. At his death, Wanstead became the property of the widowed Countess, who then married Sir Christopher Blount, Earl of Devonshire.

DYNES

The Dynes family of Great Maplestead produced a Sir John Dynes, who was Member of Parliament for Essex from 1310 to 1338. He died in 1341. In 1343 his widow confirmed his grant of land to the Hospitallers of St. John of Jerusalem in Little Maplestead. The hall built by the Dynes was replaced by one built by William Deane (q.v.).

DICKENS

Charles Dickens (1812-70), novelist, drove through Essex in 1834
on his way to Sudbury. The weather kept him indoors, with the result that Chelmsford was described as 'the dullest and most stupid
spot on the face of the earth'. Chigwell fared better with him. He
loved the village. In a letter to Forster, following a visit to the
'King's Head' in 1841, he said:
> 'Chigwell, my dear fellow, is the greatest place in the
> world. Name your day for going. Such a delicious old
> inn opposite the churchyard - such a lovely ride - such
> beautiful forest scenery - such an out-of-the-way rural
> place - such a sexton! I say again, name your day.'

The 'King's Head' figures as the 'Maypole Inn' in Barnaby Rudge,
although, as Dickens put it, he 'patched' and produced a composite
picture by introducing features from Chigwell Row, which had a
Maypole Inn.

He took a noted Pickwickian from the forest in the person of Serjeant
Arabin of High Beach, who became the original of Serjeant Snubbin,
leading counsel for the defence in the trial of Bardell v Pickwick.

DIMSDALE

Thomas Dimsdale (1712-1800), pioneer of inoculation, was born at
Theydon Garnon. His grandfather, Robert Dimsdale, practised as
a surgeon at Theydon Garnon (which then took in much of the present
town of Epping) and later at Bishops Stortford. He accompanied
William Penn on a visit to America in 1684. His father, John Dimsdale,
also practised at Theydon Garnon. Thomas followed them in the practise of medicine and surgery, and developed an interest in inoculation
which led to his being recommended by his Quaker friend, John
Fothergill (q.v.), to go to St. Petersburg in 1768 in order to inocul-
ate the Empress Catherine and her son for smallpox. The mission was
so successful that he was created a Baron of the Russian Empire by
the empress and rewarded with a present of £10,000, an annuity of
£500 a year, and miniatures of the Empress and the Grand Duke.

Dimsdale was already a wealthy man when he went to Russia. He had
inherited money from his father, and had married, as his second wife,
the well-to-do Anne Iles, with whom he lived at the Priory, Hertford,
where he raised a large family. His first paper on inoculation was
published in 1767. Seven editions followed and the work was translated into several languages.

He was elected a Fellow of the Royal Society in 1769, shortly after
his return from Russia, and continued to practise inoculation at
Hertford, where he died at the age of 88 in 1800. He was buried in
the Friends' Burial Ground at Bishops Stortford.

DODD

Dr. William Dodd (1729-77), forger, was curate of West Ham for 15
years (1751-66), and published several literary and philosophical
works during the period. He appears to have been something of a
dandy. Horace Walpole said that he 'preached very elegantly in the
French style'. He is said to have been nicknamed the 'macaroni
parson'. In 1763 he was appointed chaplain to the king; but was
struck off the list of royal chaplains in 1774 for improper solicitation
of preferment from the Lord Chancellor. His weakness for the ladies

and extravagant style of living led him into debt, and to meet these
he forged a bond for £4,200, which he signed with the name of his
former pupil, Lord Chesterfield. Numerous petitions for clemency
were presented on his behalf. The whole of the money was repaid by
influential friends, and when a sentence of death was passed on him,
Dr. Johnson tried to get it commuted to transportation; but Dodd was
executed in 1777 - not, however, before he had managed to produce
his last work: Thoughts in Prison. It was said that as two well-born
brothers had recently been executed for forging a bond, it would not
be appropriate to reprieve a mere curate. Dodd's widow spent the
rest of her life at Ilford.

See P. A. FitzGerald: A Famous Forger, Dodd Collection in
                      Stratford Central Library.

DOUBLEDAY

Henry Doubleday (1808-75), naturalist, was the son of a Quaker
grocer who set up in business at Epping in 1770 in premises that
had previously been the 'Black Boy' inn. He was educated at a nearby local school conducted by a highly respected Quaker schoolmaster,
Isaac Payne. Both Henry and his younger brother, Edward, assisted
their father in the shop; but Edward left home in his early twenties
to travel in America collecting insects, birds and botanical specimens. On his return he became an assistant in the Zoological department of the British Museum. He died in 1849, one year after his
father.

Henry carried on the grocery and hardware business built up by his
father, but proved a poor business man, and in 1871 some of his
natural history collections had to be sold to pay off his debts. By
this time his collections were well known. In 1851 Edward Newman,
editor of the Zoologist, had written:
    'In this country the art of bird-stuffing has, in a limited
    number of hands, attained great excellence ... in this
    no-one has surpassed Henry Doubleday; there is a great
    truthfulness in his birds that defies criticism.'

Doubleday kept up observations of 25 common summer migrants for
18 consecutive years. His records were published in Birds of Essex,
by Miller Christy (q.v.), another Essex Quaker naturalist. Of even
greater scientific value was his contribution to entomology. His
Synonymic List of British Lepidoptera was published in instalments
between 1847 and 1850, and immediately established his reputation
as a naturalist of more than common note. He was one of the original
members of the Entomological Society, and contributed his first
scientific paper to The Entomologist, a journal edited by Edward
Newman, yet another Quaker naturalist. In it he described his method
of collecting moths from sallow-blossoms, which was then unique.
In 1838 he published A Nomenclature of British Birds, in which he
attempted a uniform system of ornithological nomenclature.

Apart from visits to Fellow naturalists, Doubleday seldom left home.
Between 1846 and 1873 he slept away only twice. All his specimens
were obtained by 'sugaring' trees in Epping Forest and even nearer
home. In a letter to The Entomologist in 1875 he wrote:
    'There is a row of seventeen lime trees in the field adjoining
    my garden, and I have sugared the trunks for more than thirty
    years in every month, except the four winter ones.'

Doubleday's financial worries reached a climax in 1866 when a local bank in which he had invested much of his savings closed down. Five years later he had a nervous breakdown and spent a few months in the Quaker Mental Hospital, The Retreat, York. A few friends relieved his distress by creating a trust to ensure a small income for him. He died at Epping in 1875, and was buried behind the Friends' Meeting House.

DRINKWATER

John Drinkwater (1882-1937), poet, was born at Leytonstone in 1882. His father was a schoolmaster there at the time. His family had been settled for generations in Oxfordshire and Warwickshire; but Essex celebrated his connection with Leytonstone in 1938 with a bronze tablet unveiled by his widow in the Public Library.

DYKE

Jeremy Dyke of Epping (d. 1639), a moderate Puritan divine, was described by Thomas Fuller (q.v.) as being,
> 'one of a cheerful spirit ... He had also a gracious heart, and was very profitable in his ministry ... He was one peaceable in Israel. And though no zealot in the practice of ceremonies, quietly submitted to use them.'

Dyke was vicar of Epping, and when Laud ordered the communion table to be set at the east end of the chancel and there railed off, he obeyed part of the order by putting a rail round the table, but left it standing in the middle of the chancel - as it still is at St. Osyth - believing that it should be used as God's table for a meal and not as an altar for sacrifice. He preached before parliament in 1628. Several of his published works ran through five or six editions.

EDWARD

In Manners of England in the 13th and 15th Centuries, there is a story of Edward I recognising his washerwoman, Matilda of Waltham, among the bystanders when he attended a deer hunt at Fingringhoe. Riding up to her he wagered a fleet hunter that she would not ride it to the chase and be in at the death. Matilda accepted the challenge and won the bet. The king had to pay her forty shillings to ransom the horse, which would probably be worth about that sum in those days.

EDWARDS

George Edwards (1693-1773), the Stratford naturalist, was educated at Leytonstone and Brentwood before being apprenticed to a tradesman in Fenchurch Street, London. In 1716 he gave up his plans for a career in business and set out on a series of travels, on which he spent most of his time drawing such natural objects as attracted his attention by their significance in an undisturbed environment. In 1733 he became librarian to the Royal College of Physicians on the recommendation of Sir Hans Sloane, and studied the volumes in his care to such good effect that he became one of the foremost ornithologists of his day. In his studies he frequently conferred with Dr. John Fothergill at Upton (q.v.) and Captain Raymond of Valentines, Ilford. His History of Birds, begun in 1743, was continued to a fourth volume published in 1751. Gleanings of Natural History appeared in 1758, and was followed by a second volume in 1760, and a seventh and last in 1764.

In all, Edwards provided engravings and descriptions of more than 600 subjects in Natural History. He was a Fellow of the Royal Society, of the Society of Antiquaries, and many other learned bodies both at home and on the Continent. At his death he was buried at West Ham, but his gravestone has gone.

·ELIOT

John Eliot (1604-1690) of Nazeing, 'The Apostle to the Indians', was born at Widford, Hertfordshire, and is commemorated there by a stained glass Window in the parish church, unveiled by the American Ambassador in 1895. When he was three years of age his family re-moved to Nazeing in Essex. At Cambridge he came under the influence of Thomas Hooker (q.v.), and when Hooker took 'Cuckoes', Little Baddow in 1629, Eliot joined him as assistant. Together they attracted the congregation which became the nucleus of the Independents at Little Baddow.

Eliot emigrated to America in the ship 'Lyon' in 1631 and settled at Roxbury, Mass. (See Pynchon), where he established a ministry that continued for nearly 60 years until his death in 1690. He began ministering to the Indians in 1646, preaching to them under an oak tree in their own language. His great work was the translation of the Bible into the language of the Indians to whom he ministered.

See W. Winters: Trans. R. Hist. S x 267

ELIZABETH

Elizabeth I visited at least 24 Essex houses during her Progresses through eastern counties. There may have been more. Most acc-ounts are unreliable because they fail to appreciate that the Progress planned for 1579, which took in several houses in east Essex, was cancelled (probably on account of the plague) and a shorter one sub-stituted. See Morant MSS, vol. 42. Essex Record Office. The 24 were:

Ardern Hall, Horndon-on-the-Hill, the home of Thomas Rich, visited 8 August 1588. This house was demolished about 1730 when the pres-ent Ardern Hall was built.

Audley End, Saffron Walden, the home of Thomas Howard, 4th Duke of Norfolk, visited September 1571 and July 1578. This was Lord Chancellor Audley's house, not the mansion built c. 1615 by Thomas Howard, 1st Earl of Suffolk.

Belhus, Aveley, the home of Edward Barrett, visited 9-10 August 1588.

St. John's Abbey, Colchester, the home of the Lucas family, visited 26-30 July and 1-3 August 1561. The Benedictine abbey of St. John the Baptist at Colchester came into the possession of the Lucas family in 1547.

Copt Hall, Epping, the home of Sir Thomas Heneage, visited 19-20 July 1568. This was the second of three Copt Halls. It was newly built when the queen visited and can hardly have been completed. This house, built in 1564-68, was replaced by a third Copt Hall in the middle of the 18th century (See Country Life, 29 October and 5 November, 1910). The third Copt Hall was destroyed by fire, 5 May 1917.

Felix Hall, Kelvedon, probably the home of Sir Thomas Cecil at the time, visited 24-26 July 1561. The house visited was replaced by the present Felix Hall about 1760.

Gaynes Park, Theydon Garnon, the home of Sir William FitzWilliam, visited 19-20 September 1578.

Gidea Hall, Romford, the home of Sir Anthony Cooke (d. 1576) and Richard Cooke, visited July 1568 and 23-25 September 1579 in the short Progress substituted for the one originally planned.

Gosfield Hall, Gosfield, the home of Lady Mautravers, visited 19-21 August 1561. Gosfield Hall was practically new when the queen visited. It was built by Sir John Wentworth about 1545. Lady Mautravers was his daughter.

Hallingbury Place, Great Hallingbury, the home of Henry, 11th Lord Morley, visited 25-26 August 1561, and 11-16 August 1576. The house visited was replaced about 1771.

Havering, the royal palace which was part of a queen's jointure, was visited on many occasions and was the starting point of most of the Progresses. No part of it remains. A plan by A. W. Clapham, F.S.A., appears in the Architectural Review, 1911, pp. 192-3.

Hedingham Castle, the home of John, 16th Earl of Oxford, visited 16-19 September 1561. The castle in which the queen was entertained was destroyed less than 40 years after the visit. The main keep-tower remains.

Horham Hall, Thaxted, the home of Sir John Cutte, visited 5-14 September 1571 and 7-11 September 1578. Parts of this fine house, built by Sir John Cutte, remain in good preservation. The Great Hall, with its beautiful mullioned window and lantern, is one of the best examples of Tudor architecture in the county.

Ingatestone Hall, the home of Sir William Petre (d. 1572) and his widow, Dame Anne, visited 19-21 July, 1561, and possibly in 1579. Ingatestone Hall was built by Sir William about 1540.

Leez Priory, Little Leighs, the home of Lord Chancellor Rich and Robert, 2nd Lord Rich, visited 21-25 August 1561 and 16-17 September 1571. Leez was built on the site of the demolished priory by Lord Rich about 1537. Much of it was demolished in 1753, but about two-thirds of the south and west sides of the outer quadrangle and the gate-house of the inner quadrangle remain.

Loughton Hall, the home of John Stonard, visited 17-19 July 1561 and 19-20 September 1578. The old hall was destroyed in 1836 in the fire described by Dickens in Barnaby Rudge. It had been refronted during Queen Anne's reign. The present hall was built in 1879.

Mark Hall, Latton, the home of James Altham, visited 14-16 September 1571 and 22-23 July, 1578.

Moulsham Hall, Chelmsford, the home of Sir Thomas Mildmay, probably visited September 1579. When Thomas Mildmay had completed the house built soon after acquiring the estate in 1550 it was described as the largest esquire's house in Essex. This house was demolished about 1730, when a new house was built by Benjamin (Mildmay) Earl Fitzwalter, which in turn was demolished about 1810.

Moyns, Steeple Bumpstead, the home of Thomas Gent, visited 1-2
September 1578 (another visit that has been presumed rather than
proved). If the queen did visit Moyns it must have been the older
house on the site. The present house, although a splendid piece of
Elizabethan architecture, was not begun by Thomas Gent until about
1580. It was unfinished when Norden wrote in 1594.

New Hall, Boreham, then a royal palace, visited 21-24 July 1561,
September 1579 and on other occasions. Although only a fragment
remains of the palace begun in 1500 and greatly enlarged by Henry
VIII, it has great interest through being almost entirely original.

Ongar Castle, the home of Mrs. Morris, visited 9-10 August 1579.
This was an imposing mansion of brick, built by Thomas Morris about
1550, on the summit of the mound thrown up in the 12th century for
Richard de Lucy's castle. It was pulled down in 1744, when another
house was built on the mound. This also has disappeared.

Rookwood Hall, Abbess Roding, the home of Wistan Browne, visited
September 1571, 18-19 September 1578, and 10-12 August 1579.
This house had been built about 1523, probably by Wistan Browne's
father. It has gone.

St. Osyth's Priory, the home of Lord Darcy, visited 30-31 July 1561.

Wanstead, the home of Robert Earl of Leicester, visited July 1561,
May 1578, August 1578, and probably on other occasions. The manor
of Wanstead was granted by Lord Rich to Robert Dudley, Earl of
Leicester, in 1577. It is probable that he lived there for some time
before buying the property.

That so many of these houses had been built during Elizabeth's reign
is eloquent testimony to the stimulating effect she had on her people.
The most famous visit, of course, was not to a great house, but to
The Camp Royal at Tilbury when the Armada threatened in 1588.
Upwards of 900 horse soldiers had been ordered to assemble at
Brentwood on the 27 July 1588. Leicester himself had ridden across
the county from Wanstead to Chelmsford on the 25th to arrange for
the 4,000 men assembled there to proceed to Tilbury.

'They be,' he reported to Walsingham, 'as forward men, and as willing to meet with the enemy as ever I saw.' Unfortunately he had to
add that they had 'brought not so much as one meal's provision of
victual with them; so that, at their arrival here there was not a
barrel of beer, nor load of bread for them.' The surrounding country
had to be scoured for provisions before the troops from London could
be received. The operation was evidently successful, and as a final
touch Leicester hit on the idea of inviting the queen to visit the Camp
and address the men. It was not an easy decision to reach, and some
delay was inevitable. On the 8 August, however, she reached Ardern
Hall and spent the night there. The following morning she rode into
the camp with the Lord Lieutenant and the Lord Chamberlain in attendance, and with Leicester leading her horse she inspected the
troops and delivered the famous speech, containing the words:

'My loving people, I have always placed my chiefest strength
and safeguard in the loyal hearts and goodwill of my subjects;
and therefore I am come amongst you, as you see, at this
time, not for my recreation or disport, but being resolved,
in the midst and heat of the battle, to live and die amongst
you all, to lay down for my God, for my kingdom and for my
people, my honour and my blood, even in the dust. I know I

have but the body of a weak and feeble woman, but I have
the heart and stomach of a king, and a King of England too
... Rather than any dishonour shall grow by me, I myself
will take up arms, I myself will be your general.'

ELLIOT

Henry Lettsom Elliot (1831-1920) was presented to the living of
Gosfield in 1871 and remained there till his death 49 years later,
devoting himself to the study of heraldry. He compiled An Armorial
Index for the County of Essex, Arranged as an Ordinary in four volumes. This fine production, representing a lifetime's work, was
presented by his family to the Essex Archaeological Society.

ELWES

John Elwes (or Meggot) (1714-89), miser, acquired his parsimonious
habits in order to ingratiate himself with his uncle, Sir Harvey Elwes,
of Stoke-by-Clare, Suffolk. He used to call at an inn at Chelmsford
and change into the ragged clothes that he knew would be approved by
his uncle. On Sir Harvey's death he inherited the whole of his property on condition he changed his name from Meggot to Elwes.

Despite his miserly habits, he continued to gamble all his life, sometimes sitting up all night, with thousands of pounds at stake, in the
company of some of the most profligate rakes of the age. On leaving
the table he would walk out to meet his cattle being brought to Smithfield market, where he would barter with butchers for the last shilling. He frequently walked the 17 miles from Smithfield to his home,
Theydon Hall, to save the coach fare.

See E. Topham: The Life of the late John Elwes

ERCONWALD

St. Erconwald (or Erkenwald), believed to have been the son of the
East Anglian prince, Anna, founded two monasteries, one at Chertsey,
the other at Barking, with himself as abbot of one, and his sister,
Ethelburga, abbess of the other. In 675 he was consecrated Bishop
of the East Saxons, which included Essex, Middlesex, and the Deanery of Braughing in Hertfordshire, with St. Paul's as his cathedral
church. At his death in 693 he was buried at Barking; but in 1140 or
1148 his body was re-interred in a sumptuous shrine in St. Paul's.

ESSEX

The Saxon Kings of Essex were:

Erchwine,	c. 527
Sledda,	c. 587
St. Sebert,	c. 597
Saxred,	c. 614
Sigebert I	c. 617
Sigebert II	c. 623
Sigebert III	c. 655
Sigeric & Sebba	c. 663
Sigenard	c. 693
Offa	c. 700
Selred	c. 709
Swithred	c. 738
Sigeric	c. 792
Sigered	c. 799

ESSEX

The descent of the earldom of Essex has been:

1. Geoffrey de Mandeville, created 1140. His great-niece married Geoffrey FitzPeter, Earl of Essex 1199. Through his daughter, Maud, the earldom passed to:

2. Humphrey de Bohun, created Earl of Essex by the second creation, 1236. Eleanor de Bohun married Edward III's son, Thomas, Duke of Gloucester, who was murdered at Calais, 1397. Her daughter was the mother of:

3. Henry, Viscount Bourchier, created Earl of Essex by the third creation, 1461. The second Bourchier earl died in 1539 and the earldom was granted to:

4. Thomas Cromwell, created Earl of Essex by the fourth creation, 1540, who was thus the first Earl of Essex not connected with the 1st Earl, Geoffrey de Mandeville.

5. In 1543, Lord Parr, who had married but repudiated the Bourchier heiress, was created Earl of Essex by the fifth creation. The countess's cousin:

6. Walter Devereux, Viscount Hereford, who succeeded her as the Bourchier heir, was created Earl of Essex by the sixth creation, 1572. His son, Elizabeth's favourite, who was beheaded in 1601, was the father of the father of the parliamentary 'Great Lord Essex'.

7. Arthur, Lord Capel, was created Earl of Essex by the seventh creation in 1661. He chose the title because his wife was a great-niece, though not an heiress, of Elizabeth's favourite. His descendants in the earldom can claim that they derive the title through connection with the families of Devereux, Bourchier, Plantagenet, Bohun, and Mandeville, who have held the earldom of Essex, with one intruder, since its creation in 1140.

ESSEX

Henry de Essex (grandson of Suene), lord of Rayleigh and 54 other lordships in Essex, stood high in the favour of Henry II until the War with the Welsh in 1157, in which he bore the king's standard. He lost the royal favour by panicking when he found himself ambushed throwing away the standard and crying out that the king had been killed. For his cowardice in 1157 he made amends by conspicuous bravery at Toulouse two years later, which fully justified the king's clemency towards him for his former weakness. The Chronicle of Brakelond relates how he fought a duel with Robert de Montfort and suffered defeat. He was believed dead and taken to a nearby abbey for interment, but revived and took the habit of the Order. He died c.1196 after more than 30 years in the Cloister. As Fuller put it: 'Between shame and sanctity he blushed out the remainder of his life.' At his defeat all his possessions had been confiscated by the king. Alice, his widow, who was a sister of Aubrey de Vere, afterwards married Richard FitzRichard, lord of Warkworth in Northumberland and Clavering in Essex.

EUDO (DAPIFER)

Eudo Dapifer, Governor of Colchester Castle and builder of the Keep, held 20 manors in Essex at Domesday. He was seneschal, or steward, in the household of William the Conqueror and his sons, and was in attendance when William died in Normandy in 1087. When William Rufus hurried over to England to claim the throne on his father's death, Eudo was with him. He is said to have been the person who obtained for him the keys of the Royal Treasury at Winchester, and to have secured possession on the king's behalf of the castles of Dover, Pevensey, and Hastings. For these services he was granted command of Colchester, which would then be seen as an ancient walled town with fortifications that could be adapted to meet the needs of the new order. Eudo lost no time in building the magnificent Norman keep. In 1096 he founded the abbey of St. John, laying the first stone himself at Easter, 1097. When he died in Normandy in 1120 he bequeathed to St. John's Abbey the manor of Brightlingsea. He was buried in the abbey church. His only daughter married William de Mandeville, mother of Geoffrey de Mandeville, 1st Earl of Essex (q.v.).

EVELYN

John Evelyn, the diarist, visited Audley End in October 1654. He found it 'a mixt fabric 'twixt antiq. and modern, but observable for its being compleately finish'd, and without comparison is one of the stateliest palaces of the kingdom'. The hall he thought 'faire, but somewhat too small for so august a pile'. The gallery he found 'the most cheerfull, and I thinke one of the best in England; a faire dining-roome, and the rest of the lodgings answerable, with a pretty chapell'.

He was there again on 23rd July 1670 and 13th September 1677. On the 2nd September 1669 he called on the Earl of Norwich 'at his house in Epping Forest'.

On 8th July 1656 he found Colchester 'a faire towne, but now wretchedly demolished by the late siege, especially the suburbs, which were all burnt, but were then repairing'. He was shown the place where Sir Charles Lucas and Sir George Lisle were shot. 'For the rest, this is a ragged and factious towne, now swarming with Sectaries. Their trading is in cloth with the Dutch ... It is also famous for oysters and eringo-root, growing here about and candied for sale.'

Dedham he found 'a pretty country towne'. On returning homeward he passed near Chelmsford and saw New Hall, Boreham, 'a faire old house built with brick', with a fine avenue of limes, which he particularly admired.

On 16th March 1683 he,
> 'went to see Sir Josiah Child's prodigious cost in planting walnut trees about his seate, and making fish-ponds, many miles in circuit, in Epping Forest, in a barren spot, as oftentimes these suddainly monied men for the most part seate themselves ... I din'd at Mr. Houblon's, a rich and gentile French merchant, who was building a house in the Forest, neare Sir J. Child's ... it will be a pretty villa, about 5 miles from Whitechapell.'

This was James Houblon (q.v.), to whom there are many references in Pepys.

Evelyn was an Essex landowner himself for six years. He purchased the manor of Great Warley in 1649, but sold it in 1655 when he found that taxes were 'so intolerable that they eate up the rents, etc., surcharged as that county has been above all others during our unnatural war.'

EVERARD

The Everard family settled in mid-Essex in the time of Henry III. The first Everard of Langleys, Great Waltham, was Thomas, who came into possession of half the estate in 1515, after marrying the daughter of John Cornish. Thomas Everard had six sons and three daughters. At his death he was succeeded by his son, Richard, to whom the other half of Langleys was conveyed in 1529, bringing the whole of the estate into the possession of the family. At his death in 1561, Richard had estates in Great Waltham, Felsted, Rayne, Little Dunmow, Good Easter and High Easter. His eldest son, Anthony, who was knighted along with many other gentlemen of Essex in 1603, did not succeed because he died in 1614, three years before his father. This was the Sir Anthony who has a noble monument to his memory in Great Waltham church, with an alabaster effigy of himself fully attired in armour, and an effigy on a pedestal of his first wife, Anne (Barnardiston), who died in 1609. He married as his second wife a daughter of Sir Anthony Felton of Playford in Suffolk, also named Anne.

Richard Everard, the father of Sir Anthony, was succeeded by his third son, Hugh, who was High Sheriff of Essex in 1626. He died in 1637. His son, Sir Richard, was created a baronet by Charles I in 1628. His first wife was Joan, daughter of Sir Francis Barrington (q.v.). By her he had several children, including his successor, Sir Richard, the 2nd baronet, who died in 1694. He was succeeded by Sir Hugh, the 3rd baronet, whose three sons all distinguished themselves in the service of their country. The youngest, Morton, was killed in the 'Hampshire', while fighting under Lord Maynard, his kinsman; the second, Hugh, was lost with his ship and crew on the Goodwins in the great storm of November, 1703, leaving Richard, the eldest son, to succeed as 4th baronet in a somewhat reduced and saddened family when the 3rd baronet died in 1706. The 4th baronet became Governor of North Carolina and had a distinguished career; but he inherited an estate so encumbered with debts that he and his mother, Dame Mary, were forced to sell Langleys to Samuel Tufnell (q.v.) in 1710. The Everard baronetcy became extinct at the death of Sir Hugh, the 6th baronet, in 1745.

EWER

Isaac Ewer (d. 1650), regicide, joined the parliamentary army in 1642 and rose to the rank of colonel of foot although 'at first but a serving man'. He was prominent at the siege of Colchester in 1648, and a member of the council of war that decided the fate of Sir Charles Lucas and Sir George Lisle. At the end of the same year he was entrusted with the custody of the king, whom he received 'with small observance'. He died of the plague in Ireland soon after the surrender of Waterford. In his will, dated 1649, he describes himself as of Hatfield Broad Oak, Essex. He owned properties at Great Waltham, Great Leighs and Boreham, all of which were confiscated at the Restoration.

FABYAN

Robert Fabyan (d. 1513), historian, was a member of the Drapers'
Company of London and alderman of the City ward of Farringdon
Without. In 1498 he was commissioned to hold Newgate and Aldgate
against Cornish rebels encamped on Blackheath. He resigned as
alderman in 1503 in order to evade the expense of becoming mayor.
His will, however, proved him to have been a wealthy man, and his
shrinking from the mayoralty is odd, because he had the reputation
of being 'of a very merry disposition', and one who'used to entertain
his guests with good victuals as with good discourse.' Moreover,
his historical writings show him to have been one who delighted in
pageantry.

Fabyan married the daughter of a rich Essex clothier named John
Pake. Stephen Fabyan, one of his ancestors, owned property in
Halstead, and in 1404 acquired the manor of Jenkins. There were
several branches of the family settled in the Coggeshall neighbourhood, Robert Fabyan himself lived at Theydon Garnon. His New
Chronicles of England and France, a work based on records made
by monks, was used by John Richard Green in his Short History of
the English People.

FANSHAWE

Members of this eminent family, associated in Essex with Barking
and Dagenham, held the office of King's Remembrancer for nearly
150 years. The first was Henry (1506-68), who came to London in
1523 as a younger son of Henry Fanshawe of Fanshawe Gate in
Derbyshire, to seek his fortune. He became a clerk in the Exchequer
Office. In 1557 he purchased the manor of Jenkins in Barking. Four
years later he obtained the lease of Dengie Hall for 600 years. He
received the grant of the office of Remembrancer in 1561 and before
his death in 1568 secured the reversion to his nephew, Thomas (1533-
1601), who purchased Ware Park in Hertfordshire in 1576, and by
his first wife founded the Ware branch of the family; by his second
wife he established the Jenkins (Barking) and later the Parsloes
(Dagenham) lines.

Parsloes was purchased by Sir William Fanshawe (d. 1634) in 1619,
and the estate remained in the family for over 285 years. The first
four owners held the office of Auditor to the Duchy of Lancaster.

Thomas (1569-1665), eldest son of the Henry who bought Jenkins and
settled at Barking, was created a viscount in 1661, as a reward for
his support of the Royalist cause. The viscountcy continued through
five generations until the death of the 5th viscount in 1716.

Sir Richard Fanshawe (1608-1666), brother of the 1st viscount, was
Secretary of War to Prince Rupert and a distinguished classical
scholar. He published translations of Horace, Virgil, and other
poets. The letters he wrote while Ambassador to Spain and Portugal
were published in 1702. His wife's Memoirs, published in 1676, achieved a wide public. Sir Richard was buried at Ware. It is much to
the credit of Dagenham, and particularly of John O'Leary, for many
years borough Librarian, that many portraits of the most distinguished members of the Fanshawe family have been preserved at Valence
House, Dagenham, to perpetuate the association of the family with
Essex.

See H. C. Fanshawe: The History of the Fanshawe Family (1927)

FERRERS

The Ferrers family held the Woodham Ferrers manor for about 16 generations from the Conquest to 1445. Their ancestor was Henry de Ferrers, a Norman who was granted 210 lordships in England, five of which were in Essex. In 1235 William de Ferrers, Earl of Derby, was granted a licence to assart and impark his wood at Woodham. Other manors held by the family were those of Stebbing and Fairsted. It was a Henry de Ferrers who obtained a charter for a market to be held every Monday at Stebbing, with an annual fair. The Woodham Ferrers manor passed by marriage into the Grey family, from whom it passed, again by marriage, into the possession of Lord Chancellor Audley (q.v.).

FINCH

Sir Heneage Finch (d. 1631), Speaker of the House of Commons, was the grandson of Sir Thomas Heneage (q.v.) of Copt Hall, Epping. He represented the City of London in parliament from 1623 to 1626. In 1623 he was knighted at Wanstead. The following year his mother (Elizabeth, only daughter of Sir Thomas Heneage) was raised to the peerage as Viscountess Maidstone, with remainder to her heirs male. This honour was bought through the interest of Sir Arthur Ingram for £13,000 and an annuity of £500, to secure which Copt Hall manor and park were mortgaged. In 1628 Viscountess Maidstone was created Countess of Winchelsea, with remainder to her heirs male. She died in 1633 and was buried at Eastwell, Kent, under a splendid monument. Sir Heneage's elder brother succeeded as 1st Earl of Winchelsea.

See Manning's Lives of the Speakers

FITCH

Edward Arthur Fitch (1854-1912), local historian, farmed on a large scale at Brick House, Maldon, where he settled in 1874. He was a Fellow of the Linnaean, Entomological and Zoological Societies, and one of the founders of the Essex Field Club, of which he was president from 1888 to 1891. For many years he was joint-editor of the Essex Review. His most important work was his History of Maldon and the River Blackwater.

FITCH, William See CANFIELD

FITZLEWES

Members of the FitzLewes family of West Horndon were prominent in county and national history during the 15th and 16th centuries. Sir John FitzLewes figures in Stow entertaining Prince Henry, Thomas Duke of Clarence, John Duke of Bedford, and Humfrey Duke of Gloucester, the sons of Henry IV, at his house in the Vintry. The family probably settled in Essex on the marriage of a FitzLewes with an heiress of the Gosham family, which had been settled at Ingrave since Edward II's reign. By 1438 there was certainly a Sir John FitzLewes at West Horndon, and from that date onwards the name appears at intervals as patrons of the rectories of Ingrave, West Horndon, and Cranham.

This first Sir John, who is referred to as Sir Lewes John, was knighted about 1438. He died in 1442. His will shows that he held land in 24 Essex parishes. His first wife was Alice, daughter of Aubrey de Vere, 10th Earl of Oxford, who brought several estates with her. His second wife was the widow of Sir Richard Hankford, and daughter of John Montacute, 3rd Earl of Salisbury. In his will he refers to nine children, and to the sons specifically as FitzLewes, which may be taken as the original of the family name. He himself had been called Sir Lewes John.

Lewes FitzLewes, son and heir of Sir Lewes John, was Sheriff of Essex and Hertfordshire in 1458 and two years later was summoned to parliament. As a near kinsman of the de Veres and supporter of the Lancastrian cause he suffered during the reign of Edward IV, and in 1471, the manors of West Horndon, Purley in Stebbing, Ingrave, Shenfield, Cranham, East Horndon and West Tilbury, and Ames, which had formed a large part of the FitzLewes possessions in the county, were granted by the Crown to Richard, Duke of Gloucester, afterwards Richard III.

The next FitzLewes, Sir Richard (c.1446-1528), came to reside at West Horndon soon after 1480, when some of the family estates were restored to him. He was knighted in 1487. He married four wives, and had children by them; but when he died in 1528 he had survived not only all his sons but all the male descendants of his father. Camden in his Britannia says that his eldest son was burnt to death along with his bride on the night of their marriage in the fire that destroyed West Horndon Hall. The story has frequently been repeated, but it cannot be true because they had a daughter, born in 1510, to whom the estates descended. She married Sir John Mordaunt, and at her death in 1543 left a son, Lewes Mordaunt, aged five.

The name then passed out of Essex history, but memorial brasses in Ingrave church remind us that in their time the FitzLeweses had formed alliances with many noble families, including those of De Vere, Mountacute, Holland, Beaufort, Nevill, Wingfield, Stonor, Lovell, Tyrell, Wake, and Mordaunt.

FITZRALPH

In the 13th and 14th centuries the FitzRalph family, associated principally with Pebmarsh, held large estates in Essex and Suffolk. Pebmarsh itself was held of the Honor of Castle Hedingham by the service of the fourth part of a knight's fee. The field in which the home of the FitzRalphs stood is still called Castle Meadow.

In 1314 Sir William FitzRalph was appointed a conservator of the peace, the title that preceded that of justice of the peace. Two years later he was commissioned to raise foot soldiers for the king's service. He probably died soon after 1322, as in 1324 his son was summoned to attend the Great Council at Westminster. In 1338 this son obtained a grant of free warren in Pebmarsh, Bures, Finchingfield, Little Wenden and other parishes. The last descendant in the male line was John FitzRalph, who succeeded to the estates in 1441. The family's connection with Pebmarsh is commemorated in the fine brass, c.1323, to Sir William FitzRalph.

FITZROY

Henry Fitzroy, Duke of Richmond (1519-36), whom Anne Boleyn and her brother were suspected of poisoning, was the natural son of Henry VIII and Elizabeth Blount, who lived at the Priory of St. Lawrence, known as Jericho, Blackmore. Morant says that the king, 'when he had a mind to be lost with his courtesans, often frequented

the Priory, when his courtiers employed the cant phrase that he had
gone to Jericho.' Henry Fitzroy was born there; but there is some
doubt about Henry's visits.

Elizabeth Blount was the daughter of Sir John Blount of Kinlet,
Shropshire. She was one of the most brilliant of the ladies at the
court of Catherine of Aragon, where she appeared for the last time
on 3rd October 1518, with Sir Francis Bryan (q.v.) as her partner.
The following summer she gave birth to 'a goodly manne child, in
beautie like to the father and the mother' at the Prior's house at
Blackmore. Henry showered honours and titles on his son, estab-
lishing a royal household for him at Pontefract. At 14 he was engaged to the only daughter of the Duke of Norfolk; but he died at the age
of 17 and was buried with the Howards at Framlingham.

See W. S. Childe-Pemberton: Elizabeth Blount and Henry VIII (1913)

FITZWALTER

Tombs at Little Dunmow preserve the memory of Walter FitzWalter
(d. 1198), who was buried with one of his wives in the middle of the
choir. Robert, his son (d. 1235), who was buried before the altar,
and Walter, last of the line (d. 1432) and his wife. The tomb chest
to the last Walter and his wife (1464) has alabaster effigies of rare
quality.

The most distinguished head of the family was Robert (d. 1235), who
was elected leader of the barons against King John and bore the proud
title of 'Marshal of the Army of God and Holy Church'. When John
accepted the terms of Magna Carta at Runnymede in 1215, Robert
FitzWalter was one of the 25 commissioned to see that its terms were
fully observed. When John appealed to Rome against Magna Carta,
and succeeded in persuading the Pope to annul the Charter and excommunicate the barons, FitzWalter offered the Crown on behalf of
the barons to Louis, son of Philip of France.

After fighting in the Fifth Crusade, FitzWalter made his peace with
Henry III. His daughter, Matilda, who was known as the 'Fair Maid
of Essex', attracted the unwelcome attentions of King John. Tradition
has it that she was murdered by poison secretly administered for her
refusal to gratify the king's illicit passion.

The FitzWalter barony was conveyed to the Radcliffe (q.v.) family by
Elizabeth, only daughter and heiress of Walter FitzWalter, 7th baron
(1400-32), with whose death the male line of the FitzWalters became
extinct. From the Radcliffe family the barony went to the Mildmays
(q.v.).

FITZWILLIAM

Sir William FitzWilliam (1460?-1534), an alderman of the City of
London who obtained a new charter for the Merchant Taylors' Company in 1502, purchased Gaynes Park, Theydon Garnon, in 1508,
covenanting to prosecute the manors out of the king's hands and to
acquit the king of the interest he had in them under an Act of 1503.
He was a Northamptonshire man who entered the service of Cardinal
Wolsey, to whom he became treasurer and chamberlain, remaining
loyal to his master after his fall. On hearing that Wolsey, while in
disgrace, had been hospitably received by FitzWilliam in Northamptonshire, Henry VIII asked him how he dared entertain so great an
enemy of the State. FitzWilliam replied that 'he had not contempt-
uously or wilfully done it, but only because he had been his master,

and partly the means of his greatest fortunes.' This reply so pleased
the king that he observed that he himself had few such servants and
promptly knighted him. Sir William FitzWilliam was Sheriff of
Northampton in 1524. By 1525 he owned the manors of Gaynes Park
and Hemnalls in Theydon Garnon, Marshalls in North Weald Bassett,
Madelles in Epping, and Arnolds and Hunts in Lambourne.

At his death in 1534, he bequeathed £500 to mend the highway between
Coopersale and Chigwell, and £100 for 'poor maids' marriage's
(Stow's Survey, ed. 1720, i p. 262). He also cancelled all debts
due to him, and forgave his debtors, writing over their names Amor
Dei Remitto - for the love of God I remit.

The second Sir William FitzWilliam (d. 1552) of Gaynes Park, son
of the first, figures little in Essex history. In 1543 he settled Gaynes
Park, Hemnalls, Madells, together with Marshalls in North Weald -
considerable estates - on his eldest son, William and his wife, Anne,
daughter of Sir William Sidney of Penshurst, on their marriage.
This third Sir William settled all his Essex estates on his wife for
life in 1569, with remainder to their second son John, and his heirs
male. The reason for this became apparent at his death.

The third Sir William FitzWilliam (1526-99) became a national figure
as Lord Deputy of Ireland, where he was closely associated with the
Earl of Essex (q.v.). His career in Ireland began with his appointment to the office of Vice-Treasurer by Elizabeth I in 1559. In 1561
he assisted Sussex against Shane O'Neill. Ten years later he was
appointed Lord Justice in Ireland, and advanced to Lord Deputy in
1572. Three years later he returned to England and was Governor
of Fotheringhay Castle when Mary Queen of Scots was executed in
1587. In appreciation of his consideration for her at the end, Mary
gave him a portrait of her son, James, afterwards James I of England.

In 1588, Sir William was reappointed Lord Deputy of Ireland, where
he remained until he retired shortly before his death.

In serving as Treasurer in Ireland, Sir William III incurred debts to
the queen amounting to £3,964. He was pardoned £1,000, but at the
time of his death had only paid off £1,185 of the balance. The debt
was inherited by his eldest son, William, and this led to a dispute
over the ownership of Gaynes Park. By the settlement of 1596 referred to above, John, not William, inherited the estate at his mother's
death in 1602. William challenged his brother's title, even going so
far as to mortgage the estate to the queen as a means of discharging
the family debt. The dispute between the two brothers was brought
before the Court of the Exchequer, which gave a decision in favour
of John. It was a decision that would have pleased his father, who had
probably settled the estate on John to prevent it falling to the Crown.

There is a monument to Lady FitzWilliam (d. 1602) in Theydon Garnon
church. By her will she endowed the almshouses for four widows still
standing. John FitzWilliam died without issue in 1612.

See FitzWilliam of Milton Papers, Northamptonshire Record Office
    Mary E. Finch: The Wealth of Five Northamptonshire Families
                   (1956)
    F. G. Emmison: Forcible Dispossession in Elizabethan Essex,
                   Essex Journal, vol. iv no. 2
                   Elizabethan Life and Disorder, 122-3
                   Victoria County History Essex, iv

FITZWIMARC

Robert FitzWimarc, a Breton who anticipated the Conquest and served under both Edward the Confessor and William the Conqueror as Sheriff of Essex, built the castle at Clavering. (See SWEYN)

FLOWER

Sarah Fuller Flower (1805-48), afterwards Sarah Flower Adams, who wrote the hymn 'Nearer my God to Thee' at Loughton, was the daughter of Benjamin Flower (d. 1829) of Harlow.

Benjamin Flower first attracted attention while editor of a Cambridge newspaper by denouncing the war with France and censuring the political activities of a certain bishop. For these subversive activities he was sent to prison for six months. This roused the sympathy of Eliza Gould, a fellow Nonconformist who shared his views and visited him in Newgate. On his release they married and settled at Harlow, where Flower set up as a printer. Benjamin and Eliza Flower had two daughters, Sarah and Eliza. Eliza was a friend of Robert Browning in youth and the family claimed that it was through Sarah's influence that Browning's first volume of poems was accepted for publication. In 1834 Sarah married William Brydges Adams, and by his encouragement became an actress. Her health proved unequal to the strain of theatrical life, so she decided to devote herself to the writing of verses, chiefly hymns, which were set to music by her sister, Eliza. On retiring from the stage she lived at Woodbury Hill, Loughton. When she died in 1849 she was buried with her sister and parents in the Nonconformist burial ground at Foster Street.

See Z. Moon: E.R. xv 151

FORSTER

A branch of the Forster family of Alnwick, Northumberland, settled at Walthamstow in the middle of the 18th century. Several members distinguished themselves as naturalists.

Edward Forster (1765-1849), a merchant in London, travelled widely in England and Wales collecting botanical specimens. He was elected treasurer of the Linnaean Society in 1816 and held the post till his death 33 years later. He published several works and contributed many articles to the journals of learned societies. The Forsters lived from 1782 at 'Clevelands', afterwards renamed 'The Chestnuts', in Hoe Street, Walthamstow. After his marriage in 1796 Edward probably lived in or near Epping. From there he removed in 1819 to Mill Cottage, Hale End, Walthamstow, an 18th-century thatched cottage in a forest enclosure, where he remained until 1832, when he removed to Beech Hall, Hale End. After two years there he removed to Ivy House, Woodford.

Among his friends were Edward Newman (1801-76), the Quaker naturalist who launched a periodical called 'The Phytologist' in 1841, and two other Quaker naturalists, George Stacey Gibson of Saffron Walden (q.v.) and Henry Doubleday of Epping (q.v.). Forster made valuable contributions to Newman's periodical and helped Gibson with his Flora of Essex, published in 1862. During these years, Henry Doubleday was his closest friend. Both were men of retiring nature, passionately devoted to the study of natural history, whose haunt was Epping Forest.

Edward Forster had two brothers, Thomas Furley (1760-1825), and Benjamin Meggott (d. 1829), who published papers in the Philosophical Magazine at intervals between 1801 and 1821, and in 1820 published a botanical work entitled An Introduction to the Knowledge of Funguses.

All the Forster brothers were interested in philanthropic work, an interest they had inherited from their father, who brought them up on the principles derived from his study of Jean Jacques Rousseau. The Forster brothers founded a Refuge in Hackney Road. Benjamin Meggott Forster died in 1829, shortly after preparing evidence in support of the Child Stealing Act. As a result of a visit to the Refuge in 1849, Edward Forster contracted the cholera from which he died. His portrait by Eden Upton Eddis, painted shortly before his death, hangs in the Rooms of the Linnaean Society.

FOTHERGILL

John Fothergill (1712-80), Quaker physician and philanthropist, was born in Wensleydale, Yorkshire. At 36 he had one of the largest practices in London. He began to practise in the poorest districts of London, but such was his devotion to duty that his reputation soon reached the ears of the well-to-do. As he himself put it, 'I climbed on the backs of the poor to the pockets of the rich.' Throughout these years his Yorkshire stamina enabled him to follow other interests, and he was elected a Fellow of the Society of Antiquaries in 1753, of the Royal Society in 1763, and in 1770 he became a member of the American Philosophical Society.

In middle life Fothergill found time to establish a large botanical garden at Upton, stocking his flower beds and hothouses with thousands of species of both hardy and exotic plants. His first purchase of land was Rooke Hall, a small estate of 30 acres that had belonged to the Rooke family from 1566 to 1666. After them it had passed through the hands of Sir Robert Smyth and his descendants until it came into the hands of Admiral Elliot, who sold it to John Fothergill in 1762. The estate was later enlarged and laid out as a flower garden surrounded by shrubberies, with a wilderness of trees beyond. A watercourse ran through the middle, with banks planted with exotic shrubs. In the glass-houses were oranges amd myrtles amid thousands. of different species of plants imported from warmer climes. Sir Joseph Banks said of it: 'In my opinion no other garden in Europe, royal or of a subject, had nearly so many scarce and valuable plants.' Only Kew could be compared with it.

Although Fothergill was kept too busy by his patients to spend much time in his garden, he maintained a high standard of care, employing 15 gardeners and four artists who were commissioned to make drawings on vellum of each plant when it was in full bloom. After Fothergill's death 2,000 of these drawings were bought by the Empress Catherine II of Russia.

Dr. Fothergill's garden was sold up at his death and the specimens dispersed. The house was enlarged and became Ham House, the home of Samuel Gurney (q.v.). It was pulled down in 1872, but the gardens are preserved by the City of London Corporation as West Ham Park, a public garden of 80 acres, which was purchased with the help of generous contributions from the Gurney family in 1874.

See R. Hingston Fox: Dr. John Fothergill and his Friends (1919)
    Fothergill: Works, iii

Katherine Fry: History of East and West Ham
Dr. Pagenstecher: Story of West Ham Park (1908)

FOWLER

Robert Copp Fowler (1867-1929), historian, was the son of a vicar
of Ulting. After Winchester and Oxford he entered the Record Office
in 1891 and eventually became senior assistant keeper. He served
as secretary to the Master of the Rolls' Committee on Manorial
Records. From 1918 to 1929 he edited the Transactions of the Essex
Archaeological Society, contributing articles of permanent value. He
also edited for the Society three volumes of the Feet of Fines of
Essex, 1327-1422, having in fact abstracted these important property
records as far as 1574. He contributed the section on Religious
Houses to the Victoria History of Essex.

FOXE

John Foxe (1516-87), martyrologist, lived at Waltham Abbey at the
height of his fame. Two of his children were baptised in the abbey
church in 1565. He was on friendly terms with the Heneage family,
who had taken up residence at Copt Hall in 1564. Lady Heneage is
known to have consulted him frequently on spiritual matters, and in
1587 his eldest son, Samuel, entered the service of Sir Thomas
Heneage (q.v.), who placed him in charge of the Royal Palace of
Havering-atte-Bower. Some time after 1594 he took up residence
at Warlies, where several of his children were born.

Samuel Foxe's daughter married Henry Wollaston of Waltham Abbey,
an active magistrate and public figure in the middle of the 17th century. Dr. Thomas Foxe, the eldest son of Samuel, married the granddaughter of Mrs. Honywood (q.v.). Like his father, he was a prominent local citizen. Farmer, the Waltham Abbey historian, tells us
that an estate was left in trust to Dr. Thomas Foxe for the repair of
the abbey church, in which he was buried. From first to last, John
Foxe's family flourished in West Essex for three centuries.

See W. Winters: John Foxe, martyrologist Trans. R. Hist. S. v
(1877)

FRANKLAND

Newport Grammar School was founded in 1588 by Joyce Frankland,
a widow, of the Rye, Stanstead Abbots (Herts.), whose son had been
thrown from his horse and killed in 1581 while riding to London. On
hearing of the accident, Dean Nowell of St. Paul's, who had many
connections with Hertfordshire and Essex, came down to sympathise
with her. 'Comfort yourself, good Mistress Frankland,' he said,
'and I will tell you how you shall have twenty good sonnes to comfort
you in these your sorrows which you take for this one sonne.'

When she died six years later she was found to have left most of her
property to found scholarships and fellowships in Gonville, Caius,
and Emmanuel Colleges, Cambridge, and Lincoln College, Oxford,
besides founding Newport Grammar School.

Joyce Frankland was the daughter of Robert Trappes of London, goldsmith. Her second husband was William Frankland, a London merchant,
whom she married in 1567. Her portrait hangs in the Combination
Room of Caius College, Cambridge.

FRY

Elizabeth Fry (1780-1845), prison reformer, sister of Samuel and
Joseph John Gurney, was the daughter of a Norwich banker. She
married Joseph Fry in 1800 and came to live in Essex in 1808 when
her husband inherited from his father the family estate at Plashet in
East Ham. Her brother, Samuel, lived at Ham House about a mile
away; her sister was the wife of Sir Thomas Fowell Buxton (q.v.).
Both Plashet and Ham House have gone, but the 80 acres of parkland
at Ham House are preserved by the Corporation of London as West
Ham Park.

At Plashet, Elizabeth Fry started a school for girls in the large
house opposite her own, where she had accommodation for 70 girls.
Her prison work began with a visit to Newgate in 1813. Four years
later she formed her association for the improvement of, female
prisoners.

In 1829 financial difficulties forced the Frys to leave Plashet. Their
next home was Upton Lane House, later called 'The Cedars', in West
Ham. It was at this house that King Frederick William of Prussia
called upon Elizabeth Fry in 1842 to tell her how much he admired
her work. From the grounds of Upton Lane House there was a fine
view across the Thames towards Greenwich Park. The Frys were
happy there. At the same time they had a summer cottage by Dagenham
Breach.

In 1839 Mrs. Fry made a tour of French prisons; in 1841 she visited
Copenhagen. She died, aged 65, in 1845 and was buried in the Friends'
Burial Ground at Barking.

FRYE

Thomas Frye of Bow (1710-62), china manufacturer, has the distinction of having established the first porcelain works in England. Born
in Ireland in 1710, he settled in England as a painter and engraver.
In 1744, while living at West Ham, he became associated with Edward
Heylin, merchant, of Stratford-le-Bow in taking out the first English
patent for the manufacture of china, which was to protect 'a new method of manufacturing a certain material, whereby a ware might be made
of the same nature or kind, and equal to, if not exceeding in goodness
and beauty, China or Porcelain Ware imported from abroad ...' The
factory in which the china was manufactured stood on the Essex bank
of the River Lea, about 200 yards east of Bow Bridge, in the parish
of West Ham.

In 1749, Frye alone took out a second patent, which describes a different process of calcination and giving a different glaze. The year
1749 is of particular interest because it is the year in which Josiah
Wedgewood completed his apprenticeship. Ten years later Frye was
obliged to retire. Living amid the heat and fumes of the furnaces had
undermined his health. After spending 12 months in Wales, trying to
recuperate, he returned to London in 1760, and there produced engraved portraits at his house in Hatton Garden, where he died. The
inscription of his tomb describes him as:
    The Inventor and first Manufacturer of Porcelain in England:
    To bring which to perfection, He spent Fifteen years among
    Furnaces, Till his Constitution was near destroyed: He,
    therefore, quitted these works and retired into Wales.

FULLER

Thomas Fuller (1608-61), church historian, came to Essex as chaplain to James Hay, Earl of Carlisle (q.v.), who presented him to the
perpetual curacy of Waltham Abbey in 1648. He quickly settled down
in the parish and applied himself to a study of its history. 'When I
consider,' he wrote, 'how many worthy words which had their first
being within the bounds of this our Parish, I may justly be ashamed
that my weak endeavours should be born in the same place.' After
six years at Waltham he published his Church History, to which he
appended his History of Cambridge and History of Waltham Abbey,
the first history of an Essex parish to be published.

The son of Fuller's marriage with Anne Roper was buried in the
chancel of the abbey church in 1654; the second child of the marriage,
Anne, born in 1653, was buried in 1655, so Waltham brought sorrow
as well as joy to its genial incumbent.

In 1653 Fuller published The Infant's Advocate, and dedicated it to
the Earl of Carlisle, 'my most bountiful patron', and Lionel Cranfield,
Earl of Middlesex (q.v.), 'my noble parishioner'. Not satisfied with
two noble patrons, he went on to name other distinguished parishioners: Edward Palmer, Henry Wollaston, and Matthew Gilly, Esquires;
John Vavasour, Francis Bointon, Gentlemen; with all the rest of 'my
loving parishioners in Waltham Holy Cross'.

Fuller had good reason to pay tribute to the Earl of Middlesex, whose
father, the 1st Earl, had built up a fine library at Copt Hall. When
Fuller came to Waltham Abbey, the 2nd Earl was his parishioner. He
died in 1651 and was succeeded by his younger brother, Lionel, 3rd
Earl, who presented his father's library to Fuller. With so much
kindness displayed towards him after his wanderings during the Civil
Wars, it was little wonder that Fuller should have remembered with
gratitude his ten years in the abbey parish to the end of his life.

See W. Addison: Worthy Dr. Fuller (1952)

GALPIN

Francis William Galpin (1858-1946), authority on musical instruments,
was born at Dorchester and educated at Sherborne and Trinity,
Cambridge. He was ordained in 1883, and began his study of old musical instruments while vicar of Hatfield Broadoak (1891-1915), where
he assembled a fine collection and wrote Old English Instruments of
Music (1910). Later he extended his interest to European instruments
and those of the Babylonians, Assyrians, and Sumerians. In old age
he studied the Sumerian language in order to ensure that his identif-
ications would be correct. For his services to musical scholarship
he was made an honorary freeman of the Worshipful Company of Musicians in 1905. Cambridge conferred an honorary degree of Doctor of
Letters in 1936. From 1938 to 1943 he was President of the Musical
Association.

In 1915, Galpin left Hatfield to become vicar of Witham, moving on to
become rector of Faulkbourne in 1921. From 1917 he was an Honorary
Canon of Chelmsford, and on his retirement he was appointed Canon
Emeritus. After his retirement came his works on ancient musical
instruments, followed, somewhat surprisingly to those who thought
of him only as an antiquary, by a study of electronic instruments:
The Music of Electricity. Canon Galpin wrote extensively on historical
subjects in Essex. He was President of the Essex Archaeological Society, in which he was greatly revered. His name is perpetuated in the
Galpin Society.

GAMBLE

John Gamble (d. 1811), writer on telegraphy and chaplain-general of the Forces, published a concise history of communication from the first beacon light to telegraphy as it was known in his day. He held the rectories of Alphamstone and Bradwell-juxta-Mare.

GARNETT

Place-names in the Roothings preserve the memory of the Garnett family, who flourished in the High Easter district during the 14th century. Sir Henry Garnett was Sheriff of Essex and Hertfordshire, 1341-2, and presented to the living of Margaret Roothing in 1322 and 1332. The first Essex Garnett was Geoffrey, 1125, and the name continued in the county until late in the 15th century. Their arms are identical with those of a Westmorland family of the same name, who were also the ancestors of the Dacre and Barrett-Lennard family (q.v.).

GASCOIGNE

George Gascoigne (1525?-77), poet and courtier, of Walthamstow, was the son of Sir John Gascoigne of Cardington, near Bedford. He entered Cambridge in 1547, was admitted to Grays Inn in 1555, and represented Bedford in parliament, 1557-59. After service with the Prince of Orange he returned to England and settled at Walthamstow, where he wrote The Tale of Hermetes, the masque performed before Elizabeth I at Woodstock in 1575. A pioneer in various forms of literature, he wrote Supposes, an adaptation of Ariosto's Suppositi, our earliest extant comedy in prose, the first satire, The Steele Glasse, and the second earliest tragedy in English in blank verse. In the Elegye, The Complaynt of Philomene, 1576, he wrote in the dedication to Lord Grey of Wilton that he had 'begone this sorroweful song, the which I began to devise riding in the high way betwene Chelmsford and London and being overtaken with a sodaine dash of Raine.' As a courtier he attended Elizabeth I on one of her Progresses. For his association with Edward de Vere, 17th Earl of Oxford (see VERE). He died at the age of 40.

GASCOYNE

Sir Crisp Gascoyne (1700-61), Lord Mayor of London, was a brewer whose place of business was in Houndsditch. In 1748 he played a leading part in persuading the Common Council to pass a measure for the relief of the orphans of the City of London. As Lord Mayor in 1752 he was the first to occupy the present Mansion House.

Gascoyne had a residence at Barking, where his four youngest children were baptised between 1733 and 1738. He purchased large estates in Essex, including the old hospital and chapel at Ilford. At his death in 1761 he was buried in Barking church, where a large monument to his memory may be seen. His father-in-law, Dr. John Bamber, a wealthy Mincing Lane physician, owned estates in Essex and built Bifrons at Barking, of which a drawing is preserved in the Guildhall Library copy of Lysons' Environs. The name, Gascoyne, was introduced into the Cecil family as the result of the marriage of a Gascoyne heiress with the 2nd Marquis of Salisbury, who took the name of Gascoyne before that of Cecil.

Both Sir Crisp Gascoyne and his son, Bamber, were verderers of Epping Forest.

GATE

The chronicle of the Gate family in Essex begins with Sir Geoffrey Gate, Governor of the Isle of Wight for six years and afterwards Marshal of Calais, who died in 1477 holding lands in High Easter, where he was buried, Dunmow, and Barnston. William, his son, died in 1485, leaving a son, Sir Geoffrey, who married Elizabeth, daughter of William Clopton, by whom he had three sons: John, Geoffrey, and William, all of whom were knighted.

When the first Sir Geoffrey died in 1526 he was succeeded by the most eminent member of the family, Sir John Gate (1504-53), Captain of the Guard, Vice-Chamberlain of the Household, Chancellor of the Duchy of Lancaster and privy councillor in the reign of Edward VI, by whom he was knighted. His service to the Sovereign began under Henry VIII, who granted Beeleigh Abbey to him at the Dissolution. In 1546 he was dispatched to Kenninghall in Norfolk to bring back the Duchess of Richmond and Elizabeth Holland in order that they might give evidence against Thomas, 3rd Duke of Norfolk and the poet Earl of Surrey. Shortly after this came the grant of the College and rectory of Pleshey; but unlike his neighbour, Lord Rich, Sir John Gate made no attempt to ingratiate himself with his new tenants. His lack of tact brought him many local enemies, particularly when he demolished the chancel of the church, selling the material, and required the parishioners to buy from him the nave of the church, which remained standing.

Among other offices held by Sir John Gate were the under-steward-ship and clerkship of Waltham Forest, and the clerkship of the forest court of Swainmote.

In 1550, Sir John, now the accommodating servant of the new Sover-eign, Edward VI, played a prominent part in preventing the flight to the Continent of the Princess Mary, which had been planned by the Emperor Charles V. In 1552 he was appointed a commissioner to sell chantry lands for payment of the king's debts. The following year, 1553, was to prove his undoing. In July of that year he accompanied Northumberland in his expedition against Mary, after having already involved himself in a plot to place Lady Jane Grey on the throne. Consequently he was charged before a special commission with being concerned in the Northumberland conspiracy. At the trial he pleaded guilty and was executed.

The Protestant supporters of Northumberland and Gate were filled with dismay when they learned that both had attended mass before the end, and that Sir John had confessed on the scaffold that he had read the Bible not for edification but for sedition, finally warning his hear-ers against reading the Scriptures controversially, as he had done, or they might find that God's mysteries were not safe playthings.

GAUDEN

John Gauden (1605-62), Bishop of Worcester and reputed author of the Eikon Basilike, was born at Mayland. He became Dean of Bocking and chaplain to Robert Rich, 2nd Earl of Warwick. At Bocking he lived in his deanery, according to Anthony Walker, 'at a rate of a thousand a year, and made the greatest figure of any clergyman in Essex, and perhaps in England at that time.' For ten years after it was published, the Eikon Basilike was accepted as the work of Charles I and was the bible of the Cavaliers. When Gauden claimed the author-ship he was Bishop of Exeter. For arguments on the authorship, see W. Addison: Essex Heyday (1949).

GENT

Moyns, Steeple Bumpstead, passed into the possession of the Gent family by the marriage of William Gent (alive in 1468) with Joan, daughter and heiress of William Moyne, whose family had held estates in Essex as early as the reign of Edward II. The Gent family had been settled at Wimbish since before 1328.

Thomas Gent (d. 1593), judge, represented Maldon in parliament from 1572, was appointed serjeant-at-law in 1584, and a baron of the Exchequer in 1586. His rise to affluence appears to have been substantially due to his holding of the lucrative office of steward of all the courts of Edward de Vere, 17th Earl of Oxford (q.v.). Notwithstanding the prohibition in the Statute of 33 Henry VIII c.24., he acted in his own county as a judge of assize. His first wife was Elizabeth, daughter of Sir John Swallow of Bocking, by whom he had a large family. He was buried at Steeple Bumpstead.

Other Gent memorials at Steeple Bumpstead include a large plain sarcophagus erected in 1834. In 1864, Moyns was bought by a collateral relation, Major-General Cecil St. John Ives, and the estate came back into the descendants of the family that had held it since Norman times.

GEPP

The Rev. Edward Gepp (1855-1929), compiler of the Essex Dialect Dictionary, was the elder son of the Rev. E. F. Gepp, vicar of High Easter, 1849-1903. He was educated at Colchester Royal Grammar School, Felsted School (1866-74) and St. John's Cambridge. After 21 years as a master at Felsted School he succeeded his father as vicar of High Easter in 1903, retiring to Felsted in 1916. He contributed articles to both the Essex Review and the Transactions of Essex Archaeological Society.

GERNON

Robert Gernon came over with the Conqueror and held 44 manors in Essex at Domesday. The head of his barony was Stansted, and when his son exchanged the family name for that of Mountfitchet, this was added to the place-name of Stansted, now Stansted Mountfitchet. Robert Gernon founded the abbey at Stratford Langthorne in West Ham. The family had a long connection with the Forest of Essex. Richard, grandson of Robert, was Keeper of the Forest, Keeper of the King's House at Havering, and of all the royal lodges in the Forest. This office was confirmed to him by Henry II, with the custody of the castle at Hertford. He died in 1203. His son, also Richard, joined the rebel barons against King John, and in 1217 was taken prisoner. On regaining royal favour in 1236 he was confirmed in the office of Justice, or Keeper, of the royal forests. He died without issue in 1258.

See K. Fry: Some account of the Gernon Family E.A.T., v 173

GIBBS

John Gibbs (1822-92), botanist, author of A First Catechism of Botany etc., was born in London. He settled at Chelmsford as a wool-stapler and devoted his leisure to the study of botany, which he taught at Chelmsford Literary and Mechanics' Institute.

GIBBS

William Alfred Gibbs, who lived at Gilwell from c.1882 to 1904, was
the author of many poetical works modelled on Tennyson's. He also
invented a machine for drying hay. His essay, 'Harvesting Wheat in
Wet Seasons', was awarded the gold medal of the Society of Arts and
a prize of 50 guineas. For another essay, 'Harvesting Hay in Wet
Seasons', he was awarded the gold medal of the Highland Society.
His published works include: The Story of a Life, Battle of the
Standard, Harold Erle, Lost and Won, Church Porch, The World,
the Press and the Poets, Kling, Klang, Klong, and Arlon Grange.
Several of these went through more than one edition and received
high praise from contemporary reviewers.

GIFFORD, or GIFFARD

There is a brass in Bowers Gifford church to Sir John Gifford, 1348,
the last recorded member of the family, who was a son of Sir Robert
Gifford, or Giffard, of Bures, whose family was descended maternally
from the same family as William the Conqueror. The Giffards held the
manor of Bures Giffard from Hugh Bigod, Earl of Norfolk, from the
reign of Edward I.

GILBERT or GILBERD

Dr. William Gilbert of 'Tymperleys', Colchester (1544-1603), the
first electrician, was the favourite physician of Elizabeth I. His
work, De Magnete, published in 1600, laid the foundations of our
knowledge of electricity.

William Gilbert, or Gilberd as he himself spelt his name, was born
in Colchester, the son of Jerome Gilberd, who died in 1583. Most
of the books of reference erroneously give the date of his birth as
1540. It was 24th May, 1544. He was educated privately and at St.
John's, Cambridge, where he graduated in 1560. He took his medical
degree abroad, returning to England to practice in London in 1573.
After the death of Elizabeth I he served for a short time as physician
to James I. Gilbert was President of the Royal College of Physicians
in 1600, the year in which he published the great work he had been
engaged on for 30 years. He was buried in Holy Trinity church, where
a monument to his memory was set up.

Sixty years after Gilbert's death Dryden wrote of him: 'Gilbert shall
live till loadstones cease to draw'.

GILBEY

Sir Walter Gilbey (1831-1914), fifth son of Henry Gilbey of Bishops
Stortford, left an estate agent's office to become a parliamentary
agent in Westminster. On returning from the Crimean War, he founded the firm of W. & A. Gilbey, Wine Merchants, which became a limit-
ed company in 1893. In 1858 Walter Gilbey married Ellen Parish, who
bore him five sons and four daughters. Sir Walter became a prolific
writer on sport, horse-breeding, and agriculture. In 1893 he was
created a baronet. He was a generous benefactor to Elsenham, where
he made his home. In 1898 he endowed a Lectureship at the University
of Cambridge in the history and economics of agriculture. This was
later merged with other benefactions for the formation of a Professor-
ship of Agriculture.

GLADWIN

John Gladwin, who has a brass in Harlow parish church, died in 1615 aged 95. Wright says of him:

'It was to the unwearied perseverance of John Gladwin the elder, in many lawsuits (which finally terminated in his favour) with the Lord of the Manor of Harlowbury, that the copyholders are indebted for the advantage of a fine certain of two shillings per acre on all admissions to copyhold lands.'

Along with his son and Edward Bugge he had previously undertaken an action in the Court of Chancery in connection with a tenement called Old Pole and lands belonging to it in Harlow, which had been placed on trust by John Sworder during the reign of Henry VIII for the poor of the town, but which had been misapplied to other uses.

GLASSE

Dr. Samuel Glasse (1735-1812), rector of Wanstead 1786-1812, was elected a Fellow of the Royal Society at the age of 29, and in 1772 became Chaplain in Ordinary to George III. So far as Wanstead is concerned he was a vandal. He pulled down the old church and built a new one, completed in 1790. Opinions will differ on the merits of this action, but it was certainly unnecessary to melt down the old silver communion vessels and replace them with new ones.

Dr. Glasse held a Prebendal Stall in Wells Cathedral from 1791 to 1798, and the Prebendal Stall of Oxgate in St. Paul's Cathedral from 1798 till his death. Fanny Burney refers to him under date 1789:

'Tuesday, July 28th: Today, by the Queen's desire, I invited Dr. Glasse to dinner. I did not know him, and it was awkward enough ... He is gentle and placid, but rather too simpering and complacent.'

One of his last acts was to officiate at the marriage of the Tylney heiress at St. James's, Piccadilly.

See E.R. x 129

GODFREY

Sir Edmund Godfrey of Woodford (1621-78) was the victim of one of the most intriguing unsolved murders of the 17th century. He was a Kentish man who settled at Woodford, and prospered as a London coal and timber merchant at premises near Charing Cross in the middle of the century. His bravery in remaining in London during the Plague year of 1665 and the Great Fire of 1666, throughout which he continued to perform his public duties as a Justice of the Peace for Westminster, was brought to the notice of Charles II, who knighted him, and gave him a 'great silver flagon with His Majestie's Arms engraved on it'. It was in a deposition made before Sir Edmund Godfrey in 1678 that Titus Oates (q.v.) first revealed an alleged Popish plot. Shortly after this, Sir Edmund was found murdered on Primrose Hill (see The Murder of Sir Edmund Godfrey, by John Dickson Carr, 1936). A monument to his memory in the form of a tall funeral column, designed by Sir Robert Taylor, an Essex man and a distinguished architect, was erected in the churchyard at Woodford.

The Godfrey family remained in Woodford for nearly two centuries. Michael Godfrey (1658-95), son of another Michael (1624-89), who resided at 'The Rookery', which stood near George Lane station,

I. William Harvey, 1578-1657
(Reproduced from an engraving in Guildhall Library)

II. John Ray, 1627-1705
(Reproduced from an engraving in the British Museum)

III. John Morley, 1656-1735
(Reproduced from an engraving in Essex Record Office)

was one of the founders of the Bank of England. He was killed by a stray cannon ball at the Siege of Namur. In the same year (1689) Madam Anne Mary Godfrey gave a silver flagon, a silver bowl and paten to the parish church of Woodford. According to Luttrell, the news of Godfrey's death 'abated the actions of the Bank £2 per cent'.

A later member of the family, Peter Godfrey (d. 1742) is commemorated by a quasi-Corinthian column near the south-east door of the church, and by a churchyard yew, which was planted in April, 1741. It was lopped when a new church (gutted by fire in 1969) was built in 1816. Before that date it had a spread of 180 feet.

GOLDING

Benjamin Golding (1793-1863), physician, was born at St. Osyth and entered St. Thomas's Hospital, London, as a student in 1813. He is regarded as the founder of Charing Cross Hospital, built as an extension of the West London Infirmary in 1831, of which he remained a director till 1862. He gives an account of the new hospital in The Origin, Plan and Operations of the Charing Cross Hospital, London, edited by G. B. Golding (1867). He also wrote a history of St. Thomas's Hospital.

GOLDING

In the church of Belchamp St. Paul's is a brass representing William Golding (d. 1591) in full armour at prayer. The Goldings of Belchamp St. Paul's were descended from Robert Golding, a wealthy clothier who built the south chapel of Glemsford church (Suffolk) c.1470. John Golding of Belchamp St. Paul's Hall was one of the Auditors of the Exchequer early in the 16th century. His elder son, Sir Thomas, was Sheriff of Essex and Hertfordshire in 1561 and of Essex only in 1569. He was one of the Commissioners for certifying the Chantry lands in Essex and contrived to get a large share of them for himself. His sister married John de Vere, 16th Earl of Oxford and became the mother of Edward de Vere, 17th Earl (q.v.). It is here that the special interest of the family begins.

Sir Thomas Golding and the Countess of Oxford had a half-brother, Arthur, whose translations from the classics were used by Shakespeare. He was also the tutor of his nephew, Edward, and the links between Shakespeare and Edward de Vere, many of which were provided by Golding's association with both, are the major basis for Edward de Vere being put forward by the Shakespeare Fellowship as the author of Shakespeare's plays. For example, the last speech of Prospero in The Tempest is based on one of Golding's translations from the classics. Shakespeare's speech begins:
Ye elves of Hills, brooks, standing lakes, and groves:
Golding's:
Ye ayres and windes, ye elves of hilles, or brooks, or woods alone.

In 1934, Mr. Louis Thorn Golding, of Massachusetts, placed a heraldic window in Belchamp St. Paul's church in memory of Arthur Golding, who was buried in the churchyard. He also wrote a biography of his ancestor with the title: An Elizabethan Puritan etc. (1938).

GOOD

John Mason Good (1764-1827), physician and miscellaneous writer, was born at Epping, the son of a Congregational minister who moved

from Epping to Romsey. At the age of 20 John Mason Good set up as
a physician at Sudbury. In 1793 he removed to London and became
a voluminous writer. A book of the Memoirs of John Mason Good,
by Olinthus Gregory, was published in 1828.

GOODMAN

Godfrey Goodman (1583-1656), Bishop of Gloucester, 1625-43, the
only Anglican bishop to turn Roman Catholic since the Reformation,
was vicar of Stapleford Abbots, 1606-20. He claimed that during his
13 years at Stapleford Abbots and subsequent 30 years as vicar of
West Ildersley, Berkshire, he had:
    1st, not a beggar; 2nd, not an alehouse; 3rd, not a suit in
    law; 4th, not a quarrel; 5th, not an unthrift; 6th, in the
    week-days not a labouring man ever wanted a day's work;
    7th, on a Sunday no poor man dined at his own house but
    was ever invited; 8th, no man was ever presented for for-
    nication, or any great crime; 9th, no murder, robbery, or
    felony was ever committed in the parish; 10th, no man ever
    came to a violent end; 11th, no house was burnt in the parish.
He added, with good reason:
'God make me thankful for all his blessings.'

The claim is found at the end of a volume in Trinity College Library,
Cambridge, to which Goodman bequeathed his books.

There is an Essex reference in his <u>Court of King James</u> (vol. i, ch.
xv):
'The king's custom was to make an end of his hunting in his
house at Havering in Essex, at the beginning or in the middle
of September. Prince Henry did there accompany him. I was
beneficed in the next parish of Stapleford Abbots (1606-1620).
Many of our brethren the neighbouring ministers came to hear
the sermons before the king, and some of us did say, looking
upon Prince Henry and finding that his countenance was not
so cheerful as it was wont to be, but had heavy darkish looks,
with a kind of mixture of melancholy and choler - some of us
did then say that certainly he had some great distemper in
his body; which we thought might proceed from eating raw
fruit, peaches, musk-melons, etc.'

<u>See</u> Geoffrey Soden: <u>Godfrey Goodman</u>, (1948)

GOULDMAN

Francis Gouldman (d. 1688), lexicographer, was rector of South
Ockendon from 1634 to 1644. He compiled a Latin-English, English-
Latin dictionary with proper names (1664).

GRAY

Charles Gray of Colchester (1696-1782), son of a local glazier and
churchwarden of St. Nicholas, was educated at Colchester Grammar
School and Trinity College, Cambridge, before being admitted to
Grays Inn in 1724. After marrying the widow of Ralph Creffield (q.v.)
he lived at Holly Trees and interested himself in the preservation of
the Castle, which he acquired from his mother-in-law. He built the
tower and fitted up rooms to house the Harsnett Library and his own
collection of antiquities. In 1729 he was made an honorary Free
Burgess of Colchester. He represented the borough in five parliaments,
was a F.R.S. and a trustee of the British Museum. At his death at the
age of 86 he was buried in All Saints church.

GRAYE

Miles Graye, the elder (d. 1649), and Miles Graye, the younger
(1628-89), the most eminent of the Colchester bell-founders of the
16th and 17th centuries, supplied bells for more than 100 churches
in Essex alone. Miles Graye, the elder, began casting about 1600,
so was active for practically half a century. His foundry, which was
burned in the Siege of Colchester, was known by the sign of 'The
Swan with Two Necks', and stood 'below Head Street'. After his
death the business was carried on by his son, Mile Graye, the
younger.

See E.A.T., n.s. xii 256;
     E.A.T., n.s. xviii 69

GRENVILLE

George Nugent-Temple-Grenville, 1st Marquis of Buckingham (1753-
1813), statesman, assumed the names of Nugent-Temple on marrying
the elder daughter of Robert, Earl Nugent (q.v.). He was created
Marquis of Buckingham in 1784. The 1st Marquis of Buckingham and
his marchioness were generous benefactors to Gosfield and are remembered for having introduced into the village about 1790 the manufacture of straw-plait, which spread to Braintree, Bocking, and the
surrounding villages. Arthur Young reported that in 1806 the parish
of Gosfield, with a population of 453, had earned £1,700 in a single
year by straw-plaiting: 'In Braintree several shops were purchasing
as much as £70 worth of straw-plait a week.' He relates how Lady
Buckingham made straw hats fashionable by wearing one herself,
while the marquis wore one for church 'and laid it during the service
in full sight of the congregation'. The straw-plait industry reached
its peak in Essex about 1875. Less than 20 years later it was practically extinct.

Richard Temple-Nugent Brydges Chandos Grenville, 1st Duke of
Buckingham and Chandos (1776-1839), statesman, son of the 1st
Marquis of Buckingham, was created duke in 1822. He entertained
Louis XVIII at Gosfield. One of his claims to distinction is that he
is the only person to be granted five crests, one for each of his
surnames: Temple, Nugent, Brydges, Chandos, Grenville.
Gainsborough painted portraits of several members of the Nugent
family.

GREVILLE

Francis Richard Guy, 5th Earl of Warwick (1853-1924), married
in 1881 the beautiful Frances Evelyn Maynard (1861-1938), granddaughter of the last Viscount Maynard of Easton Lodge, Dunmow,
and heiress to the Maynard estates. As Lord Brooke he was M.P.
for East Somerset, 1879-85, Colchester, 1888-92, and Lord Lieutenant of Essex, 1901-19. He was chosen to succeed Lord Rayleigh
as Lord Lieutenant because of his suitability to raise a regiment of
Yeomanry in the county. His election as M.P. for Colchester was
greatly assisted by the electioneering ability of his wife. He himself
was never prominent in politics; but for many years he was the acknowledged leader of the agricultural and sporting life of the county.
In 1917 he published an interesting biography under the title: Memoirs
of Sixty Years.

Lady Warwick was one of the great Edwardian hostesses and a
personal friend of Edward VII, who was a frequent visitor to Easton
Lodge. She became a controversial figure in society after declaring
herself a Socialist.

See The Countess of Warwick: Life's Ebb and Flow (1929)

GREY

Lady Jane Grey (1537-54) had many associations with Essex and
Suffolk. Her grandmother, Mary Tudor, sister of Henry VIII, marr-
ied Charles Brandon, Duke of Suffolk. In 1535, Lady Jane's mother,
Margaret, Marchioness of Dorset, obtained from the abbot of Tilty
a lease for 60 years of the grange, demesne lands, and manor of
Tilty. This lease was confirmed and allowed in 1538. Before she
married the marquis, Lady Dorset had been the wife of William
Medley, of Whitnash, Warwickshire, and she was succeeded at
Tilty by her son, George Medley. One of her daughters by the marquis married Lord Audley of Walden (q.v.).

Henry Grey, 3rd Marquis of Dorset (Lady Jane's father), was created Duke of Suffolk on the death of his wife's male relations. He was
executed for treason in 1554.

In 1559, Elizabeth I granted the Palace of Pyrgo, near Romford, to
Lord John Grey, younger brother of Lady Jane Grey's father, and
among the Cecil Papers is a letter dated 29th January, 1563, to Sir
William Cecil thanking him for bringing his niece, Lady Katherine
Grey (see below) to Pyrgo. At his death in 1564 he was succeeded
at Pyrgo by his son, Henry, who was created Baron Grey of Groby
in 1603. One of Henry's sisters was the wife of Sir Henry Capel of
Hadham and Rayne, another was the wife of Sir William Cooke, son
of Sir Anthony Cooke (q.v.) of Gidea Hall, Romford. Lord Grey of
Groby sold the Pyrgo estates to Sir Thomas Cheke (q.v.), Secretary
of State to Edward VI.

In consequence of these connections, Lady Jane Grey had many ardent
supporters in Essex. Sir Anthony Cooke and Sir John Cheke were
imprisoned for supporting her; Henry Bourchier, Earl of Essex (q.v.)
lost his estates in her cause; Sir John Gate (q.v.) was executed for
his part in the Northumberland Plot; Archbishop Sandys (q.v.) had
to flee the country. Among those who supported her at the beginning
but later made their peace and acknowledged the claims of Mary, were
Lord Chancellor Rich, Lord Darcy, Sir William Petre, and William
Parr, Earl of Essex.

Lady Katherine Grey (1541-68), sister of Lady Jane Grey, was committed to the Tower by Elizabeth I in 1561 for having married Edward
Seymour, Earl of Hertford, without the queen's consent. When the
Plague broke out in London two years later she was transferred to
the custody of her uncle, Lord John Grey, at Pyrgo. At his death in
November 1564 she was moved for a short time to Ingatestone, where
she was in the charge of Sir William Petre. From there she was taken
to Gosfield, where she was in the charge of Sir John Wentworth for a
year and a half until her death in 1567. She was then taken to Cock-
field Hall, near Yoxford, where she died three months later at the
age of 27. The special importance of Lady Katherine Grey's marriage
lay in the fact that after the execution of Lady Jane Grey she ranked
next in succession to the throne should Elizabeth die childless.

GRIFFIN

Sir John Griffin Griffin, 4th Lord Howard de Walden, 1st Baron
Braybrooke (1719-97), of Audley End, began life as John Griffin
Whitwell, and took the surname of Griffin by Act of Parliament in
1749 after succeeding to the estates of his uncle, Edward, 3rd
Lord Griffin. He was born at Oundle in 1719, the son of William
Whitwell and Anne, daughter of the 2nd Lord Griffin. He had a
distinguished military career, rising to the rank of Field Marshall
in 1796. On the death of his aunt, Elizabeth, Countess of Portsmouth,
in 1762, he came into possession of Audley End, as sole heir to the
Lady Essex Howard, elder daughter and co-heir of James, 3rd Earl
of Suffolk, and one of the two co-heirs of Thomas, 1st Lord Howard
de Walden and 1st Earl of Suffolk (see W. Addison: Audley End,
1953). He held the estate for 35 years, during which he rebuilt the
house and transformed the grounds. After being elected six times as
M.P. for Andover, he achieved one of his great ambitions by being
confirmed in the barony of Howard de Walden in 1784. The following
year he was appointed Lord Lieutenant of Essex. His life had been
distinguished and rewarding; but as he grew older and realised that
he would have neither sons nor nephews to inherit his estate the succession became a matter of serious concern to him. His aunt's will
provided that if he died without issue Richard Neville Neville (q.v.)
or his heir should inherit the estate. Neville, however, could not
inherit the de Walden title, so in 1788 the 4th Lord Howard de
Walden was created 1st Baron Braybrooke, with remainder to Richard
Aldworth-Neville. The succession to the estates could not be disputed
as not only Lord Howard himself, but also his three brothers and five
sisters all died without issue. Lord Howard, the outstanding character in all the long history of Audley End, died in 1797 and was buried
at Saffron Walden.

GRIMSTON

Sir Harbottle Grimston (1603-85), Speaker and judge, ancestor of
the Earls of Verulam, was born at Bradfield Hall, near Colchester,
the second son of Sir Harbottle Grimston, 1st baronet. Bradfield
Hall, which overlooks the Stour Estuary, was bought from the
Waldegrave family about 1570 by Edward Grimston, son of an Edward
who had been knighted by Elizabeth I and lived to the age of 98. The
first Sir Harbottle was born in 1577, and created a baronet in 1612
after achieving a reputation as a magistrate in the county for his vigour in hunting down and punishing recusants. He was High Sheriff in
1614; M.P. for Colchester, 1626-28, and for the county, 1928-39.
He died in 1647 and is commemorated in Bradfield church.

The second Sir Harbottle, born at Bradfield Hall in 1603, was reared
in a rigidly Puritan household. In 1619 he was entered as a Pensioner
at Emmanuel College, Cambridge, the college founded by Sir Walter
Mildmay (q.v.) in 1584. Essex had another important association with
Cambridge at the time in that Samuel Harsnett (q.v.), another
Colchester man, was Vice-Chancellor. From Cambridge, Grimston
passed to Lincoln's Inn, and in 1629 married Mary Croke, daughter
of a Judge of the King's Bench. In 1634 he became Recorder of
Harwich. This was followed by the Recordship of Colchester in 1638.
He was elected M.P. for Harwich in 1628, in 1640 for Colchester.

During the Parliamentary Sessions of 1640-2 he made his mark in the
House in debates on ecclesiastical questions and presided over the

committee appointed to inquire into the escape of Charles I from
Hampton Court in 1647. He played a prominent part in negotiations
with Charles I in the Isle of Wight, which led to his being committed
to the Tower, where he remained until the end of Charles's trial and
execution.

Meanwhile his association with Colchester continued. In 1637 he
bought the house built on the site of that of the Crouched Friars and
raised a large family there. On his father's death in 1647 he succeeded as 2nd baronet, his elder brother having died many years earlier. In 1649 he resigned the Recordship of Colchester and went abroad until the political climate became more favourable to one of his
views. During these years he devoted himself to editing the reports
of his father-in-law, Sir George Croke.

In 1655 he returned to England, and the following year was elected
M.P. for Essex; but Cromwell still suspected him and would not
allow him to take his seat. So it was not until Cromwell died that
Sir Harbottle was able to return to active life. In 1660, however,
he came into his own. He was elected Speaker, and had the honour
of welcoming Charles II. In the next parliament he felt that his chan-
ces of being re-elected Speaker were slight, so he accepted the post
of Master of the Rolls, for which he was alleged to have paid £8,000
to Clarendon.

By this time he had moved out of Essex to Gorhambury, St. Albans,
purchased from a relative of his second wife, who was the daughter
of Sir Nicholas Bacon. There he died and was buried in his St.
Michael's church. With his death the title and family became extinct
in the male line. The earls of Verulam are descended from his eldest
daughter.

GURNEY

Samuel Gurney (1786-1856), philanthropist, was born at Earlham
Hall, Norwich. At 14 he was placed in the counting-house of his
brother-in-law, Joseph Fry (husband of his sister, Elizabeth), in
St. Mildred's Court, Poultry. In 1808 he married Elizabeth, daughter of James Sheppard of Ham House, which he and his wife inherited
in 1812 and made their home. In 1807 Samuel Gurney joined the firm
of Richardson and Overend, which in the course of the next few years
was to become the most influential counting-house in the world. In
the financial crisis of 1825 Overend and Gurney, as the house was
then called, was able to lend money to many London bankers in temp-
orary difficulties. Thus Gurney came to be known as 'the banker's
banker', and many firms began to deposit cash with his firm in preference to the Bank of England.

Samuel Gurney was associated with the work of his brother, Joseph
John Gurney, Thomas Fowell Buxton (q.v.) and Elizabeth Fry (q.v.)
in penal reform. In 1849 he visited Ireland to relieve the sufferings
of poor victims of the famine. His generosity to Liberia resulted in
a town being called after him in 1851. In 1853 he was a member of a
deputation sent to Napoleon III to express a desire for peace and
amity between France and England.

At his death in 1856 he was buried in the Friends' burial ground at
Barking. He left nine children and 40 grandchildren to carry on his
family's fine tradition of public service.

GUYON

Dynes Hall, Great Maplestead, was bought in 1667 by Mark Guyon, son of Thomas Guyon, a wealthy clothier of Coggeshall. Mark Guyon was knighted in 1675. In 1689 he pulled down the greater part of the house and rebuilt it, but died in 1690 before the work had been completed. His only son, William, died the following year.

HADDOCK

A 15th century memorial in St. Clement's church, Leigh-on-Sea, reminds the visitor of a family prominent in the town for over 200 years. Admiral Sir Richard Haddock (1629-1715), the best known member of the family, commanded the Earl of Sandwich's flagship, the 'Royal James', at the Battle of Sole Bay in 1672. For his bravery in this action he was presented to Charles II, who took a silken cap off his own head and set it upon Haddock's. From that time onwards he held many offices. He was knighted in 1675, appointed Commander at the Nore in 1682, and from 1683 to 1690 was First Commissioner of the Victualling Office. From that office he moved to be Joint Comm-ander-in-chief with Admiral Killigrew and Sir John Ashby in the ex-pedition against Ireland. He died in 1715 and was buried at Leigh.

His eldest son, Richard, was Comptroller of the Navy from 1734 to 1749. Nicholas Haddock (1686-1746), third and youngest son of Sir Richard Haddock, became Admiral of the Blue in 1744 after disting-uishing himself in reprisals against the Spaniards. He represented Rochester in parliament 1734-46. When he lay dying he called for his son and said to him:

'My son, considering my rank in life and public service for so many years, I have left you but a small fortune, but it is honestly got and will wear well; there are no seamen's wages or provisions, nor one single penny of dirt money in it.'

HARCOURT

Thomas Harcourt (1618-79), the Jesuit martyr whose real name was Whitbread, was born in Essex in 1618 and in 1635 entered the Society of Jesus, of which he became head. While Provincial, he refused to admit Titus Oates to the Jesuit order. When tried at the Old Bailey with four others in 1679 the witnesses against him were Oates, Bedloe and Stephen Dugdale. Lord Chief Justice Scroggs directed the jury to bring in a verdict of guilty; but the day before the execution Lord Shaftesbury offered them pardon if they would acknowledge conspiracy. They refused and were executed at Tyburn.

HARDIE

Keir Hardie (1856-1915), M.P. for West Ham South, was the illegit-imate son of a Lanarkshire farm servant and a miner named William Aitken. He had no formal education before going into the pits at the age of ten. On learning to read he became a devotee of Burns, of whom he said: 'I owe more to Burns than to any man living or dead.' After visiting West Ham to address a meeting at Silvertown in April 1890, he was adopted Labour canditate the following month, and elect-ed by a substantial majority in 1892. As he was the first successful Labour candidate his election caused a sensation, particularly when he took his seat wearing a tweed suit and a deer-stalker cap. In the election of 1894, Hardie lost West Ham South, owing to the defection of five or six hundred Irish dockers who had been influenced by local priests. They complained that he had failed to keep his promise to make Irish Home Rule the first plank of his platform. In 1900 he was elected for Merthyr, which he continued to represent until his death at the age of 59.

HARRIOT

John Harriott (1745-1817), projector of the Thames Police, was born at Great Stambridge. At 13, when his imagination was fired by reading Robinson Crusoe, his father co-operated by securing for him an appointment as midshipman in the Navy. This was the beginning of a life of adventure which he recorded vividly in his autobiography, Struggles Through Life. Harriott was a man with a conscience as well as a thirst for adventure. He was shocked on arrival at New York by the sight of white people being sold by public auction. Most of these, he discovered, were Irishmen who had given their ship's captain permission to sell them in return for their passage.

In the 1760 s, after being discharged from the Navy, he joined the Merchant Service; but in 1766 he left his ship, and for several months lived as a member of an American Indian tribe. On leaving them he obtained a military appointment in the service of the East India Company; but a wound rendered him unfit for further service. About 1781 he returned to his home district in Essex and bought for £40 Rushley Island, which in those days was covered by the sea at high spring tides. By embanking it at great cost, Harriott succeeded in adding two or three acres of good land to the county. His enterprise was recognised by the Royal Society for the Encouragement of Arts and Sciences by the award of their gold medal. In 1790, when the island was yielding a profit of £300 a year, his house and outbuildings were burnt down. No sooner had the house been rebuilt than, on 2nd February 1791, a tide a foot higher than any within living memory, flooded the whole island and he was obliged to call together his creditors, who accepted a composition of 10s. in the pound. Local sympathisers, however, came to his rescue. A sum of over £1,000 was subscribed to enable him to start again, but he decided to cut his losses and emigrate to America. There, however, he was disappointed with the facilities available for the education of his children and he returned to England, with little to show for the five years he had spent there.

About this time he applied himself to patenting an improvement in ships' pumps and began working out a scheme for a force of river police for the Port of London. After his return from America he spent some time farming, but the death of his wife again unsettled him and he went up to London and set himself up as an insurance broker. This was followed by an adventure into the spirit trade which proved unsuccessful and again he returned to farming. At last he appeared to be settled. He took an interest in local affairs, was appointed a magistrate, and started a local public library.

His ideas for dealing with theft from ships lying in the Thames crystalised, and in 1798 he and Sir Patrick Colquhoun were given permission to try out their scheme for the formation of the Thames River Police. Two years later the scheme was officially adopted. Harriott himself was appointed one of the three special justices to reside at the Police Office at Wapping.

In 1808 Harriott published his autobiography. He was still holding the resident magistrate's appointment when he died at Burr Street,

Spitalfields, at the age of 72.

Obviously he has a place in national history. For Essex his reminiscences are valuable for the information they give about conditions
in the Rochford Hundred in the second half of the 18th century. The
clergy were nearly all non-resident. He remembered only three who
were permanently in residence, and he gives an account of a petition
from the parishioners of Little Stambridge to Lord Chancellor
Thurlow asking for a resident curate to be given the living:

> 'All the 27 neighbouring parishes being in the same predic-
> ament, served by curates (three, four, and sometimes five
> churches to one curate), we have little or no relief if we
> ride to any neighbouring church.'

The same problem is dealt with in Palin's Stifford and Neighbourhood.

HARRISON

William Harrison of Radwinter (1534-93), topographer and contemporary social historian, was an Essex parson for 34 years, during
which he not only wrote his Description of England, brewed his own
beer like his neighbours and collected Roman coins as befitted an
antiquary, but also fought valiantly with 'the rascally Essex lawyers'
of his day. Harrison was presented to the Radwinter living by William
Brooke, Lord Cobham, whom he served as chaplain. In 1571 he was
given the neighbouring living of Wimbish to augment his income, but
he resigned it in 1581. In 1586 he was appointed a canon of Windsor.

Much of the value of Harrison's Description is in its racy style,
which is so redolent of the Elizabethan age as the common people
knew it. Becket, for example, figures as 'the old cocke of Canter-
burie'. Essex readers in particular must warm to him, especially
when he mentions by name such notable contemporaries as Sir Thomas
Smith of Hill Hall (q.v.), author of De Republica Anglorum, 'requiting
him with the like borrowage as he hath used toward me in his discourse
of the sundrie degrees of estates in the commonwealth of England.' He
must also have kept in touch with Alexander Nowell, Dean of St. Paul's,
who spent much time in Essex. Harrison had been one of his pupils at
Westminster School.

Harrison's Description was published with Holinshed's Chronicle in
1577. In the preface to the Description he says that he had then given
up the study of history because it was interfering with 'that vocation
and function to which I am called in the ministrie', from which we may
deduce that he was a moderate Puritan. He was a keen advocate of the
amalgamation of livings and a shrewd observer of life in general. Four
things, in particular, he says he would like to see reformed:

'1. the want of discipline in the Church;

2. the covetous dealing of most of our merchants in the
   preferment of the commodities of other countries and
   the the hindrance of their own;

3. the holding of fairs and markets upon the Sunday to
   be abolished and referred to the Wednesdays;

4. every man (with) forty acres or more of land (should
   be obliged to) plant one acre with wood or sow the
   same with oak mast, hazel, beech, and sufficient
   provision be made that it should be cherished and
   kept.'

He describes his work as a 'foule frizeled treatise', and can have
had little idea of the value it would have for future generations.
What mattered most to him was that he should be accounted profitable
in his ministry, and it is to be noted that his name does not appear in
the list of 'unpreaching ministers' compiled in 1585. In the south window of his parsonage he had painted 'the sun in his glory' with a hare
below it - a rebus on his name. Another of his works, a Great
Chronologie, has never been published, although parts of it appear
in Furnivall's edition of the Description of England. The manuscript
was at one time in the Episcopal Library at Derry.

See G. Edelen's scholarly and well-indexed edition of the Description
(1968)

HARSNETT

Samuel Harsnett (1561-1631), archbishop, was the son of a Colchester
baker. At 15 he won a scholarship to King's College, Cambridge, from
which he moved to Pembroke on winning a scholarship in Divinity. At
25 he returned to Colchester as master of his old school, but did not
settle, and after 18 months returned to Pembroke, 'chusing rather to
follow his studies at Cambridge than the painfull trade of teachyng'.
In 1597 he was inducted to the vicarage of Chigwell, where he remained until 1605, and for which he developed an abiding affection. In 1604
he was presented to the living of Shenfield, followed by presentation
to that of Stisted in 1609. From 1603 to 1609 he was Archdeacon of
Essex.

Harsnett was Master of Pembroke from 1605 to 1616, and Vice-Chancellor of the University in 1606 and 1614. It was said of him that he
'governed with a high hand'. While retaining his mastership of
Pembroke and one or two livings, he was Bishop of Chichester from
1606 to 1619, so it is hardly suprising that he should have been critic-
ised for being an absentee who mismanaged the college accounts. In
1616 the Fellows sent an 'Accusation' against him in 57 articles, for
presentation to the king, who as it happened, had recently been entertained by Harsnett at Cambridge, so although he satisfied the critics
by advising Harsnett to resign his Mastership he appointed him (1619)
Bishop of Norwich. Ten years later he was translated to the Arch- .
bishopric of York. Shortly after this his health broke down. He died
at Moreton-in-Marsh in 1631 and was buried at Chigwell, which he
had already chosen for his retirement, and where in 1629 he had
founded a school as a thank offering for his elevation to York. By his
will, he left his library to Colchester, an annuity of £6 13s. for the
maintenance of poor persons living in the almshouse at Chigwell and
24 twopenny loaves for distribution to the poor. He also left £14 a
year for maintaining a footpath five miles long from Abridge towards
London.

Harsnett was a masterful character who gloried in ritual and waged
continuous war against the Puritans. A fine brass in Chigwell church
shows him fully attired as a bishop in the garments ordered by the 24th
canon in the first prayer book of Edward VI. Considerable interest
has been shown in his Egregious Popishe Impostures, written at
Chigwell and published in 1603, from which Shakespeare took the
names of the spirits in Lear. Other parallels are given by Kenneth
Muir in Notes and Queries, vol. cxcvii.

HARVEY of Saffron Walden.

All four sons of John Harvey, a 16th century Saffron Walden rope-
maker, went to Cambridge, and two, Gabriel and Richard, became
famous. Both were oddities. Of Gabriel, a learned but pedantic
Fellow of Pembroke, it may be said that although he lacked humour
himself he added much to the mirth of the age by provoking it in others. In 1586 Edmund Spenser wrote a tribute to him; but he is now
chiefly remembered for the ridicule his pedantic pomposity inspired
in Nash, with whom he waged a famous battle of pamphlets.

Richard, Gabriel's brother, was a clergyman who dabbled in astrology and at the age of 25 published a pamphlet entitled: 'An Astrolog-
ical Discourse upon the Conjunction of Saturn and Jupiter, which
shall happen the 28th day of April, 1583, with a declaration of the
effects which the late eclipse of the Sunne is yet hereafter to worke.'
This prophecy, dated from 'my father's house in Walden, the 6th
December, 1582', went into two editions and caused widespread
alarm. The Rev. Richard prophecied that at high noon on the 28th
April gales and floods of no common order would play havoc in the
land. 'If these fall not in every point as I have wrote,' he states,
'let me for ever lose the credit of my astronomie.' If that was gen-
uinely his wish it was fulfilled, because a deluge of abuse and ridicule fell upon him when none of these things came to pass. Nash
joined in the fun: 'Would you in likely reason gesse it possible for
anie shame-swoln toad to outlive this disgrace ?' he wrote, 'It is,
deare brethren, vivit, imo, vivit - he lives, verily, he lives - and,
which is more, he is a vicar.'

John, a third son, dabbled in astrology but more cautiously. Mercy,
their sister, was rediscovered by Virginia Woolf, who in The Strange
Elizabethans, describes a scene with Mercy 'milking in the fields
near Saffron Walden accompanied by an old woman, when a man app-
roached her and offered her cakes and malmsey wine'. He had come
from Lord Surrey who had fallen in love with her.

See W. Addison: Essex Heyday (1949)

HARVEY of Hempstead and Chigwell.

The great Harvey vault at Hempstead contains between 40 and 50
family coffins. The most distinguished member of the family was
William Harvey (1578-1657), discoverer of the circulation of the
blood, who was born at Folkestone and educated at King's School,
Canterbury, and Caius College, Cambridge. During the Civil Wars,
Harvey followed Charles I. At the Battle of Edgehill in 1642 he had
charge of the princes, Charles and James. Aubrey, in his Brief
Lives, tells a delightful story which he says he had from Harvey himself. During the heat of the battle he withdrew with the princes 'under
a hedge, and took out of his pocket a book to read; but he had not
read very long before a Bullet of a Great Gun grazed on the ground
near him, which made him remove his station.' Charles rewarded
Harvey by making him Warden of Merton College.

During the Commonwealth he spent much of his time with his brothers,
one of whom was Sir Eliab, a London merchant who became wealthy.
It was at his house that William Harvey died. Sir Eliab had recently
built a vault at Hempstead, and William's body was borne in a large
funeral procession for burial there, between those of two of his nie-
ces. It had no coffin, but was 'lapt in lead'. In 1882, the tower of the
church collapsed, and this catastrophe moved the College of Physicians to take the necessary measures for safeguarding Harvey's

remains. So on St. Luke's Day, 1883, the leaden case was carried from the vault by eight Fellows and laid in a marble sarcophagus in the Harvey Chapel, with a memorial scroll and the quarto edition of Harvey's works. The bust is believed to have been modelled from a death mask.

The Harvey connection with Chigwell began in 1688, when the manor of Barringtons was sold to John Prestwood and Sir Eliab Harvey, nephew of William. He was knighted at the Restoration and represented Maldon in Parliament until his death in 1698. This Eliab bequeathed his share in Barringtons to his second son, William (d. 1731), who in 1700 purchased the remainder from Francis Comyn. A second William of Chigwell died in 1742, a third in 1763, a fourth (unmarried) in 1779, leaving Barringtons to his brother, Eliab, later Admiral Sir Eliab Harvey, who died without surviving male issue in 1830.

Sir Eliab Harvey (1758-1830), Admiral of the Blue, K.G.C.B., who commanded the 'Temeraire' at Trafalgar, was thus the direct descendant of Eliab Harvey, brother of William, the discoverer of the circulation of the blood. He married Lady Louisa Nugent, younger daughter of Earl Nugent (q.v.), was M.P. for Maldon, 1780, for Essex, 1803 to 1812, and 1820 to 1826. His title to fame is the bravery he displayed as one of Nelson's captains at Trafalgar, where he commanded the second ship in the Line. As the two great ships, the 'Victory' and the 'Temeraire', moved into battle they were so close that the second almost touched the stern of the first. At the climax, while Nelson was dying in the cockpit of the 'Victory' and a French boarding party preparing to take his ship, Harvey came up in the 'Temeraire' and shattered the French ship with a broadside. Collingwood wrote of the part of the 'Temeraire' in the action: 'Nothing could be finer. I have no words in which I can sufficiently express my admiration of it.' A celebration dinner was held at the 'King's Head', Chigwell, and in 1805 Harvey was promoted to Rear-Admiral. He was advanced to Admiral in 1819; but between the two he had been in disgrace. In 1809 he was dismissed for abuse of Lord Cochrane, and remained in disgrace for several months.

Sir Eliab was active in local affairs in Essex. He served as a magistrate and in 1785 was elected a verderer of Epping Forest. In 1818 he served on a committee appointed to examine allegations concerning encroachments of Epping and Hainault Forests. During the agricultural depression in 1816 he showed generous public spirit by reducing his rents by ten shillings an acre. At home he does not appear to have been the great man he was to the public. The harmony of his domestic life is said to have been all too frequently disturbed by his violent and uncertain temper. So much so that at times his wife doubted his sanity. Perhaps the explanation of this domestic unhappiness is to be found in his disappointment at not having a son to succeed him. His sons predeceased him. He left six daughters !

HAWKWOOD

Sir John de Hawkwood (1340-94), soldier of fortune, Froissart's 'Haccoude', was the son of a Sible Hedingham tanner. He distinguished himself at the Battle of Poitiers in 1356, gaining the favour of the Black Prince. In 1359 he earned fame as commander of 5,000 horse and 1,500 foot which became known as the White Company. With Bernard de la Salle he levied contributions for defence from Pope Innocent VII in 1360, and two years later shared in the English victory at Brignais. With his well-equipped company he placed his services

at the disposal of various Italian States, assisting Agnello to make
himself Doge of Pisa in 1364. The following year his company of St.
George ravaged the country between Genoa and Siena, pillaged the
Perugino, and in 1367 he escorted Agnello to meet the Pope at
Viterbo. In 1369 he was captured by the Pope's mercenaries, but
ransomed by Pisa. In 1374 he won a great victory for Pope Gregory
XI at Gavardo; but three years later he joined the anti-papal league,
marrying a natural daughter of Bernabo Viscounti, Duke of Milan.
From 1380 most of his energies were devoted to the defence of
Florence, where he is still honoured as the defender of Florentine
liberties.

Hawkwood was joint-ambassador for England at Rome from 1382, and
at Florence and Naples from 1385. Loaded with honours and riches
he died at Florence in 1394 and was buried in the Duomo, where he
is commemorated, proudly mounted, in a fresco by Paolo Ucello. At
the request of Richard II, leave was granted to transfer his body to
England for burial at Sible Hedingham, but it is not known whether
this was done. There is a fine monument to him at Sible Hedingham.

See J. Temple-Leader: Sir John Hawkwood (1899) E.R. xxxix 72;
E.A.T. n.s. vi 174

HAY

James Hay, 1st Earl of Carlisle, 1st Viscount Doncaster, and 1st
Baron Hay (d. 1636), courtier, was one of the Scottish nobles who
came to England with James I, whose life he was alleged to have
saved by standing knife in hand to defend the king against the Earl
of Gowrie. He married Honora, daughter and heir of Sir Edward
Denny, later Earl of Norwich (q.v.), of Waltham Abbey. At her
death the Waltham Abbey estates were inherited by their son, James,
who became 2nd Earl of Carlisle.

Hay was Master of the Wardrobe, 1613. He was sent on missions to
Heidelberg and the imperial court, 1619-20, was envoy to Paris,
1623, to Lorraine and Piedmont, 1628. After the death of his first
wife he married Lady Lucy Percy, daughter of the 9th Earl of Northumberland, whose wit and beauty were celebrated in verse by Carew,
Herrick, Suckling, Waller, and D'Avenant, and who exercised great
influence over Queen Henrietta Maria. As Hay himself was a somewhat ridiculous figure the marriage could only be regarded cynically
by those who were aware of Lady Lucy's ambitions. They did, however,
share Presbyterian zeal. Hay was said to have received from the king
gifts worth close on half-a-million pounds, yet he died penniless.

James Hay, 2nd Earl of Carlisle (d. 1660), started life as a Royalist,
but changed sides during the Commonwealth and compounded for his
estate. Unlike his father, he was a dignified figure whose courtly
address brought honour to the title. At his death without issue all the
honours conferred by James I on his father expired.

HELE-SHAW

Henry Selby Hele-Shaw (1854-1941), engineer, was born at Billericay,
the eldest of the 13 children of Henry Shaw and Marion, daughter of
the Rev. Henry Selby Hele, vicar of Grays, whose name he added to
his own. At 27 he became first Professor of Engineering at Bristol
University; in 1885 the first to hold the same appointment at University
College, Liverpool. In 1904 he left Liverpool to start a college of engineering in the Transvaal, where he became principal of the college

within a year. This was the third engineering department he set up
and all became important. His valuable inventions started in 1881
with instruments for the measuring and recording of wind velocities,
and these were followed by others in the field of apparatus for scientific experiments. To the general public, his work on vehicular transport is best known. The 'Locomotives on Highways Act, 1896', raised
questions that no-one was better qualified than he to answer. At the
same time his inventive skill was applied to problems of speed and
safety. His friction clutch was used on most vehicles for many years.
In 1885 he was awarded the Watt gold medal and Telford premium. In
later life he took great interest in professional engineering institut-
ions generally. He was president of the Institute of Automobile Engineers in 1909, president of the Institute of Mechanical Engineers in
1922. He died at Ross-on-Wye.

HELENA

St. Helena (c.242-c.330), is traditionally associated with Colchester.
According to legend, Coel II led a revolt against the Romans and made
himself ruler of Essex. Constantinus was sent to suppress the rising;
but while laying siege to Colchester he caught a glimpse of Helena and
was so affected by her beauty that he made peace with Coel, her father, so that he could cultivate her acquaintance. The Colchester Chronicle, written at the back of the Oath Book of the town, records:
  '242 A.D. Helena, daughter of Coel, born at Colchester.

  260   Constantinus, the Roman General in Spain,
                 sails to Britain, and besieges Colchester
                 (which continued to be held by Coel against
                 the Romans).

  264   The siege is raised, Constantinus betrothing
                 Helena.

  265   Constantine (afterwards Emperor and sur-
                 named the Great), son of Constantinus by
                 Helena, born before the solemnization of
                 the nuptials.'

Helena was said to have adopted Christianity when Constantine the
Great made it the official religion of the Roman Empire by the Edict
of Milan. She then undertook a pilgrimage to Jerusalem where, according to the legend, she discovered the cross of Christ. This is
commemorated in the arms of Colchester, and the earliest seal of
the bailiffs bears her image. The legend originated with Geoffrey
of Monmouth and is without foundation; but it resulted in Helena being
regarded as the patron saint of Colchester.

HELION

The Helion family of Steeple Bumpstead held land in Essex for nearly
400 years from the Conquest. The chief accession came through the
marriage of a member of the family with the heiress of the Swynbornes
of Little Horkesley. Another marriage brought them Gosfield. About
the middle of the 15th century their own heiress took their land to a
Tyrell, from whom it passed to a Wentworth. Members of the Helion
family fought at both Crecy and Agincourt.

See J. H. Round: E.A.T. n.s. viii 187

HEND

John Hend of Bradwell-juxta-Coggeshall was Lord Mayor of London
in 1391 and 1404. He was a great benefactor of Coggeshall Abbey
and rebuilt the church of St. Swithin, by London stone.

HENEAGE

Sir Thomas Heneage (d. 1595), courtier, Vice-Chamberlain to
Elizabeth I, Recorder of Colchester, was the son of Robert Heneage,
Surveyor of the Queen's Woods beyond Trent, and nephew of George
Heneage, Dean of Lincoln. He was elected M.P. for Stamford in 1553,
for Boston in 1562, for Lincolnshire in 1571, and represented Essex
in Parliament from 1585 until his death. For his loyal services to the
Crown he received from Elizabeth I grants of several properties, including Copt Hall, Epping, where he built 'a noble large house, with
a court in the middle', sometime between 1564 (when he acquired possession) and his death. Sir Thomas's was the second of three mansions.
Like the first, it stood in Waltham Abbey parish. The third was built
on an eminence in the neighbouring parish of Epping, the manor and
rectory of which were granted to Sir Thomas in 1573.

In 1577, Sir Thomas and his brother were appointed joint keepers of
records at the Tower of London. Eleven years later, when England
came under threat from the Spanish Armada, Sir Thomas was appointed Treasurer at War, an office that made him responsible for the
payment and victualling of the anti-invasion forces assembled at
Tilbury, and it was for these services that he was awarded the
Armada Jewel (see K. Neale, Essex Journal, vol. iv no..4). The
peak of his career came in 1589, when he was appointed to succeed
Sir Christopher Hatton as Vice-Chamberlain of the Royal Household.
There is evidence that the favour shown to Heneage by the queen
aroused the jealousy of Leicester, his neighbour in Essex. Sir
Thomas's local status in this Royal Forest region is shown by his
receiving in 1591, one fee-deer in virtue of his Rangership and another in virtue of his Lieutenancy, of the forest.

After the death of his first wife, Elizabeth, daughter of Sir Nicholas
Poyntz of Gloucestershire (who bore him a daughter, Elizabeth, in
1556), Sir Thomas Heneage married, in 1594, as his second wife and
her second husband, the Countess of Southampton, mother of
Shakespeare's patron, who was 20 years his senior. A good case
could be made out for the belief that Shakespeare's play, A Midsummer
Night's Dream, was written for the wedding festivities. Theseus and
Hippolyta may well have been intended to represent Sir Thomas and
the Countess.

There is much material on Sir Thomas Heneage in the Salisbury
Papers. When he lay dying, the Earl of Oxford wrote to Cecil begging
him to secure for him appointment as Lord Warden of the Forests of
Waltham and Havering, which had been held by Sir Thomas, but had
previously been held for centuries by the de Veres.

His papers were in disorder at the time of his death, and Elizabeth
pressed his widow for repayment of a loan. After the queen's death,
James I wrote to Sir Thomas Egerton:

'Whereas Sir Thomas Henneage, Knight, late Treasurer of
the Chamber, stood indebted to out late dear sister in divers
sums of money amounting in the whole to the sum of £13,300,
and had made an arrangement with Sir Moyle Finch who had
married his sole daughter and heir that if he survived and

should pay £600 a year for 13 years, he should have all
his farms, houses and lands, so as to pay the Queen's
debt first, and if any were left over Sir Thomas's own
debts ...'

Sir Thomas Heneage was thus one of the three great landowners in
the Epping district who were heavily in debt through having bought
their favours too dearly from Elizabeth I (see Smith and Fitzwilliam).

At Sir Thomas Heneage's death the Copt Hall estate passed to his
daughter, Elizabeth, wife of Sir Moyle Finch, of Eastwell in Kent,
who in 1628 was created Countess of Winchelsea, a title which descended to her son, who succeeded her in 1633. It was he who sold
Copt Hall to Lionel Cranfield, Earl of Middlesex (q.v.).

Camden says of Sir Thomas Heneage that he, 'for his elegancy of
life and pleasantness of speech, was born for the court.'

HEWETT

In the Short Blue Fleet, the Hewetts of Barking built up the largest
fishing fleet in the world. Scrymgeour Hewett settled at Barking
about 1764 and married the daughter of James Whennel, a local fish-
erman. Samuel, son of this marriage, was a man of indomitable energy who revolutionised the industry, first by introducing refriger-
ation into his boats. This was so successful that by 1833 there were
133 vessels of between 40 and 60 tons operating from Barking. His
second innovation was the introduction of the 'fleeting' system, in
which the whole fleet remained on the fishing grounds and a fast
cutter carried the catch to London.

The Short Blue Fleet was commanded by a senior skipper, known as
'the Admiral', who flew a special flag, and by special signals gave
orders for the lowering and pulling in of the nets. This system necess-
itated the redesigning of smacks, which could now be larger since
speed for bringing in the fish was no longer the main consideration.
Each of these new smacks went out with rations for six weeks, although fresh supplies to supplement the rations were brought out on
each trip by the carrier. By this means the Barking fishing industry
was transformed into a hugh concern capable of meeting the demands
of the rapidly expanding London market.

Barking reached its zenith as a fishing port about 1850, when the
Short Blue Fleet numbered about 220 vessels; but by this time skipp-
ers had been accepted as part owners. The crews were recruited
largely from orphanages, notably the Foundling School, and these
apprentices were looked after by Samuel Hewett's wife, assisted by
a staff of women.

Decline came after 1865, when the Eastern Counties Railway reached
Great Yarmouth; but Samuel recognised the change and opened a base
there. He further saw that his cutters would no longer be fast enough
and introduced steam-ships as carriers. Gradually, however, Yarmouth
proved to have greater advantages than Barking as a base, and by 1883
the Short Blue Fleet had 83 trawlers sailing out of Yarmouth. In the
meantime the railway had brought the industrial centres of Lancashire
and Yorkshire within reach, and Grimsby came to the fore with a fishing industry which to a large extent was founded by Barking fishermen.
In 1899 the last sailing smack left Barking. In the following year a
disastrous explosion at Barking brought the association of the Short
Blue Fleet with Essex virtually to an end. Roy Hewett, Samuel's

IV. Thomas Fowell Buxton, 1837-1916
(Reproduced from an engraving in Essex Record Office)

V. Joseph, Lord Lister, 1827-1912
(Reproduced from a photograph in Essex Record Office)

VI. William Morris, 1834-1896
*(Reproduced from the portrait by George Frederick Watts, R.A.
in the National Portrait Gallery)*

great-grandson, built up the fleet again, but it was found desirable
to change bases, and in 1929 the whole fleet was moved to Fleetwood
in Lancashire.

HEWITT

E. P. Strutt, in Colchester Celebrities of the Olden Times, relates
that on one occasion the Rev. Charles Hewitt, parson of Greenstead,
fell asleep in the pulpit, and when told by the clerk that all the congregation were out mumbled: 'Oh, are they ? Fill them up again, my
brave boys.'

HICKES

Sir Michael Hickes (1543-1612), secretary to Lord Burghley, had
the reputation of being 'very witty and jocose'. His Essex home was
Ruckholt, Leyton, acquired about 1598. At his death he was buried
in the chancel of Leyton church, where an elaborate alabaster monument was erected to his memory, with recumbent effigies of himself
and his widow. Sir Michael is in full armour, with the distinctive
feature of carrying in his hand a baton, to symbolise his office of
Lieutenant of Waltham Forest. Ruckholt was demolished in 1757.

HILL

Aaron Hill (1685-1750), dramatist, married a daughter of Edmund
Morris of West Ham. He was a man of fertile brain who experimented
in several novel manufactures, all of which failed. In 1713 he obtained
a patent for obtaining oil from beechmast. Another of his projects was
for a new fuel compacted of coal-dust and Thames mud. Yet another
was for repairing Dagenham Breach.

In 1738, Hill removed from a house in Petty France, Westminster, to
Plaistow, West Ham, where he planted 'near a hundred thousand
French vines'. He died at Plaistow in 1750 and was buried in the
cloisters of Westminster Abbey.

See D. Brewster: Aaron Hill, Poet, Dramatist, Projector (1913)

HOLLAND

Philemon Holland (1551-1636), who translated Camden's Britannia
into English and was known as the Translator-General of the age,
was born at Chelmsford and attended King Edward VI Grammar School
there. On leaving Cambridge he became headmaster of the Royal Free
School at Coventry, where he also practised medicine. He died at
Coventry in his 85th year and was buried in Holy Trinity church there.

HOLMAN

The Rev. William Holman (d. 1730), antiquary, was minister of the
Congregational church at Halstead from 1700 to 1730. During these
years he travelled about the county collecting material for a history
of Essex, which he assembled in 400 quarto-sized notebooks, one
for each parish. In his historical research he was assisted by
Nicholas Jekyll of Castle Hedingham, who had inherited from his
grandfather, Thomas Jekyll (q.v.), a collection of MSS, which eventually went to enlarge the Holman collection. Holman's catalogue of
the Jekyll MSS. is now in the Library of All Souls' College, Oxford.
A copy by Gough is among the Egerton MSS. in the British Museum,
a third is in the Library of the Essex Field Club (see Essex Naturalist

iii, 160-1). The Jekyll material was dispersed when it was sold by Holman's son; but the whole of it had already been assimilated by William Holman into his parish histories when he died suddenly in the porch of Colne Engaine church, although he had not completed the preparation of his work for the press.

Holman's MSS. were entrusted by his son to the Rev. Nicholas Tindal of Great Waltham, with a view to their being got ready for publication, and two parts were, in fact, issued; but lack of public interest led to the whole project being abandoned. From Tindal's hands the collection passed to Anthony Allen, a Master in Chancery, and from him to John Booth, F.S.A., of Barnard's Inn, before it was acquired by Philip Morant (q.v.) in 1750. Undoubtedly, the abundance of the material had proved an embarrassment to the scholars who had already examined it. Morant boldly set aside the arms of the families and the epitaphs that Holman had copied so assiduously and brought the historical material into manageable form by keeping it within the framework of his own plan, which was based on the descent of estates.

The Holman MSS, preserved in 22 unbound volumes, almost entirely in Holman's own handwriting, are now deposited in the Essex Record Office.

HOLST

Gustav Theodore Holst (1874-1934), composer, was born at Cheltenham the elder son of Adolph von Holst, a music teacher whose family was of Swedish origin. While still a student, Gustav Holst joined the Kelmscott House Socialist Club in Hammersmith, and there met Isobel Harrison, whom he married in 1901. Throughout his life social and musical interests remained linked, and to them was added a passion for taking long walks in the English countryside. The frugal habits of his student days stayed with him to the end of his life. He was one of the least self-indulgent of men, partly by choice and partly from principle. All these characteristics combined to make his residence at Thaxted from 1917 to 1925 the happiest period of his life. The vicar, Conrad Noel (q.v.), was his great friend. His home was The Steps, (afterwards The Manse), near the church, and under a sympathetic vicar he was able to make the Whitsuntide Festival at Thaxted a national event.

Gustav Holst dreaded popularity and never courted fame; but he enjoyed the friendship of many eminent musicians, most notable among them being Ralph Vaughan Williams. His constant companion during his later years was his daughter, Imogen, who inherited many of his gifts and personal tastes.

See Imogen Holst: Gustav Holst (1938)

HONYWOOD

The Honywood family came into Essex in 1605, when Robert Honywood, of Charing in Kent, purchased Markshall, Coggeshall, to accommodate his large family. Robert himself had 15 children, some of whom would be adults in 1605; but he had more than his own offspring to provide room for. He brought with him his mother, Dame Mary Honywood, who had married at 16 and was the mother of 16 children, all of whom had been productive. She was 77 when the family reached Markshall. When she died 15 years later in her 93rd year she left 367 descendants,

reaching to the fifth generation. Records of her piety are found in
Fuller and Foxe.

Robert was 75 when his mother died. He died seven years later at
the age of 82. His son, Robert (1587-1666), who succeeded him, was
knighted in 1632 and became a leader in the Parliamentary Army.
Local tradition maintains that the artificial lake in the grounds of
Markshall was the work of Fairfax's soldiers stationed there during
the siege of Colchester. When the Royalist garrison surrendered,
Sir Robert was placed in charge of the town, with orders to dismantle
the fortifications. He served as a Knight of the Shire for Essex in
1654 and 1656 and was one of the members of Cromwell's Upper House.

The next Honywood to enjoy more than local fame was Philip, who was
desperately wounded at Dettingen in 1742. The curious story is told
of him that he and his wife parted by mutual consent when each confessed to finding the other completely unattractive. Years afterwards,
while Gen. Honywood was taking the waters at Bath he found himself
greatly attracted by a lady who was there at the time. On enquiring
her name he was surprised to find that it was the same as his own.
It was, in fact, his wife, and they were re-united. Gainsborough,
whom he also met at Bath, painted his portrait. At his death the estate was inherited by his wife, and at her death it passed to a distant
cousin, which meant that for the first time in 200 years a direct descendant of Dame Mary had failed to provide the heir.

Honywoods continued at Markshall until the end of the 19th century;
but both family and estate went through a long decline. The last to
inherit had no option but to sell what remained.

See E.R. vii 156; xlii 109; 1 10; 1 23; 1x 99

HOOD

Thomas Hood (1799-1845), poet, lived at Lake House, Wanstead,
from 1832 to 1835. He described the house as 'a beautiful old place,
although exceedingly inconvenient, for there is not a good bedroom
in it.' Lake House had been a banqueting-hall to Wanstead House,
and for this reason had only one good room of any kind, which was
the magnificent banqueting room itself, with a chimney-piece carved
in fruit and flowers by Grinling Gibbons. In Hood's time it was already
in a state of dilapidation, but it had the attraction of extensive grounds
featuring a lake surrounded by banks of rhododendrons. Such gardens
were greatly in vogue at the time as places where friends could be
entertained and romantic fancies indulged. At Lake House Hood wrote
a three-volume novel entitled Tylney Hall, published in 1834. As a
novel it was a failure from an artistic point of view, but a success
commercially. Dickens described it as 'the most extraordinary jumble
of impossible extravagance and especial cleverness I ever saw.'
Despite what the critics said, it went through ten reprints.

Hood saw himself as a country squire at Wanstead, but the decayed
house contributed to the illnesses he suffered at this time. Its upkeep
ruined him financially. He was no more successful as a squire than as
a novelist, and his association with Essex lives now in the local references found in the rollicking stanzas of The Epping Hunt, published in
1829, before he came to live in the county.

HOOKER

Thomas Hooker (c.1586-1647), New England divine, was church
lecturer at Chelmsford for a short time from 1626 and exercised
great influence on the ministers of Essex. After being ejected from
his Chelmsford appointment he conducted a school at Little Baddow
until he was called upon by Laud to answer for his behaviour. The
2nd Earl of Warwick then provided him with a refuge in Holland,
from which he sailed in 1633 to join his many Essex friends in New
England, where he became pastor of the eighth church in Massachusetts, and the first in Newtown, later Harvard.

HOPKINS

Matthew Hopkins of Manningtree (d. 1647), witchfinder, was a
Manningtree lawyer who in 1644 became suspicious of the behaviour
of eight local women said to be practising witchcraft. He took upon
himself to prosecute them, and on obtaining sentences of death declared holy war on all witches, assuming for the purpose the title of
'Witchfinder General'. With two assistants, a woman and a Calvinist
fanatic named John Sterne, he toured the eastern counties. In Essex
alone he was responsible for the hanging of 60 poor women in a single
year. Largely as the result of his zeal, Essex has the dubious distinction of having provided far more indictments and hangings for witchcraft than all the other Home Counties put together. In 1646 Hopkins
came up against the Rev. John Gaule, minister of Staughton in Hunt-
ingdonshire, who exposed him as an unmitigated rogue. The following
year he was hanged.

HORKESLEY

Little Horkesley was held by the de Horkesley family for at least five
generations to about the middle of the 14th century, when on the death
of William de Horkesley and Emma, his wife, it passed to Robert de
Swynborne (q.v.). Oak effigies of knights, c.1250 and 1270, in Little
Horkesley church are of special interest.

HOUBLON

The common ancestor of the merchant family of Houblon in England
was Peter, a merchant of Lisle, who came as a Huguenot refugee
about 1568. His son, John, prospered as a London merchant. John's
son, James, who came to be known as 'the father of the Royal Exchange',
married Mary Ducane, a member of a Huguenot family settled at
Braxted in Essex, by whom he had ten sons. Several of these became
eminent in the City of London. Sir James was Member of Parliament
for the City in 1698; Sir John was first Governor of the Bank of
England, Lord Mayor in 1695, and one of the Commissioners of the
Admiralty.

James Houblon (d. 1700), financier, negotiated loans for Parliament,
and in recognition of these services was granted 2,000 acres of land
in Ireland. There are many references to him in Pepys. He built
Forest House, Leytonstone (demolished in 1964), and lived there
until his death at nearly 90.

One of the sons Of James Houblon of Forest House, Jacob (1634-98),
was rector of Moreton for 35 years.

The last of the Houblon merchant princes died unmarried in 1724. In
his later years he became so pessimistic about City prospects that he

diverted his investments into the purchase of land in Essex and Hertfordshire. His will directed that these estates should be held in trust for the purchase of further estates, the whole to be entailed upon his first cousin's child, Jacob, who was aged six at the time of James's death.

This fortunate Jacob was the grandson of the Rev. Jacob Houblon of Moreton. His father was Charles, a London merchant who bought Bobbingworth Hall in 1711, and died young, leaving his son in the guardianship of his brother, Jacob, rector of Bobbingworth, who was the principal trustee of the trust set up in 1724. With moneys accumulated by the trust, the Rev. Jacob of Bobbingworth purchased Hallingbury Place in 1729 as the future seat of the family. When he died unmarried in 1735 it was found that he had left his own considerable fortune to be added to that already inherited by his nephew, who was also appointed sole executor. Jacob Houblon of Great Hallingbury thus became a man of great wealth, and he married Susanna, daughter of John Archer of Coopersale by Lady Mary, sister of Earl FitzWilliam, herself an heiress.

Hallingbury was rebuilt c.1770 and became one of the great country houses of Essex, the story of which is told in The Houblon Family: Its Story and Times, by Lady Alice Houblon (1907).

HOWARD

Thomas Howard, 4th Duke of Norfolk (1536-72), was the son of Henry, Earl of Surrey (beheaded 1547) and Frances Vere, daughter of John, 15th Earl of Oxford (q.v.). His tutor was John Foxe (q.v.). In 1558 he married as his second wife Margaret, daughter and heir of Lord Chancellor Audley (q.v.). From their three sons are descended the Earls of Suffolk, Berkshire, Carlisle, and Bristol, and the lords Howard de Walden and Howard of Escrick. From one of their two daughters, the Sackvilles of Knole.

After his second wife's death the duke was allowed to hold her estates for life. He stood high in the queen's favour. In 1559 she made him a Knight of the Garter in recognition of the relationship between the Howards and the Boleyns. For a time he was the only duke remaining in England and held the lieutenancy of most counties in southern England, including Essex. In 1567 he married as his third wife, Elizabeth, widow of Lord Dacre of Gilsland. She died a year after the marriage and the duke then aspired to marry Mary Queen of Scots and place her on the English throne with himself as consort. This involved him in the Ridolfi Plot. But he miscalculated the astuteness of the queen and Cecil. The queen gave him a hint of her knowledge by warning him to 'beware on what pillow he rested his head', but he was already too deeply involved to withdraw. While visiting Audley End, Elizabeth discovered incriminating evidence, and the duke was arrested in hiding at Ashlyns, near Ongar. He was imprisoned in the Tower, and after what passed as a trial was condemned to death. Even then Elizabeth was reluctant to exact the due penalty for his betrayal of her trust. She signed several warrants for his execution and before they could be carried out revoked them. But in the early summer of 1572 Cecil convinced her that her throne would not be safe while he lived and she signed the final warrant that led to his execution on Tower Hill on 2nd June 1572.

Thomas Howard, 1st Earl of Suffolk (1561-1626) builder of Audley End, was the eldest son of Thomas, 4th Duke of Norfolk and Margaret, daughter of Lord Chancellor Audley. As Lord Thomas Howard (celebrated in Tennyson's poem The Revenge) he was already a popular hero when James I came to the English throne. He had served against the Spanish Armada and been knighted at sea by the Lord High Admiral for his gallantry. After leading the third squadron at the capture of Cadiz he was summoned to Parliament as Lord Howard de Walden. So when James created him Earl of Suffolk in 1603 he was both recognising his family's debt to the Howards and making himself popular with the English people. Shortly afterwards Suffolk further placed James in his debt by directing the search of the cellars of Parliament that led to the discovery of Gunpowder Plot.

The Great House, Audley End, reflected the proud position the Earl and his Countess expected to enjoy under the new sovereign. It was built shortly after his appointment to the office of Lord Treasurer in 1614, which occasioned James's shrewd remark: 'By my troth, man, it is too much for a king, but may do for a Lord High Treasurer.' It was not to be enjoyed for long. Two years after the completion of the house in 1616, the Earl came under suspicion of having embezzled money received from the Dutch. He was immediately relieved of office and in 1619 he and his countess appeared before the Star Chamber charged with divers offences, including misappropriation of funds, extortion and bribery. They were committed to the Tower, but after ten days were released on their undertaking to pay a fine of £30,000. The earl spent the remaining six years of his life quietly at Audley End, unable to maintain the state to which he had aspired.

Theophilus, 2nd Earl of Suffolk (1584-1640), assumed the title of Lord Howard de Walden while still a minor when his father was created Earl of Suffolk. He married Elizabeth, daughter of George Home, Earl of Dunbar, Lord Treasurer of Scotland, when he was 28 and she 11. She bore him nine children before she died at the age of 33. The 2nd earl was a friend of Prince Henry and enjoyed favour at Court. He was appointed Governor of Jersey for life in 1610. Other offices held by him were Captain of the Band of Gentlemen Pensioners and Lord Warden of the Cinque Ports. From the age of 48, if not earlier, he was a sick man. He died in 1640 at the age of 56.

James, 3rd Earl of Suffolk (1620-88), succeeded to a heavily encumbered estate at the age of 20. He had been made a Knight of the Bath at the age of six, and at 19 appointed to the command of a troop of horse. When war came in 1642 he took the Parliamentary side, but he can hardly have been surprised when his allegiance was regarded as suspect. He was impeached in 1647, along with six other peers, for levying war against Parliament, and was imprisoned in the Tower for eight months following this charge.

The Restoration, however, came in time to bring him back into favour. He was Earl Marshal at the coronation of Charles II to whom, in 1666, he sold Audley End for use as a royal palace (conveyance dated 1669). The purchase price was £50,000 of which £20,000 was left on mortgage. This was for the mansion and 283 acres of parkland. The remainder of the estate remained in the earl's possession, and as he was appointed 'Keeper of the King's House at Audley End', with Henry Winstanley of Littlebury (q.v.) as surveyor, the deal simply transferred the hugh cost of upkeep to the Crown. Moreover, the 3rd Earl's countess was the aunt of the king's mistress, Barbara Villiers, Lady Castlemaine, so personal links were strong.

The 3rd earl was Lord Lieutenant of Essex, and as Governor of
Landguard Fort played a brave part in alerting and mobilising the
county when de Ruyter's fleet sailed up the Thames in 1667. He was
said to have pressed into service every able-bodied man from
Newmarket to Harwich. When 3,000 men from 25 Dutch ships landed
at Felixstowe and the fort was attacked the earl and his men repulsed
them twice.

The 3rd Earl's third wife was Anne, eldest daughter of the Earl of
Manchester. He lived modestly with her at Great Chesterford, stead-
ily paying off his father's debts. As landowner and local magnate he
was the best of his line. His grandfather had built a house that was
to be an embarrassment to all his heirs; the 3rd earl, during his 50
years rule, built up the estate. He was the last to hold both the peer-
ages held by his father and grandfather. They had different remain-
ders: the Howard de Walden barony was by writ; the earldom with
ordinary limitation. The effect of this was that as he left two daughters and no son, the Howard de Walden barony remained vested in
the issue of his own body, the earldom descended through his uncle
Thomas's offspring until the death of the 10th Earl.

At his death he was survived by the countess, who enjoyed the income
from the estate for life, and as she outlived both the 4th and 5th earls,
the earldom again became impoverished.

George, 4th Earl of Suffolk (1626-91), brother of the 3rd earl, held
the earldom for three years only. At his death without issue he was
succeeded by Henry, 5th Earl of Suffolk (1627-1709), the third son
of the 2nd earl to hold the title. He was of little note, but figures in
the history of Audley End because in 1701 the mansion was returned
to him by the Crown on his undertaking to relinquish his claim to the
£20,000 of the 1666 purchase price still unpaid. He has another distinction in that in 1706 he was appointed Deputy Earl Marshal, to act
in the stead of the hereditary holder of the office, who as a Roman
Catholic was at that time thought unsuitable to perform the duties of
the office. In the same year his son, who was to succeed him as 6th
earl, was created Baron Chesterford and Earl of Bindon, the Howard
de Walden barony having been in abeyance since the death of the 3rd
earl.

The 5th earl spent little time at Audley End, although he was described by Macky in <u>Characters</u>, as 'a gentleman who was never yet in
business, loved cocking, horse matches, and other country sports.'

Henry, 6th Earl of Suffolk (c.1670-1718), Earl of Bindon and Baron
Chesterford, was an able administrator and a public figure. He was
M.P. for Arundel from 1695 to 1698, sat in Parliament as a Knight
of the Shire for Essex in 1705, was appointed Lord Lieutenant of
Essex in 1714, and in 1717 became First Commissioner of Trade and
Plantations (President of the Board of Trade). Much of his importance
was due to Queen Anne's decision that the hereditary Earl Marshal
was disqualified as a Catholic from acting, and her appointment of the
Earl of Suffolk to act in his stead.

By his first wife, who was a daughter of the Earl of Thomond, he had
four sons and one daughter. He died at the age of 45.

Charles William, 7th Earl of Suffolk (1693-1721), son of the 6th earl,
had no family. He settled the estate on himself and his uncle Charles,

with remainder to the Effingham branch of the family. The 7th earl
served as Lord Lieutenant of Essex; but his public career was short.
He died at the age of 29.

In leaving the estate to his uncle Charles, he passed over Edward,
who succeeded as 8th Earl of Suffolk (1671-1731), and at first disputed the settlement on his younger brother of the estate that should have
been his. Eventually, however, he agreed to waive his claim on being
allowed an annuity of £1,200 in lieu. He was a strange character.
The 7th earl was probably right in thinking him incapable of running
the estate; but if Edward was a fool, Charles was a knave.

Edward, the 8th earl, was described by Horace Walpole as a nobleman 'with great inclination to versify, and some derangement of his
intellects'. He continued:
> 'The executors of this Lord conferred some value on his
> works by burning a great number of the copies after his
> death. Indeed, the first volume is not without merit, for
> his Lordship has transplanted whole pages of Milton into
> it, under the title of Elegancies.'

Charles, 9th Earl of Suffolk (1675-1733), succeeded to the title at
Edward's death. His wife was Diana Henrietta, daughter of Sir Henry
Hobart (see below). She bore him a son, who became Henry, 10th
Earl of Suffolk (1706-45). He inherited an estate heavily burdened
with debts from a rascally father, and did little to improve the position. At his death without issue at the age of 38 the Suffolk title
passed to Henry Bowes Howard, 4th Earl of Berkshire, great-grandson of the 1st earl, and both the Berkshire and Suffolk titles have
continued in his descendants.

Henrietta Howard, wife of the 9th Earl of Suffolk and mother of the
10th, was the mistress of George II. She was the daughter of Sir
Henry Hobart of Blickling Hall, Norfolk. Her husband, was described by Lord Hervey as 'a wrong-headed, ill-tempered, obstinate,
drunken, extravagent, brutal younger brother of the Earl of Suffolk's
family'. The couple separated in 1728, three years before Charles
succeeded to the earldom, to which Charles had no expectation at the
time of the marriage. He was miserably poor, and when his debts made
life in England impossible he and his wife went to live in Hanover,
partly, no doubt, in the hope of ingratiating themselves with the future king, George I. They were said to have been so poor on arrival
that Mrs. Howard sold her hair to raise part of the cost of entertaining the Hanoverian ministers to dinner.

See W. Addison: Audley End (1953)

HOWARD

Luke Howard (1772-1864), chemist and pioneer in meteorology, made
a systematic analysis of cloud formations which he published in The
Climate of London (1818-20). In 1820 Goethe published an article on
'The Shape of Clouds According to Howard', to which he added a
commemorative poem. In John Constable's Clouds, Dr. Kurt Badt
states a case for believing that Constable's cloud studies owed much
to his reading of Howard. His business was developed by several
generations of descendants at Ilford.

HOWLETT

John Howlett (1731-1804), political economist, was presented to the living of Great Dunmow in 1771. He also held the living of Great Baddow. Howlett is remembered for his writings on the effect of enclosures on the population of rural England.

HUGHES

Sir Edward Hughes (1720?-1794), admiral, took part in the capture of Porto Bello by Admiral Vernon in 1739, served under Admiral Boscawen at the taking of Louisbourg in 1758, and under Sir Charles Saunders at the taking of Quebec in 1759. He was commander-in-chief in the East Indies during the American War of Independence. He became an Admiral of the Blue in 1793. After serving in the Navy for nearly half a century, he died at his home, Luxborough House, Chigwell. His step-son, Edward Hughes Ball Hughes (d. 1863), was a social celebrity of the day, known as the 'Golden Ball'.

HUNT

Arthur Surridge Hunt (1871-1934), papyrologist, was born at Romford, the eldest son of a local solicitor who afterwards lived at Romford Hall. In January 1896 he joined B.P.Grenfell and D.G.Hogarth in excavating for papyri in the Fayum. He succeeded Grenfell as Professor of Papyrology at Oxford. Hunt was elected a Fellow of the British Academy in 1913.

HUNT

Reuben Hunt (1836-1927), engineer, spent his entire life of 91 years in the village of Earls Colne, where he started the Atlas Engineering Works. In 1898 he enlarged Earls Colne Grammar School, founded in 1519, which was reconstituted in 1887 and moved to its present site in 1892. This was only one of the many generous gifts to his native village.

INGELRICA

Ingelrica (d. 1100), daughter of a Saxon nobleman, married Ranulph Peverel after bearing a son to William the Conqueror. Ranulph was granted 34 lordships in Essex in addition to that of Hatfield Peverel. Ingelrica founded a college for secular canons at Hatfield, which was converted into a Benedictine abbey by her son, William Peverel, Governor of Dover. At the Dissolution it was granted to Giles Leigh, whose heiresses carried it to the Alleyne family (q.v.). An ancient statue in the church commemorates Ingelrica.

INSKIP

James Theodore Inskip (1868-1949), Bishop Suffragan of Barking from 1919 to 1948, was born at Clifton, Bristol, and educated at Clifton and Corpus Christi, Cambridge. He became vicar of Leyton in 1900 and remained for seven years. From 1907 to 1916 he was vicar of Jesmond, Newcastle-upon-Tyne; from 1916 to 1919, vicar of Christ Church, Southport. In 1919 he returned to Essex as Bishop of Barking and devoted his great gifts to the service of Metropolitan Essex for the rest of his life. From 1920 to 1929 he was chairman of the West Ham and District Educational Conference. He served on many educational bodies, usually as the representative of Cambridge University, and was universally respected. His publications included The Pastoral

Idea (1905), The Harvest of the River (1930), Evangelical Influence
in English Life and The One Foundation (1933) and an autobiography,
A Man's Job (1948).

His term as bishop was a period of rapid expansion in the population
of West Essex. He met its challenge with immense zest and for 30
years was one of the most loved and revered figures in the English
Church. In Essex, his fine presence and courtly charm made a profound impression on all who knew him.

JEKYLL

Thomas Jekyll of Bocking (1570-1652), antiquary, amassed a vast
amount of material for a history of Essex, which, after being assimilated into the work of William Holman (q.v.), provided much of
the material for Morant (q.v.). Holman wrote of him: 'It is highly
fitting that his fame should live for ever that has made so many
immortal by his writing.'

Jekyll was educated for the law. He became a member of Lincoln's
Inn and Chief Clerk in the Paper Office of the Court of King's Bench.
The most important items in the Jekyll Collection were:
    A copy of the Domesday Book relating to Essex;
    An Account of Manors, etc., in Essex (1 Richard III
       to 5 James I);
    Extracts from Letters Patent (temp. John to Henry VIII);
    Licences, Pardons, and Alienations of Lands in Essex
       (Edward III to Eliz.);
    Exchanges of Monastery lands, etc.;
    Certificates of all Colleges, Chantries, etc. (Feb 14th,
       2 Edward VI);
    Extracts from the Placita de Juraris, et Assisis, et
       Coronae;
    Copies of all Essex Inquisitions post mortem (27 Henry III
       to 14 Charles I);
    Pedigrees of the Gentry of Essex in four vols.;
    Abstracts of Letters Patent (Richard I to 15 James I).

On his death in 1652 most of Thomas Jekyll's material passed into
the possession of his grandson, Nicholas Jekyll, of Castle Hedingham.
Part, however, had been acquired by the Rev. John Ouseley, who
added fresh material, and at his death in 1708, he bequeathed his
MSS. to his son-in-law, the Rev. Anthony Holbrook. For the later
history of the Jekyll material, see under Holman and Morant.

JENNENS

John Jennens, claimant to the estates of William Jennens, of Acton
Place (Suffolk), figured in the Chancery Suit used by Dickens (q.v.)
as the basis of 'Jarndyce v. Jarndyce' in Bleak House. Jennens died
at Colchester in 1769 and was buried in St. Peter's churchyard. His
tombstone bears the text: 'Through deceit they refuse to know me.'

JOHNSON

John Johnson (1732-1814), architect, was county surveyor for Essex
from 1782 to 1812. The two outstanding examples of his work are the
Shire Hall, Chelmsford (1791), with its fine County Room, and the
elegant bridge over the Can at Moulsham. The country houses designed
by Johnson were Terling Place, for John Strutt (1772-80), Hatfield
Place, Hatfield Peverel, for Col. John Tyrell (1791-5), Bradwell

Lodge, for Sir Henry Bate-Dudley (1781-6). He also enlarged The
Lawn, Rochford, and Tyrell's Hall, Thurrock. He was responsible
for the re-roofing of St. Mary's church, Chelmsford, now the Cathedral. Other works by him were the Houses of Correction, or prisons, at Chelmsford, Barking, and Halstead. His bridge across the
Stour at Dedham collapsed soon after completion, largely because
the Suffolk authority had failed to carry out the necessary preparat-
ory work on the Suffolk bank.

JOHNSTON

Andrew Johnston of Woodford Green (1835-1922), first chairman of
Essex county council and a verderer of Epping Forest, was elected
M.P. for South Essex in 1868. After his defeat in 1874 he did not
seek re-election, but devoted himself entirely to local and county
affairs. He served for a time as chairman of Essex Quarter Sessions;
but his outstanding work was for the county council, which he served
as chairman continuously for 27 years.

JOLLIFFE

Sir William Jolliffe (1660-1750), who is described on his monument in
Pleshey church as 'a steady friend, a generous relation ... and ...
a disinterested lover of his country', was the wealthy uncle of Samuel
Tufnell of Langleys (q.v.). His mother was a Boothby of Friday Hall,
Chingford (q.v.). For many years up to 1742 he was a director of
the Bank of England, an office in which he would be associated with
Sir John Houblon (q.v.), whose descendants lived at Hallingbury
Place. Sir William purchased the Pleshey estate, which adjoined
the Langleys estate at Great Waltham, in 1720. At his death he was
reputed to be one of the richest commoners in England. He never
married, and at his death Samuel Tufnell received a life-interest in
the Pleshey property, with remainder to his sons, William and George,
on condition they assumed the name of Jolliffe, which has been handed
down through successive generations of the Tufnell family. The monument to Sir William Jolliffe's memory in Pleshey church is by Rysbrack
and was commissioned by his two nephews, Samuel Tufnell and John
Jolliffe.

JOSCELYN

The Joscelyn family, who owned the manor of High Roding for 200
years, traced their descent from Egidius Jocelyn, a nobleman of
Brittany, who reached England in the reign of Edward the Confessor,
and was the father of Sir Gilbert, who returned to France and came
over again with William the Conqueror.

Sir Thomas Joscelyn (d. 1562), only son of John Joscelyn (d. 1525),
was one of the 40 gentlemen knighted at the coronation of Edward VI
in 1547. He married Dorothy, daughter of Sir Geoffrey Gate (q.v.)
of High Easter, by whom he had six sons and seven daughters. He
was the builder of New Hall, High Roding.

Richard Joscelyn (d. 1605), second son of Sir Thomas, succeeded to
the estate, the elder son having died young. John, a third son, was
secretary to Archbishop Parker and an eminent Anglo-Saxon scholar.
A successor, Robert, was created a baronet in 1665. The direct line
of the High Roding Joscelyns died out in 1770; but from the 16th century the family held extensive estates in Essex and the name is still
common.

One distinguished member of the Joscelyn family, Robert (1688?-1756), became Lord Chancellor of Ireland, and in 1743 was created Baron Newport of Newport in the county of Tipperary. In 1755 he was advanced to a viscountcy. At his death in 1756 he was succeeded by a son, Robert, who in 1771, was created Earl of Roden, of High Roding. The peerage is an Irish one; but the title was taken from the Essex home of the family.

JOSSELIN

Ralph Josselin (1616-83) of Earls Colne, diarist, was born at Chalk End, Roxwell, and brought up at Bishops Stortford, to which his father removed when Ralph was two, and Steeple Bumpstead. In 1640 he was a schoolmaster at Upminster, where he married Jane Constable, by whom he had ten children. In 1641 he became vicar of Earls Colne, a living he held for the rest of his life, although at various times he was offered the sequestered livings of Fordham, Stanway, Stisted, Thaxted, and, in 1656, Castle Hedingham. These offers testify to his popularity as a Puritan preacher; but he declined them all.

Josselin's Diary, which was published by the Royal Historical Society in 1908, records events in Essex during the civil wars from the point of view of a moderate Puritan. In 1645 he joined the Parliamentary forces, serving as chaplain to Col. Harlackenden of Colne Priory.

At the Restoration he appears to have accepted a degree of conformity An entry in the Diary reads: 'Rid to lay claim to the King's pardon before the Mayor of Colchester.' By 1680 he had even accepted the surplice, 'which I see no sin to use, and shall endeavour to live as quietly as may be to the end of my race.'

Josselin's Diary also gives lists of deaths from the plague, which show that it became worse in Essex after it had abated in London. It is useful for its records of weather, crops, food prices, and other day-to-day interests.

JUDD

Sir Andrew Judd of Colchester (fl. 16th c.) was a member of the Russian Company. He was Sheriff of London, 1544, and Lord Mayor, 1551. His widow married James Altham (q.v.) of Mark Hall, Latton, who died in 1584. In 1591 she gave £100 to the Corporation of Colchester to be used to provide wool, yarn, flax, or other merchandise for the employment of the poor of the town, the profits of such employment to be distributed among the aged and needy poor, on condition that the capital sum should be repaid to herself or her executors if at any time it remained unemployed for 12 consecutive months. She died in 1603.

KAY

John Kay (fl. 1733-64), inventor of the fly-shuttle, inherited a bay-making business at Coggeshall; but when he met with opposition from his workpeople he removed to Bury in Lancashire. The Lancashire workpeople proved to be no more amenable to his progressive ideas than their Essex counterparts had been and Kay suffered much from mob violence. For a time he lived at Leeds; but he returned to Bury and persisted with his enterprise. He appears to have been ruined by litigation necessary to protect his patent and is believed to have died in poverty in France.

KEMP

Spains Hall, Finchingfield, passed into the possession of the Kemp
family by the marriage of Nicholas Kemp with Margery, daughter of
Richard de Ispania, who was living in 1310.

Robert Kemp, sixth in descent from Nicholas, died in 1524 and was
buried in the Kemp chapel at Finchingfield under a plain altar tomb.

William (1555-1628), third in descent from Robert, married Philippa,
daughter of Francis Gunter of Aldbury, Herts. in 1588 and lived with
her at Spains Hall. In 1621, in a blind rage of jealousy, he accused
her of being unfaithful, and when he realised how unjust his suspicions had been he vowed that he would remain silent for seven years.
Nothing could persuade him to relent, even after his wife's death in
1623. To mark the years of silence he dug out a new fish pond annually. At the end of the period he was in such a state of agitation that
he became ill, and when he tried to call for help found himself power-
less to utter a sound. The shock killed him.

The inscription on his monument begins:
'Here lies William Kemp, Esq., pious, just, hospitable,
master of himself soe much that what others scarce doe
by force and penalties, he did by a voluntary constancy
hold his peace seven years.'

The property descended to his nephew, Robert, who was knighted in
1641.

The last male of the line was John Kemp. At his death without issue
the estate passed to his sister, Mary, who in 1727 married Sir
Swinnerton Dyer. In 1760 Sir Thomas Dyer sold it to Samuel Ruggles
of Bocking (q.v.) from whom it has descended to the present owner,
Sir John Ruggles-Brise, Lord Lieutenant.

See E. Vaughan: E.R. xii (1931)

KING

Henry William King (1815-92), antiquary, was one of the founders
of the Essex Archaeological Society and its secretary and editor
from 1866 to his death. The wanton destruction of sepulchral monuments in Essex at the time when so many churches were undergoing
restoration prompted him to undertake a descriptive survey of all the
churches in the county. This is recorded in five folio volumes of MS,
with all the armorial bearings reproduced in colour. King contributed
many learned articles to East Anglian and national antiquarian journals.
After holding a position in the Bank of England for 40 years he lived in
retirement at Leigh-on-Sea, where he had family connections. His wife
was a daughter of Jonathan Wood of Hadleigh Castle, and the families
of Wood and King are commemorated in stained glass windows in
Hadleigh church.

LEICESTER, Earl of See DUDLEY

LETCHWORTH

Thomas Letchworth (1739-84), quaker, was descended from Robert
Letchworth, one of the first Quakers imprisoned at Cambridge in 1660.
He came into Essex when his parents moved from Norwich to Waltham
Abbey. He was apprenticed to an Epping shopkeeper and became a dev-
out member of the Epping meeting of the Society of Friends, sometimes

sitting alone in the meeting house. In 1775 he published the Life and Writings of John Woolman, whom he describes as 'The Christian Socrates.'

LETHIEULLIER

> Your Houblons, Papillons and Lethieulliers,
> Pass now for true born English knights and squires,
> And make good senate members and lord mayors.

> Defoe's True-born Englishman

In 1694, John Lethieullier, a London merchant of Huguenot stock, purchased the Aldersbrook estate at Wanstead, part of which is now the City of London Cemetery. The following year he married Elizabeth, daughter of Sir Joseph Smart, an alderman of London, who lived at Birch Hall, Theydon Bois. In 1717 he was appointed Master Keeper of Leyton and Wanstead Walk in Epping Forest. In 1720 he purchased Cranbrook House, Ilford.

At his death his estates at Aldersbrook, Barking, Dagenham, Theydon Bois, West Ham, and Great Burstead, were inherited by his son, Smart Lethieullier (1701-60), antiquary, and a family chapel was erected at Little Ilford church. Smart Lethieullier was elected F.S.A. in 1724, but resigned in 1747. He contributed a report on the earthquake shock recorded at Aldersbrook on February 8th, 1749, to Philosophical Transactions (vol. xlvi 1751). Much of his most valuable work is found in his voluminous correspondence, collections of which are preserved in the British Museum and the archives of the Royal Society. His correspondence with Charles Lyttleton, Dean of Exeter and Bishop of Carlisle, President of the Society of Antiquaries, is in the Stowe MSS. in the British Museum (752). His letters reflect the social life of Wanstead during his period. Extracts from his History of Barking (destroyed by fire in 1857) appear in Lysons' Environs of London (1796). He contributed accounts of the Roman remains found in Wanstead Park in 1715 and 1746 to Archaeologia, and accounts of Ambresbury Banks and Roman finds at Leyton to Gough's Camden. An account of the Roman road from London to Colchester by Lethieullier appears in Morant.

In 1754 he purchased the lordship of the manor of Barking for £40,000. In the same year he became Lieutenant of Epping Forest. The inscription to his memory in Little Ilford church reads:
> 'In memory of Smart Lethieullier Esq., a gentleman of
> polite literature and elegant taste, an encourager of art
> and ingenious artists, a studious promoter of literary
> enquiries and a companion and friend of learned men,
> industriously versed in the science of antiquity and richly
> possessed of the curious productions of nature, but who
> modestly desired no other inscription on his tomb than what
> he had made the rule of his life to do justly, to love mercy,
> and to walk humbly with his God.'

LINE

The Venerable Anne Line (d. 1601), Essex martyr, was born at Dunmow. On Candlemas Day, 1601, Protestant spies broke into her house at the moment when mass was about to be celebrated. The room in which she and the priests were assembled was locked, and when the spies gained access they found nothing to confirm their suspicions. Notwithstanding the lack of evidence they carried off Mistress Line

and lodged her in prison. She was tried at the Old Bailey before
Lord Chief Justice Popham, who directed the jury to bring in a verdict of guilty of harbouring priests, and on being condemned to death
she was executed at Tyburn.

LISLE

Sir George Lisle (d. 1648), one of the chief defenders of Colchester,
was shot to death outside the castle along with Sir Charles Lucas.
Facing the firing squad he called out:
> 'Oh, how many of your lives who are now present here,
> have I saved in hot blood, and must now myself be most
> barbarously murdered in cold!. '

When he bade his executioners come nearer so that they would not
miss him, one of them replied: I'll warrant ye, sir, we'll hit you.'
'Friend, ' called back Sir George, 'I have been nearer when you have
missed me.'

He was buried with Sir Charles Lucas in St. Giles's church.

LISTER

Gulielma Lister (1861-1949), naturalist, lived all her life in one
house at Leytonstone. She was the niece of Lord Lister and the
daughter of Arthur Lister, F.R.S., with whom she collaborated
in Monograph of the Mycetozoa. After her father's death she continued in the study of the Mycetozoa and became an acknowledged
world authority on the subject, illustrating her publications with
drawings of exquisite precision. In Essex her most valuable work
was done in association with the Essex Field Club, of which she
was first lady president. She was elected a Fellow of the Linnaean
Society in 1904 and in 1929 a vice-president.

LISTER

Joseph Lister (1827-1912), founder of antiseptic surgery, was born
at Upton, the second son of Joseph Jackson Lister, F.R.S. (1786-
1869), a Quaker wine merchant who contributed to the development
of the miscroscope. Joseph Lister became Regius Professor of Surgery at Glasgow University in 1860, and in 1869 succeeded his father-
in-law, James Syme, in the chair of Clinical Surgery at Edinburgh;
but returned to London in 1877 as Professor of Surgery at King's
College, with a view to reforming the London hospitals. When he retired 16 years later, his influence had completely revolutionised sur-
gical methods and practices in British hospitals. He was elected a
Fellow of the Royal Society in 1860, and was President, 1894-1900.
In 1883 he was created a baronet. Fourteen years later he was raised
to the peerage, and in 1902 became one of the original members of the
Order of Merit.

When Lister began his great work for antiseptic surgery the mortality
rate following amputations for compound fractures was about 40%.
Seizing on Pasteur's discovery that putrefaction was the result of the
entry into wounds of living micro-organisms, he set about finding a
method of destroying these. After many experiments he found that the
best results were obtained by using carbolic acid for dressings.
Lister was an early student of bacteriology and made valuable contributions in other fields of scientific research.

LIVINGSTONE

On being accepted for missionary work, David Livingstone (1813-73),
was sent on probation to a missionary training school at Ongar, where
he remained until the early months of 1840. On one occasion, when he
was sent to preach at the Independent Chapel at Stanford Rivers, he
read the text and then found that he had forgotten every word he intended to say. When this was reported by the astonished congregation
it nearly brought his career to an end; but on further consideration
a second probationary period was granted and he was accepted. There
is a reference to Livingstone's residence at Ongar in the autobiography
of Mrs. Gilbert (Ann, of the Taylors of Ongar, q.v.).

LOCKE

John Locke (1632-1704), philosopher, was born at Wrington, Somerset,
the son of a local landowner who fought in the Parliamentary army.
He was at Westminster School under Dr. Busby at the same time as
Dryden.

From 1690 to his death in 1704 Locke lived at Otes, High Laver, with
Sir Francis and Lady Masham (q.v.), and there wrote his Treatise
on the Reasonableness of Christianity, Letters on Toleration, and
other works. He had formed a friendship with the Cudworth family at
Cambridge, and was especially devoted to Damaris, daughter of Dr.
Ralph Cudworth, who became the wife of Sir Francis Masham (q.v.).
So when Locke contracted chronic asthma as the result of living in
London, the Mashams invited him to make his home with them at High
Laver. Of the circumstances of the move, Lady Masham wrote:
        'By some considerable long visits Mr. Locke made trial of
        the air of this place, which is some twenty miles from London,
        and he thought that none would be so suitable for him. His
        future company could not but be very desirable for us, and
        he had all the assurance we could give him of being always
        welcome; but to make him easy with us it was necessary he
        should do so on his own terms, which Sir Francis at last
        assenting to, he then believed himself at home with us and
        resolved, if it pleased God, here to end his days - as he did.'

Among the distinguished men who visited Locke at High Laver was
Sir Isaac Newton, who was there in 1702.

Otes was a Tudor building with a turret over the entrance hall and a
square tower at one corner. Locke's will had bequests to the Mashams,
to every servant in the house, and £109 to the poor of High Laver.

LOCKWOOD

Amelius Richard Mark Lockwood, Baron Lambourne (1847-1928),
belonged to a family that had been Essex landowners for more than
400 years. Their seat, Dews Hall, Lambourne, was pulled down by
Lord Lambourne's grandfather, who moved to nearby Bishop's Hall.
On inheriting an estate in Surrey in 1838 the Lockwoods took the
name of Wood for many years.

Lord Lambourne, as Colonel Lockwood, represented the Epping, or
West Essex, constituency in Parliament for 25 years from 1892 until
he was raised to the peerage in 1917. He was the most popular man
in West Essex throughout his life. His jaunty air and irrepressible
sense of humour made him the centre of any company. Besides politics,
his main interests were gardens and animals. He always wore a red
carnation, and it was his passionate love of flowers that brought him

the friendship of Edward VII, George V, and Queen Mary, particularly while he was President of the Royal Horticultural Society and
had the privilege of conducting them round the society's annual shows.
He devoted equal service to the N.S.P.C.A.. In the House of Commons
he was affectionately known as 'Uncle Mark'. On Lord Warwick's
death in 1919, Lord Lambourne was appointed Lord Lieutenant of
Essex. With his death in 1928 the peerage became extinct.

LOUIS XVIII of FRANCE

Louis XVIII (1755-1824), exiled King of France, landed at Great
Yarmouth in November, 1807, on his way to Gosfield Hall, which
had been placed at his disposal by the Marquis of Buckingham (q.v.).
From Gosfield he visited the Prince of Conde (q.v.) and other exiles at
Wanstead House. On one of these visits to Wanstead a review of the
15th, the King's Hussars, was held on the Flats in the presence of
the Prince Regent and the Dukes of York, Clarence, Kent, and
Cambridge. Early in 1809 the royal household moved from Gosfield
to Hartwell House, near Aylesbury.

LUCAS

Sir Charles Lucas (1613-48), royalist, was the youngest son of Sir
Thomas Lucas of St. John's, Colchester. He served in the royalist
armies throughout the Civil War and played the leading part in the
defence of Colchester. Lucas was shot with his fellow prisoner,
Sir George Lisle (q.v.), in the castle yard and buried in the family
vault in the north aisle of St. Giles's church. He had the reputation
of being one of the best cavalry officers of his day.

LUCY

Richard de Lucy (d. 1179), Chief Judiciar at the close of Stephen's
reign, is believed to have been of East Anglian origin. He was
Sheriff of Essex and Hertfordshire under Stephen, but his chief
services were to Henry II, who dubbed him 'Richard de Lucy the
Loyal'. For 13 years he held the office of Chief Judiciar jointly with
Robert de Beaumont, Earl of Leicester. After the earl's death he
held it alone.

Lucy built himself a castle on the Saxon mound at Ongar and a church
for the people who lived in the settlement that sprang up in the outer
bailey of his castle, in which he was visited by Henry II in 1157. By
securing for his neighbours a market, or 'chipping', he laid the foundations of the market town of Chipping Ongar, which gave its name to
the Hundred formed for him about the middle of the century. Although
Lucy supported so strongly the cause of Henry II, particularly as
viceroy during the king's absence following the insurrection of 1173,
his castle was taken from him in 1176. Two years later he founded the
Abbey of Westwood at Lesnes in Kent, and in 1179 he resigned his
high offices and retired to his abbey, where he died in the same year.
His loyalty to his king had been beyond question but, had never been
blind to higher loyalties. It is worth remembering in Essex that he
boldly opposed the enforcement of the cruel forest laws, producing
evidence of the king's sanction of certain free uses of the forest and
its fish-ponds.

Lucy's castle was pulled down in the time of Elizabeth I, who in 1579
visited the new house built on the site.

MAITLAND

The Rev. John Whitaker Maitland (1831-1909), was the son of William Maitland of Woodford Hall. He was educated at Harrow and Cambridge, and after being ordained priest in 1856 spent a short time as curate at Bishop's Stortford before becoming rector of Loughton. In 1860 he married Venetia, daughter of Sir Digby Neave of Dagnams, Romford. After inheriting Loughton Hall at his father's death he was both squire and parson. Throughout his life he was prominent in public work, the value of which became obscured when he came to be somewhat unjustly cast in the role of villain in the controversy that raged over the illegal enclosures of parts of Epping Forest.

See W. Addison: Epping Forest: Its Literary and Historical Associations (1945)

MALLINSON

Sir William Mallinson (1854-1936), benefactor, obtained employment at a sawmill in North London at the age of 15 and six years later was taken into partnership. Two years later again he went into business on his own account in Wood Street, Clerkenwell. From there he moved to Great Eastern Street, where he laid the foundations of the great firm of William Mallinson, timber merchants. The first timber yard was opened in 1883. In 1885 he took nearby premises to experiment in the construction of plywood, begun in 1885. Extensions followed rapidly. In 1910 a branch of the business was established at Rotterdam. This was followed two years later with a branch in Paris followed by branches in Brussels, Nantes, and agencies in Australia, South Africa and the United States of America.

It was fortunate for Essex that William Mallinson made his home at Walthamstow, where he became a munificent benefactor. The main spring of his public life was his membership of the Methodist Church. He was a pioneer in Child Welfare work in Walthamstow, gave generously to local hospitals, and founded a trust for giving deserving local boys a University education. He was appointed a Justice of the Peace in 1901 and was chairman of the Becontree Bench from 1929. He was created a baronet in 1935 at the age of 81. His public work in Essex has been continued with generosity and distinction by his son, Sir Stuart Mallinson, who has made the White House, Woodford Green, the social centre for his generation that The Limes, Walthamstow, was in his father's time.

MANDEVILLE

Geoffrey de Mandeville, 1st Earl of Essex (d. 1144), Constable of the Tower of London, was the grandson of the Geoffrey de Mandeville who was granted 39 lordships in Essex at the Conquest. He was appointed Constable of the Tower by King Stephen, and at a date earlier than 1141 was created Earl of Essex. His wife was Rohesia, daughter of Aubrey de Vere, Earl of Oxford.

By playing a double part, first supporting one side, then the other, de Mandeville greatly increased his possessions during the struggle between King Stephen and the Empress Maud; but after intriguing once too often with the Empress he was arrested by Stephen, and deprived of the Tower and his Essex possessions at Pleshey and Saffron Walden, his capital residence. Stripped of these possessions,

he was allowed his personal freedom and is said to have dashed from
the royal presence, 'like a vicious and riderless horse, kicking and
biting'. Later he raised a rebellion in the Fens, where he lived the
life of a robber chieftain, plundering abbeys and so terrorising the
people that they would whisper to each other that Christ and his saints
must sleep that such a man should live. Finally, he was killed while
fighting against Stephen at Burwell.

Before his fall, Geoffrey de Mandeville, 1st Earl, had founded,
c.1136, a priory at Walden, which became an abbey in 1190.

The 1st Earl was succeeded by his second son, Geoffrey, the 2nd
Earl, to whom Henry II restored the de Mandeville estates and confirmed the earldom. He died near Chester in 1167, and was succeeded
by his brother, William, the 3rd Earl, who obtained permission to
fortify his castles. In 1177 the 3rd Earl made a pilgrimage to the Holy
Land, and on his return was welcomed home at a solemn service conducted by the prior of Walden, to whom he presented precious relics
collected on his pilgrimage. The 3rd Earl married the heiress of
Aumale in 1180, and acquired her lands and title. He was ambassador
to the Emperor Frederick in 1182, and took part with Henry II in the
French Wars. In 1189 he was appointed Chief Justiciar by Richard I.

The 3rd Earl died in 1190 in Normandy, where his body was buried.
His heart was brought home to Walden. As he, like his brother, died
without issue the direct line came to an end at his death.

The Essex earldom was then claimed by Geoffrey FitzPeter, who had
married the granddaughter of Beatrix, sister of the 1st Earl. Richard I
acknowledged the claim but refused to invest him. John, whose succession he helped to secure, was more friendly and confirmed him in the
title of 4th Earl of Essex.

The 4th Earl was an able administrator. He was one of the five judges
of the King's Court while Richard I was on crusade, and in 1198 was
appointed Chief Justiciar, the office previously held by the 3rd Earl.
At his death in 1213 he was succeeded by his eldest son, Geoffrey,
who assumed the surname of Mandeville. He married Isabel, daughter
and co-heir of William, Earl of Gloucester, and in his wife's right
styled himself Earl of Gloucester. He was one of the barons who reb-
elled against King John and of the 25 lords chosen to enforce Magna
Carta. He died in 1216.

William, his brother, succeeded to the Essex earldom, but when he
died without issue in 1227 the direct line failed for the second time.
William, however, had a sister, Maud, who had married Humphrey
de Bohun, Earl of Hereford. Their son, who was the sixth Humphrey
in the Bohun line, succeeded to the Essex title. (See Bohun.)

See J. H. Round: Geoffrey de Mandeville (1892)
       R. H. C. David: Geoffrey de Mandeville reconsidered   Eng. Hist.
                   Rev. LXXIX (1961)

MANWOOD

John Manwood (d. 1610), legal author, lived at Priors, Blackmore.
He was a Keeper of Waltham Forest and a Justice of the New Forest.
His treatise on forest laws, privately circulated in 1592, published
in 1598, is a standard work on forest law.

MARCONI

Guglielmo, Marchese Marconi (1874-1937), the Italian inventor of the wireless-telegraphy system, was the son of an Italian father and an Irish mother. He took out his first patent for 'transmitting electrical impulses and signals' in 1896, and in the following year formed the Wireless Telegraph Company, for which the first factory was established at Chelmsford in 1898. It was here that most of the research was carried out which enabled him in 1901 to hear in Newfoundland the first Morse messages sent across the Atlantic from his transmitting station in Cornwall. This led to the establishment of other lines of communication by wireless, for which equipment was made at Chelmsford under the direction of an eminent team of scientists. Wireless equipment for ships was followed by wireless equipment for aircraft, and after the First World War the Marconi Company, using its short-wave beam system, established a world-wide Imperial Telegraph Service. The first sound broadcast went out from Chelmsford in June 1920, when the voice of Dame Nellie Melba was heard over great distances. In 1930 Marconi was elected president of the Italian Royal Academy. At his death a state funeral was accorded him by the Italian Government. He was buried at his native town of Bologna.

MARNEY

The Marney family established themselves at Layer Marney in the reign of Henry II. Three members were knighted, one of whom, William Marney, who died in 1414, has an altar tomb in the Marney chapel. The first to achieve eminence was Henry Marney (d. 1523), Sir William's grandson. He was a member of the first council of Henry VIII, who relied much on his advice and showed his appreciation by installing him a Knight of the Garter and appointing him Captain of the Guard. Upon the attainder of Edward Stafford, Duke of Buckingham Marney was granted a large share of his lands. He was appointed Privy Seal in 1522, and the following year raised to the peerage as Baron Marney of Layer Marney.

Lord Marney's building of Layer Marney Tower has to be seen in relation to Wolsey's building of Hampton Court and Lord Chancellor Rich's building of Leez Priory in order to be fully understood. He died at his London house in 1523 while Henry VIII was celebrating the Feast of St. George at New Hall, Boreham.

John, 2nd Lord Marney, died in 1525 without male issue. The estate was divided between his two daughters and passed into other families. Consequently, the ambitious intentions of the builders were never carried out and the barony became extinct. In 1549 the widow of the 2nd Lord Marney directed her executor to bury her at Little Horkesley, and to have made a 'picture of brasse', showing her 'without her cote armoure', adding,

'And I wolle there be a scripture of brasse to shew the tyme of my decease, and of what stock I cam of, and to what men of worship I was maryed unto.'

MARSHALL

Stephen Marshall of Finchingfield (1594-1655), Puritan divine, was born at Godmanchester, the son of a poor glover. In 1608 he became church lecturer of Wethersfield in Essex and married the wealthy Susanna Castell of Woodham Walter. He was presented to the living of Finchingfield in 1625 and remained vicar for 25 years. Although a

great preacher and a political agitator who was said to influence
elections, he appears to have lived on good terms with his neighbours in Essex, possibly as the result of his wife's social influence,
which was considerable. This was shown at the marriage of one of
his daughters. Although Stephen Marshall was one of the principal
compilers of the Puritan Directory, he actually defied the law at this
marriage by conducting the service in accordance with the Prayer
Book, and not with the form prescribed by the Directory. At the con-
clusion of the service he acknowledged the offence and paid the £5
fine.

Marshall frequently preached before Parliament. He was described
by Peter Heylin as 'that great bell-wether, for a time, of the Pres-
byterians'. Certainly his influence was great. He was appointed lecturer at St. Margaret's, Westminster, in 1642; member of Westminster
Assembly in 1643. He attended Archbishop Laud on the scaffold and
was chaplain to Charles I at Holmby House and Carisbrooke, confron-
tations that must have roused mixed sentiments in both. At his death
in 1655 he was buried in Westminster Abbey; but exhumed and dis-
honoured at the Restoration. Fuller's comment on his character may
have been nearer the mark than most. He said:
   'He was of so supple a soul, that he breake not a joint,
   yea, sprained not a sinew, in all the alteration of times.'

See E. Vaughan: Stephen Marshall, a forgotten Puritan   (1909)
   F. G. Emmison: Early Essex Town Meetings   (1970)

MARTIN

Christopher Martin (d. 1621), a miller of Billericay, was one of the
three who in 1619 chartered the Mayflower and formed a company to
emigrate to New England. The other two members of the company were
Martin's brother-in-law, Solomon Prower, and their servant, John
Langerman. The winter that followed took a heavy toll on the pilgrims.
Dolomon Prower died 24th December 1620; Christopher Martin, 8th
January 1621. The tradition that Martin lived in the house opposite
the chapel-of-ease at Billericay is probably reliable.

MARTIN

Matthew Martin of Wivenhoe (d. 1749) was one of the burgesses for
Colchester in the second Parliament of George I and the second of
George II. He achieved renown as a captain in the East India Company's
service, commanding the ship 'Marlborough', which he defended successfully against three French ships of war and brought safely into port
with a cargo worth £200,000. For this he received £1,000 reward and
a medal set with 24 large diamonds. He left a large family.

MARTIN

Sarah Catherine Martin (1768-1826) was the author of the popular
rhyme based on the old tale of Mother Hubbard. When about 17 years
of age she attracted the attention of Prince William (afterwards
William IV), and he asked her to marry him. Not surprisingly, George
III disapproved, and the two parted; but in 1786 Prince William wrote
to Miss Martin's father:
   'I love her from the bottom of my heart, and only wish I had
   been in that situation of life to have married her. My best
   wishes and prayers shall always be offered up to heaven
   for her welfare.'

A month later, he wrote:
> 'I love and respect Sarah, and would make her my wife
> if possible. My best wishes and regards attend the
> dearest girl for ever.'

Sarah Martin never married. She was not, of course, the only love
of the susceptible prince, who four years later gave his heart to Mrs.
Jordan, who bore him ten children during their long association from
1790 to 1811.

Sarah Martin was buried in the family vault at Loughton.

See E.R. xxv 117

MARTIN-HARVEY

Sir John Martin-Harvey (1867-1944), actor, came of the Harvey
family of Wivenhoe, where he was born. Both his father and grandfather were distinguished designers of racing yachts and schooners.
Sir John lived as a boy at Quay House, and intended to follow the
family calling as a naval architect until he developed a preference
for the stage. After touring the provinces in Shakespeare he was
knighted in 1921. In 1932 he published an Autobiography.

MARY

The Princess Mary, afterwards Queen Mary I, was in residence at
the palace of New Hall, Boreham, at the time of Elizabeth's birth
and at various times afterwards. When she believed her life to be
in danger at the end of April or beginning of May 1550, she removed
from New Hall to Woodham Walter, near Maldon, where a boat was
kept in readiness to carry her to the Continent at short notice.

In 1551 she was living at Copt Hall, Epping, and again in trouble.
In August of that year three Gentlemen of the Household: Sir Robert
Rochester (q.v.), Edward Waldegrave, and Sir Francis Englefield,
were ordered by the Privy Council to see that the celebration of mass
was discontinued at Copt Hall. When this was communicated to Mary
she was so angry that they did not dare to press the order. For this
disobedience they were again summoned to appear before the Council.
In the circumstances they were given a second chance; but Rochester
and Waldegrave said that they would rather face imprisonment than
carry a second time such a message to the princess. Englefield said
that 'he could neither find it in his heart nor his conscience to do it'.

For this disobedience all three were sent to the Tower, and Edward,
the young king, wrote personally to express his grief that the
princess persisted in a practice that had been forbidden by the
Council. Sir William Petre, Lord Chancellor Rich, and Sir Anthony
Wingfield were commissioned to bear this message. They reached
Copt Hall on the 28th August and delivered the letter. When Mary had
read it she said quietly: 'Ah! good Master Cecil took much pains here!'

Rich told her that the king and the Council were determined that she
should not 'use the private mass or any other manner service than
such as by law ... is authorised.' Mary replied that she would rather
die than obey.

In the early part of 1553 she was again at New Hall, Boreham; but
before Edward VI's death she moved to Hunsdon, Herts. The events
following the king's death made it expedient to move away from the
Home Counties and she retired, first to Framlingham in Suffolk, and

later to Kenninghall in Norfolk. Hastily convened councils brought
her back to Framlingham, as being more capable of defence, and
affording easy access to the coast if it should be thought necessary
for her to flee. Before the end of the month, however, the tide had
turned in her favour and she was at New Hall again on the 28th July,
1553. On the 31st she left Boreham for Ingatestone Hall. On 1 August
she moved on to Havering, and the following day to Wanstead, attended by 700 gentlemen in velvet suits who went before her. Behind came
the ladies. On the evening of the 3rd she made her state entry into
London, wearing a gown of purple velvet, French fashion, with a
kirtle 'all thick set with goldsmith's work and a great pearl ... with
a rich baldrick of gold pearl and stones about her neck, and a rich
billement of stones and great pearl on her head.' Sir Anthony Browne
(q.v.) attended her. According to Wriothesley she was met at Wanstead Heath by about 5,000 horse of noblemen's servants, knights and
gentlemen. Elizabeth, with 1,000 horse carrying spears, bows, and
guns had ridden out to meet her, with all her gentlemen apparrelled
in green, 'gauded with white velvet satin taffety'.

See H. F. M. Prescott: Mary Tudor   (revised edn. 1952)
    F. G. Emmison: Tudor Secretary (1970)

MASHAM

The Masham family of High Laver derive their name from Masham,
near Richmond in Yorkshire. Sir John Masham acquired estates in
Suffolk in 1450. His descendant, William, an alderman of the City
of London, was Sheriff in 1583. The alderman's grandson, Sir William
(d. 1656), who was created a baronet in 1621, purchased the estate of
Otes, High Laver, and married Elizabeth daughter of Sir Francis
Barrington (q.v.) of Hatfield Broadoak, and widow of Sir James
Altham (q.v.) of Mark Hall, Harlow. He was related to the Cromwell
family of Hinchingbrooke, and shared their Parliamentarian sympathies, playing a notable part in the rebellion against Charles I. Both he
and Lady Masham suffered imprisonment for refusing to contribute to·
the loan levied by the king.

Sir William Masham, 1st Baronet, was M.P. for Maldon in 1623 and
1625, and for Colchester in 1640. He served as a member of Cromwell's Council of 32 entrusted with Government after the death of
Charles I.

Sir William's eldest son died before his father, so at the death of the
1st baronet, a grandson, also William, succeeded as 2nd baronet. He
died unmarried in 1663, and the title passed to a brother, Sir Francis
Masham, 3rd baronet, who represented Essex in Parliament for ten
years. His first wife was Mary, daughter of Sir William Scott, of
Rouen, by whom he had a family of eight sons and one daughter. At
her death he married, in 1685, Damaris, daughter of Dr. Cudworth,
Master of Christ's College, Cambridge, by whom he had a son, Francis
Cudworth, who died in 1723. It was through the Cudworth marriage
that John Locke (q.v.) came to High Laver.

Sir Francis Masham died in 1722, and by this date all except one of
the eight sons of his first marriage had died. The survivor was Samuel,
4th baronet, who married Abigail, daughter of Francis Hill, a Turkey
merchant. She figures in history through her association with Sarah,
Duchess of Marlborough, at the court of Queen Anne.

Sir Samuel was raised to the peerage as Baron Masham of Otes. He
died in 1758 and was succeeded by his son, the 2nd Baron Masham,
who died without issue in 1776. At his death both the barony and the
baronetcy became extinct.

Damaris Masham (1658-1708), second wife of Sir Francis Masham
of Otes, High Laver, was the daughter of Ralph Cudworth, leader
of the Cambridge Platonists. She met John Locke, the philosopher
(q.v.), in London when she was 23. 'My first acquaintance with
him,' she wrote, 'began when he was past the middle age of man and
I but young ... I had for a great part of above two years conversed
with him, and he favoured me sometimes with his correspondence in
Holland.'

In 1685 she married Sir Francis, who was then a widower with nine
children, and a year after the marriage her only son, Francis
Cudworth, was born.

From 1691 to his death in 1704 Locke lived at Otes. In 1696 a book
entitled A Discourse concerning the Love of God was published anon-
ymously. It was written by Lady Masham. Her other work (1694) was
Occasional Thoughts in reference to a Vertuous or Christian Life.
She died in 1708 and was buried in the middle aisle of Bath Abbey.
See   F. A. Keynes: Byways in Cambridge History   (1947)

Abigail Masham (d. 1734), favourite of Queen Anne, retired to Essex
at the death of the queen and died here. She began her life at court
as the result of being invited by her aunt, Sarah, Duchess of Marlborough, to assist her in waiting upon the queen. Abigail proved so
efficient in this that her Christian name became the model for all
serving women. Unfortunately the favour she enjoyed with the queen
aroused the jealousy of her aunt.

She married the 2nd Baron Masham; but was not prominent in Essex
society for a very good reason. She was involved in the faction to
bring in James Stuart, which meant that when George I came to the
throne she was obliged to live in deep seclusion, with few, if any,
social contacts. Practically nothing has come to light about her life
in Essex during the last 20 years of her life. We know, however,
that other members of her family shared her retirement because her
brother, General Hill, and her sister, Alice Hill, are both buried at
High Laver. Nothing remains of their home.

MAXEY

An altar tomb in the church at Bradwell-juxta-Coggeshall commemorates Anthony Maxey and his wife, Dorothy, daughter of Gregory
Basset, and his second son, Sir Henry, and his wife, Mildred, who
was a daughter of William Cooke of Gidea Hall (q.v.). Her mother was
Frances, daughter of Lord John Grey (q.v.), and therefore cousin of
Lady Jane Grey. Sir Henry Maxey was born in 1567 and was knighted
by James I along with many other Essex gentlemen in 1603. He died
in 1624.

Sir Henry's brother, William, a justice of the peace, has a monument
on the north wall. He used to require his family to assemble each
morning at five for prayers. His third son, William, was Major-General
of horse on the Royalist side at the Siege of Colchester. Henry, the
second son, who erected the monument to his parents, was Adjutant-
General of horse.

MAYNARD

Sir Henry Maynard (d. 1610), builder of Little Easton Hall and
founder of the Essex branch of the family, was the son of John
Maynard (d. 1556), who left Devon to settle in Hertfordshire and
was M.P. for St. Albans in 1553. Henry himself represented St.
Albans in the Parliaments of 1586, 1588 and 1597. In 1601 he represented Essex which he served as High Sheriff in 1603 and he was
one of the Essex gentlemen knighted by James I in that year. He was
Custos Rotulorum of Essex for the two years preceding his death.
His marble and alabaster tomb in the Bourchier (Maynard) chapel
at Little Easton bears effigies of himself, his wife and their ten
children. He enjoyed the favour of Cecil, whom he served as
secretary.

William, 1st Baron Maynard (1585-1640), Sir Henry's eldest son,
was created a baronet by James I in the first list of 1611 and in 1620
was raised to the peerage as Baron Maynard of Wicklow. Eight years
later he was advanced to an English barony as Baron Maynard of
Estaines Parva (Little Easton). He was Lord Lieutenant of Cambridgeshire from 1620 and of Essex from 1635. Few holders of the office
have served in more troublesome times. His first wife, who died at
the age of 20, was the daughter of William Cavendish, Duke of Newcastle. His second wife was the only daughter and heiress of Sir
Anthony Everard (q.v.) of Great Waltham. When Lord Maynard died
she complained bitterly about 'the barbarous soldiers', who had
'curdled all the summer in his blood' and had been the cause 'of his
violent fever and sudden death'. The 1st Lord Maynard has a sumptuous monument at Little Easton, on which he is represented as a
Roman commander, with his second wife as a Roman matron.

William, 2nd Baron Maynard (1622-98), married, first, Dorothy,
daughter and heiress of Robert Banastre; secondly, Margaret, daughter of James Murray, Earl of Dysart. As a Royalist he was impeached for high treason in 1647, but discharged the following year. Cromwell had him imprisoned again in 1655. When he returned to favour at
the Restoration he was appointed a Privy Councillor and Comptroller
of the Household to Charles II in which office he continued under
James II. He was Lord Lieutenant of Essex from 1673 to 1687.

The 2nd Lord Maynard's second wife was a close friend of Thomas
Ken, rector of Little Easton, 1663-5, afterwards Bishop of Bath and
Wells. She was probably the original of Hilda in Ken's epic, Edmund.

The 5th Baron Maynard was advanced to a viscountcy in 1766, with
reversion in default of male issue to his kinsman, Sir William Maynard,
Bart., who was descended from Charles, the younger son of the founder of the Essex line, Sir Henry. Charles Maynard had been an Auditor
to the Exchequer, and figures in the history of Walthamstow as lord
of the manor of Walthamstow Toni. The 1st Viscount Maynard died
unmarried at the age of 85 in 1775. At his death the title descended in
accordance with the limitation; but all other honours, including the
baronetcy, became extinct.

The 2nd Viscount Maynard died in 1824 and was succeeded by Henry,
3rd and last Viscount Maynard (1786-1865), the only son of the Rev.
Henry Maynard, rector of Radwinter and vicar of Thaxted, nephew
of the 2nd viscount. He figures prominently in Wolstenholme's plates
of the 'Essex Hunt', the fourth of which shows 'The Death' at Easton
Lodge. He had four daughters and one son, the Hon. Charles Henry,
who died in 1865, four months before his father. When the 3rd viscount

died he had been Lord Lieutenant of Essex for 40 years and had
served under three sovereigns. He played little part in national
affairs, but no landowner of his time was more highly esteemed in
Essex. At his death the Easton estate was inherited by his granddaughter, the beautiful Frances Evelyn, Countess of Warwick (q.v.),
friend of Edward VII, who is remembered as a great Edwardian
hostess with Socialist sympathies. (See Greville.)

See C. D. Saunders: Genealogists' Magazine vi (1932-4) 591;
    J. E. Ritchie, E.R. ii 40

MEAD

Isaac Mead, autobiographer, wrote the Life of an Essex Lad (1923),
in which he describes vividly rural life in the Essex of his boyhood
and youth.

MEADE

Thomas Meade, or Mede, of Elmdon (d. 1585), was a judge of the
Court of Common Pleas from 1577. He was buried under a fine altar
tomb at Elmdon. His descendants flourished for many generations at
Wenden Lofts. Joseph Mede (1586-1638), the eminent biblical scholar,
of Christ's College, Cambridge, was a member of this family.

MELLITUS

Mellitus (d. 624) was the first missionary to the East Saxons. He was
first Bishop of London and third Archbishop of Canterbury. In 604
Augustine consecrated him bishop with a special commission to preach
to the province of the East Saxons.

MIDDLESEX, Earl of See CRANFIELD

MILDMAY

The origin of the Essex family of Mildmay cannot be traced back beyond Thomas Mildmay of Great Waltham, who married Margaret Cornish
about 1465. Their son, Walter, who married Margaret Everard about
1483, held a situation in the household of Anne Neville, Duchess of
Buckingham, at Writtle. It was this Walter's son, Thomas (d. 1551),
who settled at Chelmsford, prospered, and in 1530 bought a house
called Guy Harlings in New Street, now used as Diocesan offices.

In his will, dated 1547, he described himself as a 'yeoman and merchant', and referred to the stall he used to stand behind in Chelmsford
market. His eldest surviving son, Thomas (d. 1566), became Auditor
of the Court of Augmentations, and in 1540 acquired the manor of
Moulsham, with 1,300 acres and 200 tenants, which had belonged to
Westminster Abbey. Before his death he had come into possession of
most of Moulsham and Chelmsford.

Before the end of James I's reign there were nine branches of the
family with large estates in Essex, all of whom were descended from
the Thomas who stood behind his stall in Chelmsford market less than
100 years earlier. They were: Sir Thomas of Moulsham; Sir Henry
of Woodham Walter; Sir Humphrey of Danbury; Sir Henry of Wanstead;
Sir Thomas of Springfield Barnes; Sir Henry of Little Baddow; Walter
of Great Baddow; Robert of Terling; Carew, alias Hervey, of Marks.
Despite this fertility of the family in the earlier generations, the entire male lines of Thomas's family became extinct with the death of

Carew Hervey Mildmay, of Marks, Ilford, at the age of 93 in 1784, although there were still Mildmays at Chelmsford in the 19th century.

Thomas, the auditor, built himself a mansion at Moulsham, which when completed was reputed to be the finest gentleman's house in the county, and in 1556 erected six almshouses at Moulsham, which were rebuilt in 1758 by Sir William Mildmay. Thomas was succeeded at Moulsham by his eldest son, Sir Thomas (d. 1608), who was knighted in 1566. It was during his time that Elizabeth 1 slept four nights at Moulsham in September, 1579. His wife was Lady Frances Radcliffe (q.v.), daughter of Henry, 4th Earl of Sussex. It was through this marriage that the FitzWalter barony came into the family.

Sir Thomas's third son, Henry, who succeeded to the estate on the death without issue of his elder brother in 1620, was the first to claim the FitzWalter barony; but the claim was not allowed until 1670, when Sir Henry's grandson, Benjamin, was summoned to the House of Lords as Baron FitzWalter. He was the ninth of the line at Moulsham, but only fifth in descent from the auditor. Sir Henry's claim was valid. On the death of Robert Radcliffe, 6th Baron FitzWalter and 5th Earl of Sussex (q.v.), his mother, Lady Frances, had become sole heiress. But as the Civil War had broken out before the Long Parliament had been able to consider the claim, nothing was settled. This Henry died in 1654 and was succeeded by another Henry, who also petitioned but died before a decision was reached. He was succeeded by his brother, Benjamin, who continued the claim; but was opposed by Robert Cheke (q.v.), son of Henry Cheke by Frances Radcliffe. So it was not until 1670 that the Privy Council was able to decide in favour of Benjamin Mildmay, who undoubtedly had the better claim. At his death in 1679, Benjamin, the 1st baron of the Mildmay family, was succeeded by his elder son Charles, as 2nd baron, and in 1728 by his second son, Benjamin, as 3rd baron.

Benjamin Mildmay, 19th Baron FitzWalter, 1st Viscount Harwich and Earl FitzWalter (1670-1756), who succeeded as third of the Mildmay line in 1728, served in many great offices of State. He was President of the Board of Trade, Treasurer of the Household, and Ambassador to Paris. It was he who pulled down the Moulsham house and erected a larger one designed by Signor Leon. He was created Viscount Harwich and Earl FitzWalter in 1730. From 1741 to 1756 he served as Lord Lieutenant of Essex. At his death at the age of 86 he was buried in Chelmsford church, now the cathedral, and as he left no issue the male line of his branch of the family became extinct.

The Chelmsford estates then passed to a cousin, William Mildmay, who was created a baronet in 1765, but was yet another member of the family to die without issue. Sir Walter Mildmay (1520-89), Chancellor of the Exchequer and founder of Emmanuel College, Cambridge, was the son of Thomas of Guy Harlings, and the younger brother of Thomas, the auditor. He began a career of his own at the office of the Court of Augmentations in 1540, and five years later became joint-auditor with his brother, Thomas. In the same year he started his Parliamentary career as M.P. for Lostwithiel. Two years later he transferred to Lewes, and in 1553 he was returned as M.P. for Maldon. In 1546 he married a daughter of William Walsingham, a London attorney. Her uncle was Sir Anthony Denny of Waltham Abbey (q.v.); her brother was to become Sir Francis Walsingham, the great Elizabethan diplomat. Her portrait hangs at Emmanuel.

In 1551, Thomas and Walter Mildmay were associated with Sir
William Petre and Sir Henry Tyrell in refounding Chelmsford
Grammar School, on the governing body of which members of the
family served for several generations. But Essex was not the principal centre of Sir Walter's local activities. His country house was
Apethorpe, Northamptonshire, which gave him Burghley as a neighbour. He had another house at Hackney, then a fashionable suburb.

Sir Walter's career in public finance covered a surprisingly long
period for a Tudor politician. He was Chancellor of the Exchequer
to Elizabeth I for 30 years and sat on 35 special government commissions.

In 1567 Sir Walter became involved in the affairs of Mary Queen of
Scots, although to what extent is never likely to be fully known.
Throughout he acted in close association with his Northamptonshire
neighbour, Cecil, who was his closest friend on the Council. Another
neighbour in both Essex and Northamptonshire was Sir William Fitz-
William (q.v.), of Gaynes Park, whose son married Sir Walter's
daughter, Winifred. His youngest daughter, Christian, married
Charles Barrett, son of Edward Barrett of Belhus (q:v.).

Of Sir Walter Mildmay's concern for higher learning Fuller said
that he,
    'began with his benefaction to Christ's College in Cambridge,
    only to put his hand into practice; then his bounty embraced
    the generous resolution (which the painfull piety of St.
    Paul propounds to himself, viz.) "not to build on another
    man's foundation"; but at his own cost, he erected a new
    College in Cambridge, by the name of Emmanuel.'
Of this foundation the story is told that when the queen remarked to
Mildmay: 'Sir Walter, I hear that you have erected a Puritan found-
ation,' he replied:
    'No, madam, far be from me to countenance anything
    contrary to your established laws; but I have set an
    acorn which, when it becomes an oak, God alone knows
    what will be the fruit thereof.'

In the statutes he stipulated that students from Essex and Northamptonshire, which he represented so long in the Parliaments of Elizabeth I,
were to be preferred for fellowships and scholarships.

Sir Walter died in London in 1589, and was buried in the church of
St. Bartholomew the Great, Smithfield. His eldest son, Anthony,
inherited the Northamptonshire estates; the Essex estates went to
his second son, Humphrey, who married Mary Capel. Anthony's wife
wrote of her father-in-law that he was 'a pleasantly conceited man at
his owne table;' that he 'continually would give wyse and profitable
speeches, but would never suffer any man to be evill spoken of.'

Sir Humphrey Mildmay of Danbury, the second son of Sir Walter,
was the father of a more eminent Sir Humphrey (b. 1592), the diarist.
The Capel strain in his blood may have been more potent than the
Puritan strain derived from the Mildmays. He became prominent as
a Royalist. His wife was the daughter of Sir John Crofts of Little
Saxham, Suffolk, whose 15 children were noted for their gaiety. So
gay were the girls at Little Saxham that 'going to Saxham' in Charles
II's time meant much the same as 'going to Jericho' had meant in
Henry VIII's. Endymion Porter had to promise his wife that he would
be a 'true loving husband, that will not go to Saxham'. Sir Humphrey

was a gay character, whose diary contains such Pepysian entries as,
'This afternoon I visited pretty Mrs. Oxwick (of Stratford) with much
solace, and came home to Jane.' In his gaiety, however, he anticipates
Pepys, because he belongs to the Jacobean rather than the Caroline
period. Parsons were often his cronies, and he enjoyed nothing better than getting them drunk. His diary gives a vivid account of the social life in the Essex of his day, with the Petres, the Waldegraves and
the Tyrells riding in and out of Chelmsford. He himself did not take a
prominent part in the Civil Wars, but both his sons fought on the
Royalist side and one was inside the walls of Colchester when Fairfax marched in. Sir Humphrey's diaries, Sir Humphrey Mildmay:
Royalist Gentleman, were edited by P. L. Ralph, and published by
Rutgers University Press, New Brunswick, in 1947.

Sir Henry Mildmay of Wanstead (d. 1664), Master of the Jewel Office,
was the brother of Sir Humphrey, the diarist. He had the reputation
of having enriched himself by unprincipled conduct at the Jewel Office,
and appears to have been an unreliable character generally. He was
knighted in 1617. Two years later he bought Wanstead from George
Villiers, Duke of Buckingham. Shortly after this he became M.P.
for Maldon, which he represented again after a short break from
1625 to 1660.

Sir Henry Mildmay took sides against the king in 1641 and was one of
Charles's judges in 1648-9, although he was careful not to sign the
death warrant. At the Restoration, on being called upon to give an
account of the Crown Jewels, he attempted flight, but was seized by
Lord Winchelsea at Rye and lodged at Dover. From there he was
brought to London for trial. He was condemned and sentenced to life
imprisonment, with the condition that he should be drawn on a hurdle
annually on 27th January (the anniversary of Charles I's condemnation),
with a rope round his neck, from the Tower to Tyburn and back. All
his honours and titles were stripped from him, but on his producing
a doctor's certificate that he was ruptured and could not endure such
treatment he was ordered to be transported to Tangier. He died at
Antwerp in 1664.

Sir Henry's son, Sir John Mildmay, appealed unsuccessfully against
the Wanstead estate being surrendered to the Crown on the grounds
that it had been settled on his mother as a marriage dower, and that
as she had not committed treason the estate should not be taken from
her.

See S. E. Lehmberg: Sir Walter Mildmay and Tudor Government
                                (1964)

MONCK

George Monck, Duke of Albemarle (1608-70), comes into Essex history
as owner of New Hall, Boreham. He was a Devon man whose crowded
career belongs to national rather than local history. His character
was shown early in life when he thrashed the under-sheriff of Devon
for a wrong, or imagined wrong, done to his father. Despite his services to Cromwell, who trusted him implicitly, honours were showered
on him at the Restoration, which he had, in fact, done much to acc-
omplish. In 1660 he was raised to the peerage as Baron Monck, Earl
of Torrington, and Duke of Albemarle, in recognition of his family's
descent from Richard Beauchamp, Earl of Warwick, and Arthur
Plantagenet, natural son of Edward IV. A pension of £7,000 a year
was settled on him; he was allowed to keep his Irish estates, worth

£4,000 a year, and was given the Essex estate of New Hall, Boreham, where he lived in great splendour, frequently entertaining Charles II. Pepys has a cryptic reference to a wound sustained by the Duke at New Hall under date, 28th December 1663. On that occasion he was judged to be 'a heavy dull man'.

In 1668 ill-health forced him to live quietly, and he retired to New Hall to occupy himself principally in breeding horses, in the hope that good air and diet would restore him to health; but he proved a bad patient. This was not surprising, for after a lifetime of activity he was confined to his room with dropsy until a young doctor succeeded in bringing about such an improvement in his general condition that in June 1669 he was well enough to entertain Duke Cosmo III, Grand Duke of Tuscany, who was touring the country and visited several Essex great houses. The following autumn, however, brought a relapse, and he died of dropsy a few months later. The Duke was Lord Lieutenant of Essex from 1660 to 1670.

Christopher Monck, 2nd Duke of Albemarle (1653-88), was the son of the 1st Duke by Anne, daughter of John Clarges, a farrier in the Savoy. According to Aubrey, Monck met Anne Clarges through her attendance on him as seamstress during his imprisonment in the Tower. In 1675 the 2nd Duke was appointed joint-Lord-Lieutenant of Essex with Aubrey de Vere, 20th Earl of Oxford. He was also joint-Lord-Lieutenant of Wiltshire and Lord Lieutenant of Devon. In 1685 he raised the Devon and Cornwall militia against Monmouth, and led the army that met him when he landed at Lyme Regis. Soon after the Monmouth landing, the Duke resigned his military commands and his lieutenancy commissions in Essex and Devonshire. He was appointed Governor General of Jamaica in 1687 and died there the following year.

Sir John Bramston (q.v.), in his Autobiography (pp. 205-6), gives an account of his treatment and supposed slight by James II. He entertained the king at New Hall in 1686.

At the age of 16, Christopher Monck had married Elizabeth, eldest daughter of the 2nd Duke of Newcastle; but there was no issue of the marriage. New Hall was settled on the Duchess, who in 1691 married Ralph Montagu, 1st Duke of Montagu.

See E. F. Ward: Christopher Monck, Duke of Albemarle (1915)

MONOUX

Sir George Monoux, founder of the school at Walthamstow that bears his name, was master of the Drapers' Company, and in 1514 Lord Mayor of London. He began his career in commerce at Bristol. The source of his early fortune was shipping. His next venture was into banking, and his wealth increased rapidly. He settled at Walthamstow, then a small village on the edge of Epping Forest, where he built and endowed almshouses as well as the school, which was founded in 1527.

MORANT

Philip Morant (1700-70), historian of Essex, was a younger son of Stephen Morant of Jersey. He came to England to attend Abingdon Grammar School. From there he went to Pembroke College, Oxford. After two years as preacher to the English church at Amsterdam his long connection with Essex begain in 1724, when he became curate to Nicholas Tindal (q.v.), vicar of Great Waltham, with whom he remained until 1732. During this period he published work which attracted

the attention of Edmund Gibson, Bishop of London, who had himself
published the English translation of Camden's Britannia in 1695 and
an edition of the Anglo-Saxon Chronicle in 1692. Encouraged and
advised by the bishop, Morant applied himself to historical research
to such good effect that since his day practically all the county histories of Essex have been based on his work.

In 1732 Morant again went to Amsterdam for a short period, returning
to become incumbent of the livings of: Shellow Bowells, 1733-4;
Broomfield, 1734-8; Chignal-Smealey, 1735-43; St. Mary's Colchester,1738-70; Wickham Bishops, 1743-45; Aldham, 1745-70.
Although it was an age of pluralism, he never held more than two
livings at one time. He is associated principally with the livings of
Aldham and St. Mary, Colchester, which he held until his death. He
was always a dutiful parson, particularly in keeping church records
up-to-date. An example of this is shown in an entry in his handwriting
in the Chignal-Smealey parish register:
 'The Rev. Tho. Cox, Rector of this Parish, neglected, for
 several years, to register the Baptisms, Weddings, and
 Burials; but Tho. Emberson, Clerk of this Parish since
 1713 happened, out of curiosity, to keep an exact list of
 them. Out of his List, therefore, all from 1706 as may be
 discern'd have been transcribed by me, Philip Morant,
 rector.'

In 1739 Morant married Anne, daughter and heiress of Solomon
Stebbing of Brook House, Great Tey. Their only daughter, Anna
Maria, married Thomas Astle, Keeper of the Records at the Tower
of London, an association that was to prove valuable to Morant during
his lifetime and to the public after his death.

When Morant went to Colchester in 1738 no history of the borough had
been written, but a vast amount of material had accumulated and to this
Morant applied himself with immense energy for ten years, sifting and
sorting until in 1748 he was able to publish his first major work, The
History and Antiquities of Colchester. During these ten years he also
found time to write many brief biographies for the Biographica Britannia. All these 'lives', with the exception of the one on Stillingfleet,
which he did not sign, can be identified by the signature 'C', presumably for Colchester.

His History and Antiquities of the County of Essex was published over
the period, 1760 to 1768. The basis of this great work was the Holman
MSS. (q.v.) printed, which Salmon (q.v.) was preparing for the press
when he died in 1742. Morant had a poor opinion of Salmon as editor
and went back to Holman, on whom Tindal, who introduced him to Essex
history, had relied. The abundance of the material collected by Holman
had proved an embarrassment to previous students; but Morant had already shown his mastery of detail in his history of Colchester. For
Public Records he was able to draw on the transcripts of Thomas
Jekyll of Bocking (q.v.), supplemented by the transcripts made by the
Rev. John Ouseley of Springfield.

After the death of his wife in 1767, Morant went to live in London with
his daughter and son-in-law. This led to his being appointed to succeed
Richard Blyke in preparing the Rolls of Parliament for the Press. He
died three years later and was buried beside his wife in the chancel of
the church at Aldham. He was a man of attractive personality, and with
his well-powdered wig and gold-headed cane was a familiar figure in
Colchester during the middle years of the 18th century. He was elected

a Fellow of the Society of Antiquaries in 1755, and was generally esteemed both for his learning and kindly nature.

Morant's grandson, Thomas Astle, married in 1801, Susannah Brogden. Their only son was killed in 1821. Their only daughter, Louise, married Charles Robert Sperling of Stansted Mountfitchet, whose son, Charles Brogden Sperling, inherited Dynes Hall, Great Maplestead. His son, Charles Frederick Denne Sperling, J.P., M.A., F.S.A., was a well-known Essex antiquary and authority on heraldry in his day.

After his father-in-law's death, Thomas Astle had the Morant MSS. carefully bound. They were unfortunately divided for a time; but eventually most of them found their way to the British Museum. Morant's library was purchased from Astle's executors in 1804 for the Royal Institution, his MSS. are now deposited in the Essex Record Office.

MORLEY, Barons <u>See</u> PARKER

MORLEY

John Morley of Halstead (1656-1735), land-jobber, was the first of the long line of estate speculators and 'developers' who made fortunes in Essex; but his claim to be remembered rests not on this so much as on his association with several eminent poets and men of letters of his day. Morley was the son of a Halstead butcher. The craft of money-making he learned from Sir Josiah Child (q.v.), who had an estate at Halstead and bought his meat from the Morleys, whose shop was near the church gate. One day Child advised John Morley to buy East India Stock. Morley replied that he would rather buy fat sheep; but he was eventually talked into buying £100 worth. This rose in value so rapidly that four or five months later it was worth £160, and when it reached the £200 mark he recovered the amount originally invested, leaving £100 with the Company. Morley tells us that he entrusted his profit with his wife, 'assuring her that he would not venture it any more.' But as he didn't need the money in his business he bought property with it and before long the butchery business became secondary to the property dealing.

The attraction of Morley's character is that although he became a man of wealth and the friend of landowners and several eminent men of letters and politicians, he never gave himself airs. To the end of his life he killed a pig in Halstead market once a year to show that he had not forgotten his trade. His home in his affluent days was Blue Bridge House, on the Colchester road, where the arms of the Butchers' Company may still be seen along with the date, 1714.

Morley's principal friend among the great was the poet, Prior, who was a frequent visitor to Blue Bridge House and composed the inscription in Halstead church to Morley's friend, Samuel Fiske, 'by descent a gentleman, by profession an apothecary.' Prior, who lived at Down Hall, Hatfield Broad Oak, refers to Morley as 'Squire Morley' in 'The Ballad of Down Hall'. Other literary friends were Alexander Pope and John Day.

Morley gained the acquaintance of these men of letters through his rich patron, Robert Harley, 1st Earl of Oxford, for whom he acted when Harley purchased Down Hall for Prior's use. It was said that Morley arranged the marriage of Harley's son and heir, Edward, afterwards 2nd earl, with Lady Henrietta Holles, heiress of the Duke of Newcastle, in 1713, and got £10,000 for bringing it off.

In 1716 Morley had his portrait painted by Sir Godfrey Kneller. In 1722 he received a grant of arms; but he had already placed the arms of the Butchers' Company over his front door and on the vault he had prepared for himself in the Bourchier chapel in Halstead church. This tomb was later removed to make way for pews and now stands outside the east window.

MORNINGTON, Earls of See WELLESLEY

MORRIS

William Morris (1834-96), poet, artist, craftsman and social reformer, was born at Elm Lodge, Walthamstow. Six years after his birth the family removed to Woodford Hall, which then had 50 acres of parkland and a 100 acres of farmland sloping down to the River Roding. The hall stood near the church and had a private doorway into the churchyard. Opposite the church stood the village stocks and pound. The scene was entirely rural, and the Morris family brewed their own beer and made butter in the dairy. Epping Forest was all around them and had a profound effect on William's infant mind.

When he was 14 his father died and the family returned to Walthamstow to make their home at Water House, which stands in what is now Lloyd Park. The fascination of Epping Forest and the villages round it continued to influence him, and the contrast between the Forest and rapidly developing London suburbs stimulated the romanticism and mediaevalism that throughout his life formed the background for his dreams of a happier society. This contrast is a feature of West Essex that has affected many poets and artists, but none more creatively than Morris.

On leaving Marlborough he had tuition from the Rev. F. B. Guy, who was then a young curate at Walthamstow, and was later to achieve an eminence of his own as headmaster of Forest School.

Morris must always have a prominent place in the study of Essex genius, because in his work it found such characteristic expression. The penetration of the ancient untamed forest into the workaday world of the 19th century has its counterpart in the mingling of mediaevalism and socialism in such works as A Dream of John Ball and News from Nowhere, as well as in his designs for furniture, wall-papers and painted glass. He saw what artificial ways of life were doing to the free spirit of man. Today he is associated with the arty-crafty movement; but this is entirely foreign to his vigorous and forthright genius. Walthamstow understands William Morris better than places more popularly associated with the art world ever can, and keeps alive his memory.

MORTIMER

The arms of this noble family are to be found in many Essex churches, notably in the window at Great Bardfield. The manor of Bardfield Hall descended from the De Burghs to Philippa of Clarence, heiress to the throne, who in 1368 married Edward Mortimer, 3rd Earl of March (1351-81), who is represented in glass at Thaxted. At the time of the marriage the bridegroom was 17, the bride 13. When her father, Duke of Clarence and Earl of Ulster, died, her vast estates were added to the Mortimer estates. At 22, the earl was appointed Marshal of England and Ambassador to France. At 26 he carried the sword and spurs at the coronation of his cousin, Richard II. He rebuilt the nave of Great

Bardfield church, and the transepts, south aisle, and porch at
Thaxted. His arms appear on the tower at Dunmow and on the fonts
at Shalford and Bures.

MOTT

An Essex family of this name played a distinguished part in county
life for at least 600 years. In the 13th century the name occurs at
Bradfield. From the 14th century to the 17th it was located chiefly
at Shalford and Braintree. Sherne Hall, Shalford, was a seat of
the family towards the end of this period. Members of the Mott family
contributed to the Armada Fund.

MYDDELTON

Sir Thomas Myddelton (1550-1631) of Stansted Mountfitchet, Lord
Mayor of London, was born at Denbigh Castle, where his father was
governor. He was a brother of Sir Hugh Myddelton. An original member of the East India Company and of the New River Company, Thomas
Myddelton made a fortune as a merchant. He was knighted in 1603, and
during the same year became an alderman of the City of London. He
was Lord Mayor, 1613-14. Today he is remembered for having published the first popular edition of the Bible in the Welsh language. At
his death at the age of 81 he was buried at Stansted under one of the
finest Jacobean altar-tombs in England. It bears the arms of the City
of London and of the Grocers' Company, of which he was a member.

Another fine tomb at Stansted commemorates Hester Salisbury, daughter of Sir Thomas by his second wife. His son, Sir Thomas (1586-
1666), was a distinguished parliamentarian, who was entrusted with
the command of forces sent to bring North Wales into subjection. After
taking several towns he had to retreat when the Welsh brought in Irish
reinforcements. Later he crushed the Royalists of North Wales at
Montgomery in 1644. In 1659 he took up arms in support of Charles II
but was defeated by Lambert. What Stansted thought of this we do not
know; but in 1644 the parish subscribed to a fund 'to reduce North
Wales to the obedience of Parliament'.

The Myddeltons were lords of the manor of Stansted Mountfitchet for
seven generations until it was sold in 1710 to Thomas Heath.

NASSAU

The founder of the English branch of the family was William Henry de
Zuylestein de Nassau (1641-1708), bastard son of a Prince of Orange
and cousin of William III, who in 1695 raised him to the peerage with
the titles of Baron Enfield, Viscount Tunbridge, and Earl of Rochford.
He married Jane, daughter and heiress of Sir Henry Wroth of Durance,
Enfield, by whom he had four sons and five daughters.

William Henry de Nassau, 2nd earl (d. 1708), fought under Marlborough
and carried the dispatches announcing the victory of Blenheim. He was
killed in battle two days after succeeding to the earldom.

Frederick, 3rd earl (1682-1738), brother of the short-lived 2nd earl,
married Bessie Savage (d. 1746), natural daughter and heiress of the
famous rake, Richard Savage, 4th Earl Rivers (q.v.). She brought
St. Osyth's Priory to her husband after an Act of Parliament had confirmed the succession in 1721. Before this the 3rd earl had lived in
Holland. On his wife's succession he returned to England and built the

greater part of the present Priory House. Richard Savage, the poet,
claimed to be the illegitimate son of the 4th Earl Rivers. When his
claim was rejected he wrote:

Hail Rivers! hallow'd shade, descend from rest;
Descend and smile to see thy Rochford blest;
Weep not the scenes through which my life must run,
Though Fate, fleet-footed, scents thy languid son.

William Henry, 4th earl (d. 1781), courtier, became lord of the bedchamber to George II in 1738. In 1748 he was appointed Vice-Admiral
of the Coasts of Essex. The following year he went as envoy to the
King of Sardinia. On his return he held a succession of offices at
court. The monument to his memory in St. Osyth's church records
that he was Ambassador to the Court of France, 1763; Ambassador
to the Court of Vienna, 1768; Secretary of State to George III, 1776.
On two occasions George III stayed at the Priory as his guest.

The 4th earl was Lord Lieutenant of Essex from 1756 to 1781. He is
believed to have introduced the Lombardy poplar into England, some
of the earliest being planted at St. Osyth. At his death he left three
illegitimate children, but no legitimate issue. In addition to his estates
in the east of the county he owned the Loughton Hall estate, inherited
from his Wroth ancestors; but this he sold in 1745 to William Whitaker,
an alderman of the City of London. By his will he left all the Essex
estates of which he died possessed in trust for his 'natural or reputed
son, commonly called Frederick Nassau.' The mother of this heir was
Anne Labbee, or Johnson, of the parish of St. George, Hanover Square,
who was living with him at the time of his death, and 'of whose fidelity,
friendship, and affection', he wrote, 'I have constant proofs, and who
deserves more than I am able to give.' She died on the day on which
the will was proved.

The titles went to his nephew, the 5th and last Earl of Rochford, who
died unmarried in 1830. With his death the earldom became extinct.

NEVILLE

During the reign of Edward III the lordship of Clavering passed into
the possession of the family of Neville, lords of Raby and earls of
Westmorland. John de Neville held the manor of Great Totham in the
13th century. He succeeded his father as justice of the King's Forests,
but was removed from office in 1244. He died the following year and
was buried at Waltham Abbey.

NEVILLE

Richard Aldworth Neville, 2nd Baron Braybrooke (1750-1825), was
the son of Richard Neville Aldworth-Neville, of Stanlake, Berkshire.
He took the name of Neville in 1782, then in 1797 exchanged it for that
of Griffin on succeeding to the barony of Braybrooke. He was M.P.
for Grampound, 1774-80; Buckingham, 1780-82; and for Reading in
four successive Parliaments from 1782 to 1797. In 1798 he was appointed Lord Lieutenant of Essex, and for the remainder of his life
was the leading figure in the social and political life of the county.
He died at his Berkshire seat in 1825, and was succeeded by his son,
Richard Neville, 3rd Baron Braybrooke (1783-1858), first editor of
Pepys and historian of Audley End, who in 1819 married Lady Jane
Cornwallis, eldest daughter of Charles, 2nd Marquess Cornwallis,
the marriage that brought the valuable Cornwallis collection of furniture and portraits to Audley End on the death of the 2nd marquess.

Lord Braybrooke's interest in Pepys was aroused by his coming upon
the diary in the library of Magdalene College, Cambridge, to which
the owners of Audley End were hereditary Visitors, at the time when
diaries had come into fashion. Of the £2,200 paid for the copyright,
£1,000 went to endow an annual benefaction at the college, £1,000
towards building a new Master's Lodge. The History of Audley End
was published in 1836, and in 1842 the 3rd Lord Braybrooke published at his own expense, The Private Correspondence of Lady Jane
Cornwallis (1581-1659).

Richard Cornwallis Neville, 4th Baron Braybrooke (1820-61), inherited his father's antiquarian and biographical interests, but died
without issue at the age of 41 after holding the estate for only three
years. He abandoned the use of the name of Griffin, which by the
terms of a will all who came into the estate were to assume, and reverted to the sole use of the name Neville. Although he contributed
little to the history of the estate, he was an enduring place as a scholar. His chief works are: Antiqua Explorata, the report of excava-
tions during the winters of 1845 and 1846 and the spring of 1847 in
and about the Roman station at Chesterford; Sepulchra Exposita, an
account of the opening of barrows near Saffron Walden; Saxon
Obsequies, illustrated by ornaments and weapons discovered in a
cemetery near Little Wilbraham, Cambridgeshire, and learned articles on similar subjects published in Archaeologia and the Archaeological Journal. His collections are now at Cambridge.

Charles Cornwallis Neville, 5th Baron Braybrooke (1823-1902), brother of the 4th baron, held the estate for 40 years and lived the life
of a country squire at Audley End, serving the county well in many
public offices, but never aspiring to be a national figure except as a
noted breeder of Southdown sheep and Jersey cattle. In 1842 he lev-
elled the lawn in front of the house and laid a cricket pitch. His wife
was a daughter of the 3rd Viscount Hawarden.

At the death of the 5th baron there was again no son to succeed and
the estate passed to his 75 years old brother, the Rev. Latimer
Neville (1827-1904), Master of Magdalene College, Cambridge, who
for 50 years had been rector of the remote country parish of Heydon
on the Essex-Cambridgeshire border. When he became 6th Baron
Braybrooke, he was the third of the 3rd baron's sons to inherit the
title. At his death two years later he was succeeded by his son, Henry
Neville, 7th Baron Braybrooke (1855-1941), who held the title and
estate for 37 years until his death at the age of 86. Both his sons,
Richard Henry Cornwallis Neville, 8th Baron Braybrooke (1919-43),
and Robert George Latimer Neville (1920-41), were killed during the
Second World War, and the title and estate passed to their cousin,
Henry Seymour Neville, 9th Baron Braybrooke, son of Grey, younger
brother of Henry the 7th baron.

See W. Addison: Audley End (1953)

NEWMAN

Richard Newman Harding Newman, of Nelmes, near Hornchurch, is
considered the founder of the Essex Hunt. His portrait by Romney,
'The Pink Boy', rivals Gainsborough's 'Blue Boy'. Arthur Young was
not an admirer of fox-hunting and referred to Newman's hounds as
'not quite so useful as the cow that supplied them with a pailful of new
milk daily through the summer.'

NIGHTINGALE

Florence Nightingale (1820-1910), pioneer of hospital reform, was
the great-granddaughter of Samuel Smith, who amassed a fortune as
a London merchant and devoted it to humanitarian purposes. His son,
William Smith, of Parndon Hall, near Harlow, went through much of
the fortune he inherited from his father in collecting pictures and
fighting lost causes. As a member of Parliament for 46 years he
fought continuously to relieve the weak and oppressed, championing
the causes of Dissenters and Jews, and fighting for better conditions
for sweated factory workers. He was a prominent abolitionist. Throughout his long life he enjoyed remarkably good health. At 80 he
wrote that he had 'no recollection whatever of any bodily pain or illness'. Apparently not one of his ten children shared his altruistic
principles; but his daughter, Fanny, who inherited his physical
stamina and lived to the age of 92, married William Edward Nightingale, and became the mother of Florence Nightingale.

NOEL

Conrad Noel (1869-1942), Socialist vicar of Thaxted, was the son of
the Victorian poet, Roden Noel, and a grandson of the 1st Earl of
Gainsborough. On leaving Cambridge and taking Holy Orders he became curate to a Socialist vicar of Newcastle-upon-Tyne. From Newcastle he went to St. Mary's, Primrose Hill, to assist Percy Dearmer,
whose concern was to bring back to the services of the Church the
beauty that had been lost at the Reformation.

As secretary of the Church Socialist League, Noel became a militant
pioneer of the brand of Christian Socialism associated with Frederick
Dennison Maurice. When the League was disbanded he was presented
to the living of Thaxted by the Countess of Warwick and remained there
for the rest of his life, finding inspiration in the pageantry of the Middle Ages, and particularly in the Sarum Missal. Gustav Holst (q.v.),
became a parishioner and contributed to the musical life of the church.
Mrs. Noel revived Morris dancing in the town, and a parish life unique
in the 20th century came to revolve round the dynamic personality of
the unconventional vicar, who created his biggest sensation by hoist-
ing the 'red flag' in the church. When critics complained about his mix-
ing of politics and religion he replied that, 'politics, in the wider sense
of social justice, is part and parcel of the Gospel of Christ, and to ig-
nore it is to be false to His teaching.'

He remained true to his early inspiration throughout the 32 years of
his incumbency. Towards the end of his life he suffered from diabetes,
which produced at the end almost total blindness. On his tombstone
were carved the words: 'He loved Justice and hated Oppression.'

NOEL-BUXTON

Noel Edward Noel-Buxton, 1st Baron Noel-Buxton (1869-1948), politician and philanthropist, was the second son of Sir Thomas Fowell
Buxton, 3rd baronet. His mother, Lady Victoria Noel, was the daughter of the 1st Earl of Gainsborough. Lord Noel-Buxton was brought
up at Warlies, Upshire, Waltham Abbey, one of a family of ten, and
educated at Harrow and Trinity College, Cambridge. While working
at the family brewery at Spitalfields he became concerned about the
poverty in the neighbourhood and joined the Christian Social Union,
adopting politics as a means to achieve social reform and justice.
While M.P. for North Norfolk - Buxton country - he was appointed

Minister of Agriculture in 1924, and piloted an important bill on agricultural wages through Parliament. In 1929 he returned to the same office, but the following year was obliged to retire through ill health. When he was raised to the peerage his wife was elected for his Norfolk constituency.

Among his philanthropic interests was the 'Save the Children Fund', of which he was president from 1930 to 1948, and the establishment of the Noel Buxton Trust for public and charitable purposes.

NORTH

Francis North, 2nd Baron Guildford (d. 1729), who was described by Bishop Burnet as 'fat, fair, and of middle stature, a mighty silly fellow', was a son of Lord Keeper North, from whom he inherited Harlowbury. He was Lord Lieutenant of Essex from 1703 to 1705.

The 1st Baron of Guildford bought Harlowbury in 1617. It was held by three generations of the North family. The 2nd Lord Guildford built the gallery in All Saints' church, Harlow.

NUGENT

Robert Nugent, Earl Nugent (1702-88), politician and poet, became Comptroller to Frederick, Prince of Wales, in 1747. He was created Lord of the Treasury in 1754, and was Vice-Treasurer for Ireland, 1760-5 and 1768-82. From 1766 to 1768 he held office as President of the Board of Trade. In 1766 he was raised to the peerage as Viscount Clare and Baron Nugent. Ten years later he was created Earl Nugent.

Earl Nugent is chiefly remembered for his success in marrying rich widows, a habit that prompted Horace Walpole to invent the word 'Nugentize'. It was the second of these marriages that brought him into Essex.

In 1736 Nugent married Anne Knight, widow of John Knight of Gosfield Hall. The marriage proved slightly embarrassing because Mrs. Knight had recently erected a large marble tomb in the north aisle of Gosfield church, near the hall pew, with an inscription commemorating her first husband's virtues. Nugent objected to this, so she had it enclosed. The Knight marriage brought Nugent a seat in Parliament and a large fortune Arthur Young wrote:

'Gosfield, in my opinion, merits much attention from the circumstance of having been formed about sixty years by the late Earl Nugent before the spirit of decoration took place: he did it himself. The lake is a happy effort and just what Brown would have executed. The plantations are so disposed as to attract the eye in every direction and, were the hedges cleared of pollards for a few miles around the village, the woods would be seen as a very magnificent outline on every side.'

Besides laying out the grounds, Nugent rebuilt the south-west front of the house.

After a time Lady Nugent saw through her husband and they separated. She reverted to her former name of Knight, but assumed the title of Lady. She was still Lady Nugent; but had no right to the title of Lady Knight. She died in 1756.

Nugent's third wife was Elizabeth, widow of the 4th Earl of Berkeley. Again he acquired a fortune with a wife, and again he failed either to give or receive happiness. Separation inevitably came along in due course, and Nugent derived perverse satisfaction from disowning the second of the two daughters born during the marriage.

Oliver Goldsmith, who visited Gosfield in 1771, celebrated his friendship with Nugent in the poetical epistle The Haunch of Venison. At his death in 1788 Nugent was buried at Gosfield. He was fittingly described as 'a jovial and voluptuous Irishman, who had left Popery for the Protestant religion, money and widows.' The honours and offices that came to him were mainly in return for moneys lent to the Prince of Wales and never repaid. Even his contemporary fame as a poet was suspect. The authorship of his 'Ode to William Pulteney', his most admired work, was said to have been bought from Mallet, who was widely believed to have written it.

The title and estate passed to his son-in-law, George Grenville, who had assumed the names of Nugent-Temple in 1775 on marrying Nugent's elder daughter.

See GRENVILLE

OATES

Captain Lawrence Edward Grace Oates (1880-1912) of Gestingthorpe was a member of Captain Scott's Antarctic expedition which reached the South Pole in January, 1912. He died in tragic but heroic circumstances. A brass tablet in the parish church of Gestingthorpe records that 'on the return journey from the South Pole ... when all were
> beset by hardship, he, being gravely injured, went out into
> the blizzard to die, in the hope that by so doing he might en-
> able his comrades to reach safety.'

Scott and his companions left Tilbury on 1st June, 1910, and successfully located the South Pole, but during the return journey they were overtaken by a blizzard. Scott wrote: 'I do not think human beings ever came through such a month.' Two of his four companions had already died, and he was sheltering with the remaining two with only two days food supply left. Three or four days later all three had perished. The bodies were found in the tent by a search party on 12th November, 1912.

Oates was the elder son of William Edward Oates of Gestingthorpe Hall. Of his end, his chief wrote:
> 'He was a brave soul. He slept through the night, hoping not
> to wake, but he awoke in the morning. It was blowing a blizz-
> ard. Oates said: "I am just going outside and I may be some
> time." He went out into the blizzard and we have not seen him
> since. We knew he was walking to his death, but though we
> tried to dissuade him we knew it was the act of a brave man
> and an English Gentleman.'

The search party carved on a rough tablet his name and 'Hereabouts died a very gallant gentleman, R.I.P.' He was 32.

See L. C. Bernacchi: A Very Gallant Gentleman; E.R. xviii 57

OGBORNE

Elizabeth Ogborne (1759-1853), historian of Essex, was born at Chelmsford, the daughter of Mrs. Jane Jackson and Sir John Eliot,

Bart., physician to the Prince of Wales. Sir John died unmarried at
Brocket Hall, Hertfordshire, in 1786, bequeathing an annuity to 'Miss
Elizabeth Jackson, daughter of Mrs. Jane Jackson, Tea Dealer, of
Tottenham Court Road.' Elizabeth married John Ogborne, the engraver
in 1790. In 1813 the Ogbornes lost their only child at the age of 20,
and it was to assuage their grief that they undertook the history of
Essex. In old age Mrs. Ogborne was a pensioner of the National Benevolent Institution. She was a precise, neat little person, somewhat affected in manner, who adopted an old-fashioned style of dress and felt
acutely the poverty that 'brought her down in the world', and restrict-
ed her rather high-flown social pretentions.

OGLETHORPE

General James Edward Oglethorpe (1695-1785), whose virtues are
eulogised in a long inscription on his monument at Cranham. was
granted a charter in 1732 to settle undischarged debtors in America,
where he founded the colony of Georgia with money voted by Parliament. The early years were full of problems, both in organising the
settlers and in securing the defences of the colony against the Spaniards in Florida. On returning to England in 1743 he married Elizabeth, only daughter and heiress of Sir Nathan Wright, of Cranham
Hall, which he made his home for the rest of his life. He served under
Cumberland during the Jacobite rising of 1745 and in later years became a figure in the London life that revolved around such well-known
personalities as Dr. Johnson, Horace Walpole, Burke and Hannah
More. General Oglethorpe was lord of the manor of Fairstead.

OSYTH

Osyth, a Saxon saint whose name is perpetuated in the Essex coastal
village, was the daughter of Redwald, the first Christian king of the
East Angles, and his wife, Wilburga, daughter of Penda, king of the
Mercians. As a child she was placed in the care of St. Modwen at
Pollesworth in Warwickshire. According to legend, while carrying
a book from St. Edith, sister of King Alfred, to St. Modwen she fell
into a river and was drowned; but after three days she was restored
to life by the prayers of St. Modwen. After being reunited with her
parents she was betrothed and married to Sighere, king of the East
Saxons. But before the marriage was consummated she took the veil
and Sighere, accepting her vocation, gave her his village of Chich
and founded an abbey there, with Osyth as abbess.

In 653, a band of Danish pirates under Inguar and Hubba landed near
Chich, and after they had burnt and laid waste the surrounding countryside they attacked the abbey, calling on the nuns to accept their pagan
gods. When Osyth refused she was beheaded, and, according to the
legend, she immediately took up her head and bore it to the church of
St. Peter and St. Paul at Chich. At the place of her martyrdom a
fountain of clear water gushed out, which was later said to have mir-
aculous healing properties.

The 1st Earl of Oxford's countess was a generous benefactress of the
nunnery. Her son wrote a life of the saint, who was held in great veneration in East Essex. When the abbey was dissolved in 1539 its properties were granted to Thomas, L rd Cromwell (q.v.).

OXFORD, Earl of See VERE

PALIN

William Palin (1803-82), divine and local historian, was born at
Mortlake, Surrey. He came to Essex as curate of Stifford in 1833.
The following year he became incumbent of the living and remained
rector of Stifford till his death 48 years later. In collaboration with
his daughter he compiled Stifford and its Neighbourhood, Past and
Present, a description of 20 parishes in south Essex, which was
published in 1871, and was followed in 1872 by More About Stifford
and its Neighbourhood. Both are mines of information about the social
history of south Essex.

PALMER

William Palmer (1633-1710), founder of Palmer's School, Grays
Thurrock, was the son of Edward Palmer, a City merchant who bought the manor of Grays in 1637. Morant's account of the family is
unreliable. Edward Palmer was twice Master of the Haberdashers'
Company, and was one of the founders of the Honourable Artillery
Company. He died in 1638, leaving two daughters and William, who
was only five. Apparently, his father's business interests were taken
care of until he was ready to take charge himself.

Our knowledge of William Palmer is sketchy; but he was living at
Stifford in 1669, and it was in this year that he married his second
wife. Neither marriage produced children, so in 1706, when over 70,
he founded a Trust to endow the Free Schools that bear his name. He
died at Stratford, West Ham, in 1710.

It is odd that so little is known about this important local benefactor,
lord of the manor of Grays, owner of waterside property at Grays
and in London, founder of an important school. He has no monument,
and no entry of his burial has come to light. A silver paten at Grays
Thurrock bears his arms and the date 1685. It was undoubtedly his
gift, and not that of a vicar of the same name to whom it has been attributed. At his death the school was built opposite the church at Grays,
and there it remained until 1871. In 1876 the endowment was extended
to girls.

PARKER

The Great Hallingbury branch of the Parker family left Norfolk for
Essex early in the 14th century. The barony of Morley came to them
in 1489, when Henry Parker (1476-1556) became 8th baron on the
death of his uncle, Henry Lovel. As a boy he entered the royal service through the Household of the Lady Margaret Beaufort, mother of
Henry VII. He became a favourite of Henry VIII, and was present at
the Field of the Cloth of Gold and many other State occasions. In 1523
he was sent as Ambassador to the court of Ferdinand, Archduke of
Austria, and while travelling in Germany met Durer, who sketched
the portrait of him that is now in the Durer Collection in the British
Museum.

The 8th Baron Morley was one of the judges at the trial of Anne Boleyn,
whose brother, George, Lord Rochford, had married his daughter,
Joan. After Anne Boleyn's execution he appears to have retired from
court and devoted himself to study and the administration of his estate.
He died, aged 80, in 1556 and was buried in Great Hallingbury church.

His only son, Henry, died in 1553 during his father's lifetime. The 8th
baron was consequently succeeded by his grandson, Henry, 9th baron,

who lived until 1577, when he was succeeded by Edward, 10th baron, who married Elizabeth, only daughter and heiress of William Stanley, Lord Monteagle, fifth son of Thomas, Earl of Derby. At his death in 1618 he was succeeded by his son, William, 4th Baron Monteagle and 11th Baron Morley (1575-1622), who was summoned to the Parliament that was to meet in 1605, and it was to him that the famous letter was sent which led to the discovery of Gunpowder Plot. Although a Protestant in 1605, the 11th Lord Morley was closely related to most of the leading Roman Catholic families of England. His wife was Elizabeth, daughter of Sir Thomas Tresham, and the letter he received in November, 1605, was from his brother-in-law, Francis Tresham.

The Great Hallingbury estate continued in the Parker family till the death of Thomas, Baron Morley and Monteagle, in 1697. With his death the title became extinct and the property passed to Sir Edward Turner, Speaker of the House of Commons, whose son sold it to Jacob Houblon in 1727.

PARNELL

James Parnell (1636-56), Quaker martyr, was born at Retford. He formed a deep attachment to George Fox, visiting him in prison at Carlisle. After suffering imprisonment himself at Cambridge, Parnell came to Colchester and on 4th July, 1655 was allowed to speak in St. Nicholas's church. After ten days at Colchester he moved to Coggeshall, where he was arrested in the name of the Protector, charged with heresy and thrown into Colchester Castle. The keeper of the prison was a cruel man named Nicholas Roberts, who forbade him even the privilege of exercising in the castle yard. His cell was a chamber in the wall of the castle, 12 feet from the ground, to which he had to scramble from a six-foot ladder propped against the wall. As the result of hardships suffered at Colchester, Parnell died at the age of 19. He is now revered as the Quaker pro-martyr.

PARR

The last of the Bourchier earls of Essex (q.v.), left a daughter, Anne, who married Sir William Parr of Kendal, brother of Queen Katherine Parr. Despite the unhappiness of the marriage, William Parr was created Earl of Essex in his wife's right in 1543, the year of Henry VIII's marriage with his sister. He died without heir in 1571 and for the sixth time the earldom of Essex came to an end in the male line, although Anne, in whose right her husband had claimed the title, had several children by a man named Hunt, all of whom were declared illegitimate by Act of Parliament.

The earldom was again revived on the distaff side. Henry Bourchier, father of the Anne named above, had a sister, Cicely, who married John Devereux, and their great-grandson, Walter, in 1572, received the Garter and was created Earl of Essex.

See DEVEREUX

PAYCOCKE

The house called Paycockes at Coggeshall, and brasses in the church of St. Peter ad Vincula, preserve the memory of a family of wool merchants prominent in the town in the 15th and 16th centuries. A Thomas Peacock was king's bailiff of the Witham Hundred in 1371. He may have been of the family; but the Paycockes of Coggeshall were a branch of the family that had been settled at Clare in Suffolk as early as 1296.

The first Paycocke of Coggeshall appears in the middle of the 15th century. John Paycocke, who died in 1505, left to Thomas, his youngest son, 'my house lying and bielded in the West Street of
> Coggeshall, afore the Vicarage ... to have and to
> hold to hym his heyers and assignes for ever more.'
Paycocke's fine house is an outstanding example of Tudor domestic architecture. The family merchant mark, an ermine's tail, is seen on the carved beams of the chimney, and on the band of carving along the front of the house, along with other Tudor devices.

Thomas Paycocke (d. 1518), whose will is an important social document, was a generous and sympathetic employer, who took a personal interest in the lives of his workpeople. He was a benefactor of the Crutched Friars at Colchester, took a benevolent interest in the abbey at Coggeshall, and left money to the churches of Bradwell, Pattiswick, and Markshall as well as to several churches along the Suffolk border. He was buried along with other members of his family before St. Katherine's altar.

The ownership of Paycockes, now the property of the National Trust, can be traced from the Thomas who died in 1518, to John, who died in 1584, and was, according to the parish register, 'the last of his name in Coxall'. It was later owned by members of the Buxton family (q.v.).

See E. Power: The Paycockes of Coggeshall (1920)

PEARSON

Wietman Dickinson Pearson, 1st Viscount Cowdray (1856-1927), was born in Yorkshire, the grandson of the founder of a family engineering firm in which he was responsible for railways, electrical installations, harbour and other works in Mexico. He was made a baronet in 1894, a baron in 1910, and created Viscount Cowdray in 1916. In 1910 he was appointed High Steward of Colchester, the borough he had represented in Parliament since 1895. Lord and Lady Cowdray bought Colchester Castle and presented it to the borough. Later Lord Cowdray bought Holly Trees mansion and its estate in order to add to the museum amenities of the castle, the house and park. He received the freedom of Colchester in 1919, and in 1922 the same honour was accorded to Viscountess Cowdray, who succeeded her husband as High Steward in 1927.

PENN

William Penn (1644-1718), founder of Pennsylvania, was the son of Admiral Sir William Penn, who had a country house at Wanstead. John Aubrey, in Brief Lives, describes a religious experience that came to Penn while a boy attending Chigwell School:
> 'He was mighty lively, but with innocence; and extremely
> tender under rebuke; and very early delighted in retire-
> ment; much given to reading and meditating of the script-
> ures ... The first sense he had of God was when he was
> 11 yeares old at Chigwell, being retired in a chamber
> alone.'
Aubrey adds that his schoolmaster 'was not of his persuasion'. There is a tradition that Penn developed his running powers at Chigwell; but the authority for this is not known.

After leaving Chigwell School at the age of 12, Penn had private
education for a time before being sent in 1660 to Christ Church,
Oxford. While still a youth he came under the influence of a Quaker
named Thomas Loe, who eventually brought him into the Society of
Friends. Quaker influences affected his attitude towards official
religious services at Oxford. His refusal to attend college chapel
was reported to his father, who advised, according to Pepys, his
removal to Cambridge. In 1661, however, he was sent down without
taking a degree. His father was so angry that he turned him out of
his house for a time, but relented and sent him on the Grand Tour
in the hope that this would cure him 'of being religious in too original a way'.

Penn founded a school in Philadelphia, the Penn Charter School,
and in 1949 a 17th century sundial was presented to it by Friends
of Chigwell School. In return, Chigwell received a cutting from a
descendant of the famous Shackamaxon elm, under which Penn signed
his treaty with the Indians.

PEPYS

On 27th February, 1660, Samuel Pepys visited Audley End and was
impressed by the ceilings, chimney-pieces and 'form of the whole'.
He drank the king's health and played on his flageolette in the cellar,
'there being an excellent echo'. Afterwards he inspected the ancient
almshouses, where he drank from 'a brown bowl, tipt with silver ...
at the bottom was a picture of the Virgin and the Child in her arms
done in silver': this now famous mazer bowl sold for £22,000 in 1971.

On 7th March, 1666, he records that the following day the king and the
Duke of York were to visit Audley End with a view to buying it from
the Earl of Suffolk. On 7th October of the following year he was again
'mighty merry' there himself, but was less favourably impressed by
the house than he had been on his first visit.

Pepys reported that the Plague was raging in Colchester in July 1666
and threatened to 'quite depopulate the place'.

Among local persons who figure in the Diary are Sir William Batten
of Walthamstow (q.v.), Sir William Penn of Wanstead (q.v.), Sir
Josiah Child (q.v.) and Sir Robert Brookes. It is from Pepys that
we learn that Sir William Penn considered buying Wanstead House
from Sir Robert Brookes. Pepys wisely advised against the purchase.
Others who figure in the Diary are Sir John Minnes, Sir Anthony
Deane (q.v.), Thomas Fuller (q.v.), Sir Harbottle Grimston (q.v.)
and Sir William Hickes of Leyton (q.v.).

Essex has a special interest in the Diary because its first editor was
the 3rd Lord Braybrooke, see Neville.

PERRERS

Alice Perrers (d. 1400), mistress of Edward III, was probably a member of the Hertfordshire family of that name, although her enemies dismissed her as being of low birth. She began her career at court in the
service of Philippa of Hainault sometime before October 1366. When
the queen died in 1369 she was already the king's mistress and at once
assumed almost regal power, even sitting in courts with the King's
judges and directing that the findings should be in favour of those who
gave her the largest bribes. Among the manors bestowed on her by the

king were those of Steeple, St. Lawrence, and Gaynes in Upminster.
Her fall came when the Commons rose against her in 1676. She was
then banished and her lands forfeited. Her exile, however, was of
short duration. Later in the same year the king died and Alice returned to power.

The sentence of banishment was confirmed by the first Parliament of
Richard II, only to be revoked after her marriage with William de
Windsor, a soldier of fortune, in 1379. De Windsor was well able to
recover for her some of her lost estates, as we know from the Pipe
Rolls of 1380, which record how in rewarding him for his services
in France there was a:

> 'Grant in fee simple to William de Wyndsore, who is married
> to Alice de Perrers, of lands and tenements which she acqu-
> ired whilst single, and those which others acquired to her
> use forfeited by the judgement in Parliament against her.'

Sir William died in 1384. In 1400 Alice made her will, directing that
she should be buried in the parish church of Upminster on the north
side, before the altar of Our Lady the Virgin.

PETRE

The founder of the Essex family of Petre was Sir William Petre
(c.1505-72), Tudor Secretary and diplomat, builder of Ingatestone
Hall. In 1535 Petre, who was a Devon man, was appointed one of the
Visitors of the Monasteries under Thomas Cromwell. Three years
later he obtained a 40 year lease of the manor of Ingatestone from the
Abbess of Barking, and when the abbey was dissolved he bought the
land from the king and built himself a house there. To this original
estate he added large neighbouring estates in mid-Essex, and became
a man of influence in the county as well as in the State. His first wife
was Gertrude, daughter of Sir John Tyrell of Little Warley Hall. She
died in 1541, while Ingatestone was being built, leaving two infant
daughters. His second wife was Anne, widow of John Tyrell of Heron
Hall (q.v.)., and daughter of William Browne, Lord Mayor of London
in 1521.

Sir William Petre was Chancellor of the Order of the Garter, Secretary of State to Henry VIII, Edward VI, Mary, and was frequently consulted on high affairs of state by Elizabeth and her principal minister,
Cecil. Tudor Secretary, by F. G. Emmison, county archivist of Essex
for 30 years, is the most detailed and perceptive study of one who had
a unique place in the service of four Tudor Sovereigns.

Among Petre's principal benefactions was the virtual refounding of
Exeter College, Oxford, his own college. He died at Ingatestone Hall
and has an imposing monument in the church, probably by Cornelius
Cure, the Crown mason.

Sir William was succeeded by his only son John, 1st Baron Petre
(1549-1613), Lord Lieutenant of Essex, 1575-1603, who was created
Baron Petre of Writtle in 1603. In 1570 he married Mary, eldest daughter of Sir Edward Waldegrave of Borley. He was knighted in 1576,
three years after buying West Horndon Hall, which became the principal seat of the family.

The 1st Baron Petre left three sons and one daughter when he died in
1613. Next in the line was his eldest son, William, 2nd Baron Petre
(d. 1627), and in his turn Robert, the 3rd baron (d. 1637). Robert
left three sons, William, John, and Thomas, each of whom succeeded
to the title.

William, 4th Baron Petre (1622-84), came into national history by being accused by Titus Oates (1678) of complicity in the Popish Plot for the invasion of England. In 1683 he wrote to Charles II protesting his innocence, but he died in the Tower of London a few months later after five years' imprisonment.

An account of a visit to Thorndon Hall in the time of the 4th Lord Petre is found in The Travels of Cosmo de Medici, the 3rd Grand Duke of Tuscany.

John, the second of the three sons of the 3rd Baron Petre, succeeded in 1684 as 5th baron. At his death without issue he was followed by his brother, Thomas, the third son of the 3rd baron as 6th Baron Petre. He held the title for 21 years and found favour with James II. His cousin, Father Edward Petre (1631-99), was the king's confessor. Another source of influence came through his marriage with a daughter of Sir Thomas Clifton, of Lytham, Lancashire, one of the most influential Roman Catholics in the north of England. The 6th Lord Petre succeeded the 20th Earl of Oxford as Lord Lieutenant of Essex. His only son was the 7th Baron Petre.

The 8th Baron Petre (1713-42), was one of the leading botanists and gardeners of his day. Under his rule Thorndon was becoming the horticultural centre of England; but he died at the age of 29 in 1742 of smallpox. Thorndon was partly rebuilt by Leoni for the 8th Lord Petre, who was described by the botanist, Peter Collinson, as having the presence of a prince.

Robert Edward, 9th Baron Petre (1742-1801), had the house pulled down and (c.1763) commissioned James Paine to build a Palladian mansion on a site one mile to the north. The grounds were laid out by 'Capability' Brown, and Thorndon became a great social centre. Despite its owner's Roman Catholicism (and the fact that he was the grandson of the Jacobite Earl of Derwentwater), George III was entertained at Thorndon in 1778, and it may well have been his friendship with the Royal Family that enabled the 9th baron to play so successful a role in the movement for Catholic Emancipation, which eventually resulted in the Catholic Relief Acts of 1872 and 1891. In a portrait by Romney, the 9th baron is shown pointing to the plans for Thorndon Hall. He suffered less than some members of his family for his loyalty to Rome, but he had his disappointments. Perhaps the one he felt most keenly was that, having raised and equipped a body of 250 men for the defence of the county in 1798, his son, because he was a Roman Catholic, was not allowed to command it. The 9th lord was, however, Grand Master of the Freemasons of England, and took great pride in that.

Today, with four centuries of residence in the county, the Petres can claim to be the oldest noble family in Essex. The present baron is the 17th, and the family has now returned to its original home, Ingatestone Hall.

PLUME

Thomas Plume (1630-1704), benefactor of Maldon, was vicar of Greenwich, where Pepys records hearing him preach, from 1658 to 1704, and Archdeacon of Rochester from 1679-1704. He endowed a chair of astronomy and experimental philosophy at Cambridge. To Maldon, his birthplace, he bequeathed a valuable library which is housed in a building attached to the old tower of the ruined church of St. Peter. Plume was a benefactor of Maldon Grammar School, and gave £200 to build a workhouse for the poor of the town, together with £1,000 to establish a factory for weaving sack-cloth to employ the inmates.

POUND

The Rev. James Pound of Wanstead (1669-1724), astronomer, was presented to the rectory in 1707 by Sir Richard Child. He had previously been in the service of the East India Company as a medical chaplain. While at Wanstead he devoted himself to the study of astronomy, especially to the satellites of Jupiter and Saturn. He was assisted in his studies by his nephew, the Rev. James Bradley (1693-1762), who discovered the aberration of light and was referred to by Newton as 'the best astronomer in Europe'.

POYNTZ

Members of the Poyntz family were lords of the manor of North Ockendon for nearly 300 years from a date near the beginning of the 14th century, when the first Nicholas Poyntz arrived. They are commemorated by monuments in North Ockendon church. The earliest of these is a brass with effigies of William Poyntz and Elizabeth, his wife. The next is a brass inscription to John Poyntz, who like many of this distinguished family was a member of the Royal Household. Two of the poetical epistles of Sir Thomas Wyatt, the elder, are addressed to him. He was 'Sewer to Queen Katherine of Aragon' at the Field of the Cloth of Gold. This John Poyntz who died without issue, was the subject of a portrait by Holbein. He was succeeded as lord of the manor by his brother, Thomas, whose heir, Gabriel, was the last of the Essex line. One member of the family is named in Shakespeare's Henry IV.

Gabriel Poyntz (d. 1608), who has a magnificent tomb at North Ockendon, was High Sheriff in 1577 and 1589. He was knighted in 1604. His wife was Etheldreda, daughter of Peter Cutts of Debden. Gabriel was responsible for several monuments to his family.

The most interesting Poyntz inscription in North Ockendon church is to Thomas, father of the last of the line. It recalls the part he played at the Reformation while living as a London merchant at Antwerp, where he gave hospitality for a year to William Tyndale, the translator of the Bible. It was at the door of Thomas Poyntz's house that Tyndale was seized by Thomas Cromwell's emissaries and carried off into Austria, where he was condemned to be burnt for heresy. For exerting himself in the cause of Tyndale, Poyntz was condemned to the same death, but he escaped from prison, and, as mentioned above, lived to succeed his brother, John, at North Ockendon.

PURCHAS

Samuel Purchas (c.1575-1626), writer of travels, was born at Thaxted. While at St. John's College, Cambridge, he 'first conceived with this travelling genius whereof without travelling he hath travelled ever since.' In 1604 he was presented by James I to the living of Eastwood, and there his interest in the adventures of mariners was increased. For the rest of his life he devoted much of his time to the collection of the narratives published in Purchas his Pilgrimes, and other works, culminating in the 1626 issue in five volumes of Hakluytus Posthumus or Purchas his Pilgrimes,

contayning a History of the World in Sea Voyages and Lande Travells,
etc. Among the travels recorded are those of Andrew Battell, who
sailed from Leigh in 1589 and returned 21 years later in 1610, while
Purchas was at Eastwood, bringing with him tales of Central Africa
and South America. Accounts of Purchas's last days agree that he
ran into financial difficulties; but while one report states that he
died in a debtors' prison, another states that he was saved from this
by the kindness of Charles I, who presented him with the revenues of
a deanery in the last year of his life.

PYNCHON

William Pynchon (1590-1662), founder of Springfield, Massachusetts,
was born at Springfield, Essex, the elder son of John Pynchon (d.1610),
whose family owned land at Writtle, Widford, Broomfield, and other
nearby villages. He married Anna, daughter of William Andrew (or
Andrews) of Triwell, Northants. and had one son and three daughters
when in 1630 he left Essex for New England to settle, first at Dorchester, later at Roxbury, near Boston. The Pynchon family was
included in the Heralds' Visitations of Essex in 1612 and 1634, and
one of William's cousins married Richard Weston, later 1st Earl of
Portland and Chancellor of the Exchequer (q.v.) of Skreens, Roxwell.

Pynchon sailed out with the Winthrop fleet to join the Massachusetts
Bay Company, in which he quickly established himself as a prosperous
fur-trader. Within a short time of his arrival he was appointed a magistrate and treasurer of the plantation. In 1635 he appears as one of
the 11 members of the commission for military affairs established by
the General Court. Throughout these early years he played the role
of a wise and moderate counsellor, constantly advising caution when
more zealous settlers like Hooker (q.v.) and Eliot (q.v.) wanted to
adopt policies which in Pynchon's opinion would inevitably lead to war.
At the same time he helped the settlement to build up a trading post and
establish itself on a firm basis of law and sound government.

After 22 years in Massachusetts, Pynchon returned to England to live,
first at Hackney, later at Wraysbury, Bucks., where he died. His
closest friend in Massachusetts, John Winthrop (q.v.), Governor and
historian of New England, had died in 1649.

John Pynchon (1626-1703), son of William, was born at Springfield,
Essex, and emigrated with his father. He was elected town-treasurer
of Springfield, Mass: in 1650, shortly before his father's return to
England, and served as a magistrate there for 21 years. He shared
in all his father's interests, continuing his commercial enterprises
by laying out new plantations on the banks of the Connecticut River,
expanding the family interests in the fur trade, and generally following
in his father's footsteps until he had become the principal landowner
and fur-trader in Western Massachusetts. To these interests he added mining amd milling ventures, and finally established a reputation as
a military leader in defensive actions against Indian and French mar-
auders.

The Pynchons kept an account of cases in which they adjudicated from
1639 to 1702. The record has great historical value as evidence of the
shrewd administration of Colonial justice at grass-roots level.

See Joseph H. Smith: Colonial Justice in Western Massachusetts
                           (Harvard (1961)

PYRTON

The Pyrtons succeeded the Bourchiers at Little Bentley and remained there until the 17th century. Sir William (d. 1490), who is commemorated in a brass in the parish church, was Captain of Guisnes in Picardy.

QUARLES

Francis Quarles (1591-1644), poet, was born at Stewards, Romford, the son of James Quarles, Clerk to the Green Cloth and Surveyor General of Victualling to the Navy, two lucrative offices. On leaving Cambridge, Francis was entered as a student at Lincoln's Inn. In 1613 he was in the retinue of four gentlemen in the train of the Earl of Arundel at the marriage to the Elector Palatine of the Princess Elizabeth, to whom he became Cupbearer. Among other offices held by Quarles were that of secretary to Archbishop Ussher and City Chronologer.

In 1618 he married Ursula Woodgate, by whom he had 18 children. Several baptisms and burials are recorded in the parish registers of Roxwell, where he made his home.

Quarles spent two years composing his Emblems, many of them written while staying at Brent Hall, Finchingfield, with his friend, Edward Benlowes. He became one of the most widely-read religious poets of his age. There are several references to Essex persons in his verses - for example, the elegy on the death of the wife of Sir William Lucky, daughter of Sir Gamaliel Capel of Rookwood Hall.

RADCLIFFE

The association of the Radcliffe family with Essex began with the marriage in 1444 of Sir John Radcliffe of Radcliffe Tower in Lancashire and Elizabeth, only child and heir of Walter, 7th Lord Fitz-Walter of Woodham Walter. His son, also John (1452?-96), was summoned to Parliament in 1485 as Baron FitzWalter. He took part in Perkin Warbeck's conspiracy, was attainted in 1495 and beheaded the following year.

Robert Radcliffe, his son (1483-1542), obtained the reversal of his father's attainder in 1506 and gained the favour of Henry VIII. He was created 1st Viscount FitzWalter in 1525, 1st Earl of Sussex at the Field of the Cloth of Gold in 1529. In 1540 he was appointed Great Chamberlain.

Henry, 2nd Earl of Sussex (1506?-57), supported Mary in 1553. Little is known of his public work, but he is remembered for being given leave by Mary to wear his 'cappe, coyf, or night cappe' in her Royal Presence.

Thomas, 3rd Earl (1526?-83), came to prominence as the result of his part in suppressing Wyatt's rebellion. In 1556 he was appointed Lord-Deputy of Ireland, where he proved a vigorous administrator, although he failed to subdue Shane O'Neill (see FitzWilliam). After his return he suppressed the Northern Rebellion in 1569, showing more leniency in dealing with the rebels than the queen thought right. Elizabeth rewarded his services in 1573 with the grant of New Hall, Boreham, where he died without issue in 1583 and was buried in the church. His widow, Frances, aunt of Sir Philip Sidney, founded Sidney-Sussex College, Cambridge, under her will dated 1596. The pheon, the heraldic symbol of the Sidneys, is the college badge.

At the 3rd earl's death the Boreham estate passed to Henry, 4th Earl of Sussex (1530?-93), who was M.P. for Maldon, 1555. He was succeeded by his only child.

Robert, 5th earl (1569?-1629), who acted as Earl Marshal in 1597 and 1601, was one of the peers commissioned to try the Earl of Essex in 1601. The 5th earl held several offices in Essex. He was Governor of Harwich and Landguard Fort, and Lord Lieutenant of Essex for 20 years from 1603. In 1626 he was Bearer of the Orb at the Coronation of Charles I. His presence at Court meant that most of his duty as Lord Lieutenant fell on his two deputies, Sir Francis Barrington (q.v.) and the 1st Lord Maynard (q.v.). The 5th earl sold New Hall to George Villiers, Marquis of Buckingham (afterwards Duke) in 1622 and resigned the lord lieutenancy. In 1625, however, he was reappointed to hold the office jointly with the Earl of Warwick. This he considered a slight, but continued in office until his death in 1629. He was buried at Boreham. His friend, Sir Walter Mildmay (q.v.), was one of the executors of his will.

With the death of the 5th earl (his four children having died before him), the viscountcy and earldom of Sussex passed to his kinsman, Edward Radcliffe, at whose death the titles became extinct. There are fine effigies of the 1st, 2nd and 3rd Earls of Sussex in Boreham church.

RAMPSTON

Robert Rampston of Chingford is commemorated by a brass (1589). He was the son of Rowland Rampston, who bought the manors of Gowers and Buckerells in Chingford in 1544, and uncle of Rowland Rampston, who has a brass at Great Parndon. Rowland of Great Parndon was Robert Rampston of Chingford's heir. The Rampston family founded charities and are commemorated by brasses in a considerable number of parishes in south-west Essex.

See Mill Stephenson: Monumental Brasses

RAMSEY

Dame Mary Ramsey, who founded Halstead Grammar School in 1594, was the daughter of a Bristol merchant named Dale. Her husband, Sir Thomas Ramsey, was Lord Mayor of London.

RAY

John Ray (1627-1705), naturalist and founder of the modern study of botany, was born at Black Notley, the son of the village blacksmith. He was educated at Braintree Grammar School, Catherine Hall and Trinity College, Cambridge, of which he became a Fellow. In 1658 he began his botanical tours of England and Wales in the company of his friend and former pupil, Francis Willoughby. His first published work (1660) was a county flora of Cambridgeshire. In 1662 Ray and Willoughby resolved to compile a systematic description of all animal and plant life, Ray to be responsible for the plants. As a Dissenter, Ray was obliged to resign his Fellowship when the Act of Uniformity came into force. Friends came to his aid and he was enabled to travel on the Continent to study the flora of Western Europe. In 1667 he was elected a Fellow of the Royal Society.

In 1671 he married Margaret, daughter of John Oakley, of Oxford-shire, by whom he had four daughters. After Willoughby's death in 1672, Ray applied himself to completing and editing his friend's work. For two years he lived at Faulkbourne Hall, the home of Edward Bullock. After his mother's death he removed to Dewlands, Black Notley, the house he had built for her. Ray's Dewlands stood until 1900, when it was burnt down and replaced by a new house.

Ray's greatest work, the History of Plants, was published in three volumes in 1686, 1688, and 1704. In it he described and classified more than 11,000 species. All he received for the work was £5, al-though it remained a standard work for more than 200 years. His bio-grapher, Charles Raven, says of Ray:

'His greatness is that in a time of transition and universal turmoil he saw the need for precise and ordered knowledge, set himself to test the old and explore the new, and by dint of immense labour in the field and in the study laid the found-ations of modern science in the many branches of zoology and botany.'

See C. E. Raven: John Ray

RAYLEIGH, Barons See STRUTT

RAYMOND

Sir Thomas Raymond (1626-83), judge, of Downham, was the son of Robert Raymond of Bowers Gifford. In 1679 he was knighted and rai-sed to the Bench. The same year he became a Baron of the Exchequer. The following year he passed, first, to the Court of Common Pleas, later to the King's Bench. Roger North relates of him that two old women who were tried before him at Exeter for witchcraft were con-victed, and one of them hanged, because he failed to point out to the jury how irrational their confessions were. Sir Thomas was buried in Downham church.

Robert, 1st Baron Raymond (1673-1733), judge, son of Sir Thomas, was admitted to Gray's Inn in 1682, when he was only nine. His father who died nine months later, was determined to see him a member during his own lifetime. He is remembered for his Reports, which begin in 1694, when he was 20, and extend over the 38 years to 1732, the year before his death. They were published in 1743 and have been reprinted several times under the editorship of distinguished lawyers.

He sat as M.P. for Bishop's Castle in the Parliaments of 1710 and 1714. In 1710 he was knighted and appointed Solicitor General; in 1720 he became Attorney General, in 1724 a judge of the King's Bench, and in 1725 Chief Justice. He was raised to the peerage in 1731 as Baron Raymond of Abbots Langley in Hertfordshire, in the church of which there is an elaborate monument to his memory.

REBOW

The Rebows of Wivenhoe Park, a family of Flemish extraction, settl-ed at Colchester in the middle of the 17th century and maintained their connection with the borough for nearly 300 years. In 1685, John Rebow, who bought Colchester Castle, received a grant of arms. His son, Isaac, made a fortune out of South Sea Stock and was knighted by William III. He served as Recorder of Colchester and M.P. His grand-son, Isaac Lemyng Rebow, married the daughter of Captain Martin,

who owned an estate at Wivenhoe. Their son, Isaac, married his
cousin, Mary Martin of Alresford Hall. They had no son, but left
three daughters. The eldest of these married, in 1796, General
Francis Slater, of Chesterfield, who took the name of Rebow. He
died in 1845 and again there was no male heir. In 1835 the general's
daughter had married, as her second husband, John Gurdon of Norfolk,
who also took the name of Rebow. He died in 1870. By his second wife,
who was the fourth daughter of the 2nd Earl of Norbury, he left an
only son, Hector John Gurdon-Rebow, who was mayor of Colchester
in 1885. He died at Woodhall Spa in 1931, aged 85.

RENDALL

Canon G. H. Rendall, who died at Dedham in 1945 aged 93, came to
Essex after being headmaster of Charterhouse, 1897 to 1911; principal of University College, 1890 to 1897; vice-chancellor of Victoria
University, 1890-1894. He will be remembered in the county for his
Dedham in History and Dedham Described and Desciphered. He will
also be remembered for his conviction that Edward de Vere, 17th
Earl of Oxford (q.v.) was the author of the sonnets, classical poems,
and certain plays attributed to Shakespeare. His reasons for this belief are propounded in Shakespeare's Sonnets and Edward de Vere,
and Personal Clues in Shakespeare's Poems and Sonnets. Among his
pamphlets on the subject are Shakespeare in Essex and East Anglia,
and Shakespeare's Handwriting and Spelling.

REPTON

Humphry Repton (1752-1818), landscape gardener, was born at Bury
St. Edmunds. He built up a large practice, to which his two sons,
John Adey and George Stanley, contributed architectural features.
This successful venture followed two business schemes in which he
lost a fortune, and was interesting in that he came to gardening with
little more knowledge than he had gained through studying botany as
a hobby. He was so resourceful in his landscaping that he came to be
employed by landowners all over England, providing beautifully-prod-
uced reports, known as 'Red Books', on his commissions for wealthy
clients. The special features of these was the incorporation of a flap,
which could be raised to enable comparisons to be made between the
garden before and after his proposed treatment.

Repton did work in Essex at Rivenhall Place; Claybury Hall, Woodford; Stubbers, North Ockendon; Hill Hall, Theydon Mount; and
Woodford Hall. He lived for the last 45 years of his life in a cottage
at Hare Street, Romford.

See J. C. Loudon: Humphry Repton , (1752-1818)

REYNOLDS

James Reynolds was the name of two judges, father and son, during
the reign of George II. The family lived at Helions Bumpstead and
was known for its Royalist sympathies.

RICH

Richard Rich, 1st Baron Rich of Leighs (or Leez) Priory (1500-68),
Lord Chancellor, rose to wealth and power at the Dissolution of the
Monasteries. He was appointed Solicitor-General in 1533. Two years
later he obtained the profitable office of Chirographer of the King's

Bench. In 1537 he became Speaker of the House of Commons. In 1548 he reached the peak of his political career when he was constituted Lord Chancellor and raised to the peerage.

His connection with Essex arose from his privileged position as Chancellor of the Court of Augmentations at the Dissolution. He acquired, as they became available, Leighs Priory itself, where he built himself a fine house, 100 manors in the county and 20 advowsons. As he held the office from 1536 to 1544 he was able to take his pick, or as Fuller put it, when the abbey lands passed through his hands many of them 'stuck to his fingers'.

Rich represented Essex in Parliament - first, as M.P. for Colchester, later for the county - from 1529 to 1548, the year of his elevation to the peerage. He only remained Lord Chancellor for three years. The period 1551 to 1553 was a tricky one for him. He lost the lord chancellorship when his involvement with the Duke of Somerset came to light. In 1553, like many other Essex public men, he signed the proclamation in favour of Lady Jane Grey; but when he saw how events were turning he quickly took Mary's side, welcoming her personally on her arrival in Essex and demonstrating his loyalty by becoming active in persecuting Protestants.

In later life he retired to Leighs, and by charitable works gained local credit. His most valuable benefactions were the founding of Felsted School in 1564 and the endowing of the Rich Almshouses. Felsted's original schoolhouse is still preserved, but it went out of use as a schoolroom in 1866.

At his death at Rochford Hall, his other Essex estate, he was buried in Felsted church, where in 1621 his grandson set up a splendid monument to him. This has recently been restored.

Robert, 2nd Baron Rich (1538-81), was created a Knight of the Bath at Elizabeth's coronation. He was one of the judges who tried Thomas Howard, Duke of Norfolk (q.v.), for his complicity in the Ridolfi Plot. His successor, Robert, 3rd Baron Rich (d. 1619), married Penelope Devereux (q.v.), daughter of Walter Devereux, 1st Earl of Essex, and the Stella of Sidney's _Astrophel and Stella_.

The 3rd Lord Rich married as his second wife Frances, daughter of Sir Christopher Wray, Lord Chief Justice. She was the widow of Sir George St. Paul. Chamberlain in the _Letters_ (21st December, 1616) wrote:

> 'The Lord Rich, after much wooing and several attempts in divers places, hath at last alighted on the Lady Sain Poll, a rich widow in Lincolnshire.'

Her wealth is thought to have enabled her husband to purchase the title of Earl of Warwick for £10,000 from James I.

Robert, 2nd Earl of Warwick (1587-1658), son of the 1st earl by his first wife, took a prominent part in the colonisation of the Bermudas and the settlement of the New England colonies. He was M.P. for Maldon before succeeding to the earldom in 1619. On returning to Essex from New England he became the leader of the Puritan party in the county, raising forces for Parliament at the outbreak of the civil wars. Soon after this he gained control of the Fleet and was appointed Lord High Admiral under the Long Parliament.

The 2nd Earl of Warwick was appointed Lord Lieutenant of Essex with Robert Radcliffe, 5th Earl of Sussex (q.v.) in 1625, and sole holder

of the office in 1629; but after boldly opposing the payment of Ship
Money and the revival of the forest courts in Hainault and Waltham
Forests he was replaced as Lord Lieutenant by Lord Maynard (q.v.)
in 1635. Again, however, he became Lord Lieutenant after a lapse
of seven years, and this time the lieutenancy of Norfolk was added,
together with an appointment as Captain General of London and the
adjacent counties. He served as Speaker of the House of Lords in
1642 and again in 1648.

As the second earl applied the whole force of his dominant personality to persuading the Navy and Militia to support the Parliamentary
cause he was the target of Royalist attack, and Leez suffered assault
by troops under Lord Goring and Sir Charles Lucas (q.v.). Between
1,000 and 2,000 men, including about 100 horse, arrived at the gates
on the morning of 10th June, 1648. The story of the siege is vividly
told by the earl's steward, Arthur Wilson, whose account concludes:
> 'So we lost some horses, two brass guns, a great part
> (though not half) of our arms, barrels of powder, some
> match and bullet and, after drinking some twenty hogs-
> heads of beer, one hogshead of sack, and eating up all
> our meat and killing at least one hundred deer in the three
> parks about the house, we were rid of our ill guests.'

The great 2nd Earl of Warwick died at Warwick House, Holborn, in
1658 and was buried at Felsted. Edmund Calamy, the elder (q.v.),
preached the funeral sermon. With him the family had reached the
summit of its glory. Leighs, or Leez, was then so fine a seat that a
lady who saw it said to Warwick: 'My lord, you had need make sure
of heaven or else, when you die, you will be a great loser.'

His grandson and heir, Robert, married Frances, youngest daughter
of Oliver Cromwell; but he predeceased his grandfather, leaving no
issue.

Charles Rich, 4th Earl of Warwick, who succeeded on the death of
the 3rd earl at the age of 23 in 1659, was the second son of the 2nd
earl. He married Mary Boyle (1625-78), the youngest of the seven
daughters of Richard Boyle (1566-1643), 1st Earl of Cork. She is
remembered for her diary, which formed the basis of an autobiography,
both of which survived in a manuscript and were the sources for the
Life by Charlotte Fell Smith (q.v.). Their only son died young, so
when the 4th earl died in 1673 he was without issue, and the title became extinct in the Rich family.

RIDLEY

The family firm of Ridley, corn millers, maltsters and brewers, was
founded early in the 19th century by Thomas Dixon Ridley, who established himself as a miller with water mills on the Chelmer. In the
1840s brewing and malting were added to the interests of the business.
The company, T. D. Ridley & Sons, was incorporated in 1906, and
the Ridley sign on scores of characteristically Essex inns quickly became a familiar part of the Essex scene.

RIGBY

Richard Rigby (d. 1730), financier, rebuilt Mistley Hall with profits
acquired by speculation in South Sea Stock. Horace Walpole described it as 'the charmingest place by Nature and the most trumpery by
Art' that ever he saw. His son of the same name (1722-88), who held

the office of Paymaster General to the Forces from 1768 to 1784,
extended both buildings and grounds. In 1784 he retired to Bath and
let Mistley to the 4th Viscount Galway, who had married the daughter
of Daniel Matthews of Felix Hall, Kelvedon. Lord Galway left Mistley
in 1792. Later it passed into the possession of the Baron Rivers of
Sudeley. Rigby's house was demolished about 1844.

ROCHESTER

The Rochester family were Essex landowners in Tudor times, notably
at Terling. In 1547, Sir Robert Rochester, a devout Roman Catholic,
was Comptroller of the Household to Mary. In August 1551 he was
summoned to appear before the Council and ordered to ensure that the
saying and hearing of mass at Copt Hall, Epping, where the Princess
Mary was residing, was discontinued. He did not, and perhaps could
not, carry out the order and on the 23rd August he again appeared
before the Council. This time he flatly refused to obey the order,
boldly stating that he would rather go to prison than carry such a
message to his mistress. The following day he was lodged in the
Fleet prison, and a week later removed to the Tower.

The following March he was released, and at Mary's request allowed
to resume his duties as Comptroller. On Mary's accesion to the throne
in 1553 he was reappointed Comptroller of the Royal Household, elected a Knight of the Shire, and created a Knight of the Bath. For the
remainder of his life he was one of the queen's most trusted advisers.
When Elizabeth was imprisoned in the Tower, and a warrant was prepared for her execution, it was Sir Robert Rochester who interceded
with the queen on her behalf. He died in 1557 and was buried in the
Priory church of the Charterhouse at Sheen.

ROCHFORD, Earls of See NASSAU

ROE

The family of Roe, or Rowe, gave three Lord Mayors to London within 40 years: 1. Sir Thomas, of Highams Hall, Walthamstow,
                   Lord Mayor in 1568
              2. Sir William, Lord Mayor in 1590
              3. Sir Henry, Lord Mayor in 1607

The most eminent member was Sir Thomas Roe (1580-1644), great-
grandson of the Sir Thomas who was Lord Mayor in 1568, grandson
of Sir Henry, Lord Mayor in 1607, and son of Robert Roe of Leyton,
where he was born. Sir Thomas Roe became a courtier at the end of
Elizabeth's reign. He was knighted by James I in 1604, served as political adviser to Elizabeth, Queen of Bohemia, and was Chancellor of
the Order of the Garter. His activities fall under the two headings of
adventure and diplomacy, which were then so happily combined. One
of his earliest adventures was to explore the Amazon, penetrating up
river for a distance of 300 miles, which was further than any European traveller had gone before. He was sent by the Board of the East
India Company, who bore all the expenses of the mission, as the fully
accredited Ambassador to the Great Mogul, as the Emperor was then
called. An account of the venture is found in The Embassy of Sir
Thomas Roe to the Court of the Great Mogul, which William Foster
of the India Office edited for the Hakluyt Society in 1899. It covers
the years 1615-19, and is based on Roe's journal and correspondence.

On returning to England he was elected M.P. for Cirencester; but
his stay was short. On his way home from India he had visited Persia,
so in view of the great success of his earlier mission, which may be
said to have laid the foundations of British India, he was sent in 1621
as Ambassador to Ottoman Porte, where he remained for seven years,
improving relations between England and the East, and among other
things persuading Bethlen Gabor, prince of Transylvania, to join the
Protestant alliance. Before he returned to England from this mission
he had succeeded in liberating about 700 slaves. He brought home as
a present to the king the MS. of the Bible known as the <u>Codex Alex-</u>
<u>andrinus</u>. Roe's own MSS. are in the Bodleian.

On his way home in 1628 he called on the Princess Elizabeth, by then
Queen of Bohemia. During the following year, 1629, he visited
Gustavus Adolphus, King of Sweden, and was able to mediate successfully between the kings of Sweden and Poland. For these services
he received a present of £2,000 from Gustavus.

In 1640 Roe was elected M.P. for the University of Oxford, but again
his Parliamentary career was short. This time he was sent on a mission as Ambassador extraordinary to Ratisbon, where the Emperor
Ferdinand remarked that 'he had known many plenipotentiaries, but
he never knew a real Ambassador till he met with Roe.'

This was his last embassy. On his return the king gave him the manor
of Woodford, where he died in 1644 and was buried in the parish church

Roe was a friend of Ben Jonson, who was also friendly with Roe's
neighbours, the Wroths of Loughton Hall (q.v.). He has lines:
> Roe, and my joy to name, thou'rt now to go,
> Countries and climes, manners and men to know.

Sir William Roe, his uncle, owned land at Epping. He was godfather
at the christening of John Foxe, grandson of the martyrologist, in
1593.Sir William rebuilt the old manor house of Benstedes, Walthamstow. He died in 1596 and has a brass in St. Mary's church, Walthamstow.

Sir Thomas was also a friend of Sir Walter Raleigh, whom he visited
in the Tower and of Raleigh's cousin, Sir Edward Denny (q.v.) of
Waltham Abbey.

At Roe's death it was said of him:
> 'Those who knew him well have said that there was nothing
> wanting in him towards the accomplishment of a scholar,
> gentleman or courtier, that also as he was learned so was
> he a great encourager and promoter of learning and learned
> men.'

There is a portrait of Sir Thomas Roe by M. J. Van Miereveldt in
the National Portrait Gallery. A copy by Robert John Boss hangs in
the Reading Room of Leyton Public Library.

<u>See</u>: Sir William Foster: <u>England's Quest of Eastern Trade</u> (1923)

ROGERS

John Rogers, vicar of Chigwell and Prebendary of St. Pancras, assisted Tyndal in translating the Scriptures into English. For preaching
a sermon at Paul's Cross in which he exhorted the people to stand fast
in the faith they had been taught 'in King Edward's days', he was condemned to death in 1555. A Pardon was offered him at the stake if he
would recant; but he refused and suffered martyrdom.

ROUND

The Round family came into Essex in 1726, when James Round (d.1745) bought the Birch Hall estate and rebuilt the hall. This fine Georgian house was pulled down by Charles Gray Round and replaced by a great house of Portland stone, which in turn was demolished about 1955.

John Horace Round (1856-1928), historian, was the son of John Round, lord of the manor of West Bergholt, Suffolk. His maternal grandfather was Horace Smith, one of the authors of Rejected Addresses. Despite bad health he took first-class honours in Modern History at Balliol. His scholarship was profound. He had no equal in his day in the scientific study of original documents and charters; but his passion for controversy and bitter destructive criticism gained him many enemies.

Most of Round's work is scattered through the journals and transactions of learned societies. He planned no large-scale works, but papers published separately were collected into such volumes as Geoffrey de Mandeville, Earl of Essex; Feudal England; The Commune of London; and Peerage and Pedigree. His critical examination of pedigrees, which destroyed several claims to ancient noble ancestry, led to his being given in 1914 the specially created office of honorary historical adviser to the Crown in peerage cases.

Round contributed twelve introductions to Domesday to Victoria County Histories. His editing of Pipe Rolls and Calendars of Records, in which he delighted, earned high praise. Unfortunately, his intolerance, which doubtless arose out of his passion for accuracy, and might even have been praiseworthy in a scholar, amounted in him to a serious defect of character. His vitriolic attacks on Professor Freeman showed his petulance and bitterness at their worst. It is much to be regretted that he refused to write the history of Colchester, on which he was an authority, for the 'Historic Towns' series, simply because Freeman was the editor. It should, however, be remembered that he suffered all his life from appalling health. He was a distinguished president of the Essex Archaelogical Society.

RUGGLES-BRISE

The Ruggles family originated in Clare, just over the Suffolk border. Spains Hall, Finchingfield, was bought in 1760 by Samuel Ruggles of Bocking, a wealthy clothier, whose brother, Thomas Ruggles, married Ann, daughter of Joshua Brise of Cavendish, Suffolk. At Samuel's death, Spains Hall passed to his nephew, the son of Thomas and Ann. This nephew was Thomas Ruggles (1737?-1813), then of Clare, a justice of the peace who became deeply concerned with the plight of the agricultural workers of north Essex at the time of the 1795 crisis, which led to the adoption of what became known as the Speenhamland System for the relief of the poor. In a book entitled The History of the Poor (1797), Ruggles expressed his firm belief 'that, in no instance, through any breadth of country, did the additional increase the poor received to their income, from wages, gratuitious donations, and parochial relief, approach the increased price of bread'. This work went through three editions. Thomas Ruggles also wrote critically of the legal profession in a book entitled The Barrister, or Strictures on the Education Proper for the Bar, and he contributed a paper on the ducal family of Devonshire to Archaelogia. He was a lifelong friend of Arthur Young (q.v.), who had been at school with him at Lavenham. Ruggles contributed to Young's Annals of Agriculture.

Thomas Ruggles was succeeded by his eldest son, John, who com-
bined the name of Brise with his own, assuming it by royal licence
in 1827 on succeeding to the Suffolk estate. His only son, Sir
Samuel Ruggles-Brise (1825-99), married Marianne Weyland,
youngest daughter of Sir Edward Bowyer-Smijth, 10th baronet, of
Hill Hall, Epping. He was M.P. for the Eastern Division of
Essex, 1865 to 1883. His son was Archibald Weyland Ruggles-
Brise (d.1939), who was succeeded by his eldest son, Col. Sir
Edward Archibald Ruggles-Brise, Bart. (d.1942). M.P. for
Maldon, 1922-3 and 1924 until his death, who was created a baro-
net in 1935. He married twice. His first wife was Agatha, elder
daughter of John Henry Gurney, of Keswick Hall, Norfolk. His
second wife was Lucy Barbara, daughter of the Right Rev. Walter
Ruthven Pym, Bishop of Bombay. Sir Edward's successor in the
baronetcy was Col. Sir John Ruggles-Brise (b.1908), who succeeded
Sir Francis Whitmore as Lord Lieutenant.

Sir Evelyn Ruggles-Brise (1857-1935), prison reformer, was born
at Spains Hall, the second son of family of five sons and seven
daughters. The father was Sir Samuel Ruggles-Brise (1825-99); his
mother, the fourth daughter of Sir Edward Bowyer-Smijth of Hill
Hall, Epping, later an open prison for women. He was appointed to
the Home Office in 1881, and from 1884 to 1892 served as private
secretary to four Home Secretaries. In 1895 he became chairman of
the Prison Commission, and held the office until he retired twenty-
six years later in 1921.

Ruggles-Brise felt strongly that young offenders between the ages of
sixteen and twenty-one should not be treated in the same way as adult
prisoners, and in 1901 borstal training was introduced on his
initiative, with the emphasis on training rather than mere detention.
Over the gateway at the original Borstal, near Rochester, is an inscription which reads:
　　'He determined to save the young and careless from a
　　wasted life of crime. Through his vision and persistence
　　a system of repression has been gradually replaced by
　　one of leading and training. We shall remember him as
　　one who believed in his fellow men'.
In 1924 he published Prison Reform at Home and Abroad.

　　See:　Shane Leslie: Sir Evelyn Ruggles-Brise: A memoir of the
　　　　　　　　　　　　Founder of Borstal (1938).

RUSSELL

Sir William Russell (1641-1703) bought Stubbers,North Ockendon, in
1689. The estate took its name from William Stubbers, who lived there
from 1438 to 1483; but it was William Coys who had made it famous.
Russell, an alderman and sheriff of London, who had been knighted in
1679, settled at Stubbers, and in the manner of his age proceeded to
write a book of good advice to his son. The following are a few
characteristic examples of his all too worldly wisdom:
　　'Let your love be guided by reason, not fancy.'
　　'An only child is commonly most advantageous; for
　　she possesses not only all her parents' love; but all
　　their estate.'

Sir William's homily was published in 1815 by his great-grandson, John
Russell. Each page of his account-book is headed:

'Laus Deo'; each yearly balance concludes:
'Soli Deo Gloria'.
A good story is told of him that he lent large sums of money to
Charles II, who appeared to forget the debt. So Sir William offered
Nell Gwynn one hundred guineas to extract the money from the king
on his behalf. Charles was too smart for them:
> 'Tell me, Nell,' he said; 'how much has he offered you?'
> 'Just one hundred guineas,' she replied.
> 'Well,' said the king, 'I'll give you two hundred to say no more
> about it'.

Sir William was buried at St. Dunstan's-in-the-East.

SACKVILLE

The Sackville family owned Mount Bures from the 12th to the 16th
century.

Charles Sackville, 6th Earl of Dorset and Earl of Middlesex (1638-
1706), son of the 5th Earl and Frances, daughter of Lionel, 3rd Earl
of Middlesex (see Cranfield), came into Essex on succeeding to the
Copt Hall estate, Epping. Charles II dined there in 1660, William III
in 1698, and Princess Anne (afterwards Queen) in 1688, when her life
was believed to be in danger. According to Macaulay, the escape came
one night when:
> 'At dead of night she rose, and, accompanied by her friend Sarah
> (Churchill) and two other female attendants, stole down the back
> stairs in a dressing gown and slippers. The fugitives gained the
> open street unchallenged. A hackney coach was waiting for them
> there. Two men guarded the humble vehicle. One of them was
> Compton, Bishop of London, the princess's old tutor; the other
> was the magnificent and accomplished Dorset, whom the extremity
> of public danger had roused from his luxurious repose. The coach
> drove instantly to Aldersgate Street..... there the princess
> passed the night. On the following morning she set out for Epping
> Forest. In that wild tract Dorset possessed a venerable mansion,
> the favourite resort, during many years, of wits and poets.'

Charles Sackville of Copt Hall was the Earl of Dorset who wrote the
song:
> To all you ladies now at land
> We men at sea indite; etc.

The earl and his friends were a wild set (See: W. Addison: Epping
Forest), and there were many riotous assemblies at Copt Hall while
he was there. It was also used as a retreat for poets who wanted to
retire for a time in order to write. Thomas Shadwell wrote the first
Act of The Squire of Alsatia there. While serving as Lord Chamberlain of the Household, 1689-97, the earl spent most of his time away
from Court at Copt Hall. He sold the estate in 1701, when he retired
to Knole, taking most of the best furniture and pictures with him. He
was succeeded at Copt Hall by Thomas Webster, M.P. for Colchester.

SALMON

Camden described Leigh as 'a pretty little town stocked with lusty
seamen'. Among the best known of these seafaring families were the
Salmons, who were already there in the twelfth century. Their
memorials are to be seen in the old parish church. One member of

the family was installed Master of Trinity House in 1588 - Armada
year. His son married a sister of Lancelot Andrewes, Bishop of
Winchester. When he died in 1641, aged seventy-four, a fine monument to his memory was erected in the church.

SANDYS

Pedigrees of the Sandys family are given in the Visitation of
Cumberland, 1615, and the Visitations of Essex, 1558 and 1612; but
they are unreliable. The most distinguished member of the family
closely associated with Essex was Edwin Sandys (1516-88), Archbishop of York, 1577-88, and builder of Edwins Hall, Woodham
Ferrers, a manor which had belonged to the family from the beginning of the century. He was born at Hawkshead in the Lake District,
and educated at St. John's College, Cambridge. From 1549 to 1553
he was Master of Catherine Hall, serving as vice-chancellor of the
University in 1553. When Edward VI died that year, Sandys boldly
proclaimed Lady Jane Grey queen in the name of the University. For
this he was thrown into prison; but helped to escape by a sympathetic
gaolor. On his release he made his way to the house of his step-
father at Woodham Ferrers; but within two hours of his arrival warning came through that his place of hiding had been discovered and he
would be arrested the same night. Leaving hurriedly, he went to the
house of a ship-master named Mawer, who had undertaken to get him
out of the country. Mawer lived at Milton, near the thriving little
port of Leigh, and there forty or fifty mariners gathered to welcome
Sandys and hear him preach. Such was his affect on them that they
all vowed to risk their lives to protect him. The story is told by
Foxe in The Book of Martyrs.

He fled by way of Antwerp to find refuge in Strasbourg, where he
was joined by his wife and child, both of whom died there. At
Strasbourg he had two distinguished companions, both supporters of
Lady Jane Grey and both Essex men: Sir John Cheke (q.v.) and Sir
Anthony Cooke (q.v.). All three returned to England on Elizabeth's
accession and enjoyed favour. Sandys became Bishop of Worcester
in 1559. After eleven years he became Bishop of London, and from
there he went to York as archbishop in 1577. Throughout these years
he used Edwins Hall as his country home, and in view of his support
for Lady Jane Grey it is interesting to remember that the Woodham
Ferrers manor had been held by Lady Jane's family. Elizabeth
Ferrers, who inherited the estate from her grandfather in 1445,
married Sir Edward Grey of Ruthin. Their son married Elizabeth
Woodville, who married as her second husband, Edward IV, from
whom Lady Jane Grey was descended.

In 1581, Sandys was the victim of a vulgar conspiracy to discredit
him. While conducting a Visitation he lodged at the Bull Inn,
Doncaster, where his hostess was Ann Sisson, who had formerly
been a servant in the archbishop's palace. After Sandys, who was
then 65, had retired for the night, Mistress Sisson took him his
usual hot drink, but instead of leaving him with it, promptly threw
off her dress and crept naked into his bed. Her husband then
entered the room, and when he saw his wife in bed with the archbishop he drew his dagger and sent a serving man to summon Sir
Robert Stapleton, another guest for the night, to witness the scene.
Stapleton, who was subsequently suspected of having hatched the
plot, advised the archbishop, whom he knew well, to bribe Sisson,

and the terrified archbishop agreed. This led to the usual systematic
blackmail and in all cost the archbishop £700 in the two years that
followed. In 1583 he decided that the time had come to put a stop to
the extortion, even if it meant putting his good name in question. So
he reported the whole affair to the queen and Burghley, saying that
he would rather resign than submit further. Eventually the case came
before the Star Chamber and Sir Walter Mildmay delivered a long
speech, stating the

> 'foule and horrible facte, the some whereof is, that by ... most
> detestable practice an impudent harlott was conveyed into the
> chamber, yea into the bedd of the Archbishop, to bring upon
> him this horrible slander and abuse'.*

All the confederates were suitably punished; but the enmity of
Stapleton, a Yorkshire landowner, continued to be an embarrassment
to the archbishop to the end of his life. Cecily, the archbishop's
widow, continued to live at Edwin's Hall, where an attempt was made
to murder her in 1594 (Emmison: Elizabethan Life: Disorder, 121-2).
Her magnificent monument is in the chancel of Woodham Ferrers'
church.

Sir Edwin Sandys (1561-1629), son of the archbishop by his second wife,
had a varied career as a prebendary of York, 1582-1602, M.P. for
Andover and later for Plympton, and the companion of Cranmer in
travels abroad. He was knighted along with so many others in 1603,
and the following year became M.P. for Stockbridge. Gradually he
built up a reputation as a champion of unpopular causes and stickler
for principle. From 1617 he was closely associated with the government of Virginia, where he organised the colony and is now credited
with having played a major part in bringing about its prosperity, although at the time he was suspected of designing to establish a Puritan
Republic in America. Charges were, in fact, preferred against him
and for a time he was imprisoned in the Tower.

Sir Edwin's official association with Virginia ended in 1621. In the
same year his brother, George (1578-1744), accompanied Sir Thomas
Wyatt there and was nominated a member of the Council when the Crown
assumed government in 1624. He was a gentleman of the Privy Chamber
to Charles I and a well known poet and translater in his day.

SAVAGE

Richard Savage, 4th Earl Rivers (1660-1712), second but only surviving son of Thomas, 3rd Earl Rivers, inherited estates in the east of
the county through his great-grandfather, Viscount Savage, who
married Elizabeth, daughter and heiress of the 3rd Lord Darcy (q.v.).
When Viscount Savage died in 1635, his widow coveted the Rivers'
title, and in 1641 she was created Countess Rivers for life. Lady
Rivers was a proud Roman Catholic, whose home at St. Osyth was
attacked by a Roundhead mob in 1642. After wrecking the Priory the
mob pursued the Countess to her house at Long Melford; but she had
already been warned of their approach and had escaped to Bury St.
Edmunds. Her losses in the two houses were estimated to have
amounted to between 100 and 150 thousand pounds. She died in 1650.

Richard Savage was M.P. for Wigan in 1681 and the first English

*Sloane MS 326, fols.56-70, and
Harl. MS 6265, fols.89-92, and
Harl. MS 4990, fols.80-85.

nobleman to desert James II when the Prince of Orange landed.
Certainly he attended King William in all his campaigns and served
also under Queen Anne. In 1711 he was sent as Envoy Extraordinary
to Hanover, with a commission to assure the Elector that Queen
Anne intended to leave the succession to the English Crown secured
to his family.

In 1712 he was appointed Master-General of the Ordnance and General
and Commander-in-Chief of the Queen's land forces in Great Britain.
He was one of Harley's circle and a member of the 'Saturday Club'.

At his death without a son, the heir to the earldom was John Savage,
a Roman Catholic priest and canon of Liege. He never assumed the
title and at his death all the titles of the family became extinct.

Dean Swift described the 4th Earl Rivers as 'an arrant knave', and
said of him:

> 'He has left a legacy to about twenty paltry old whores by
> name, and not a farthing to any friend, dependent or
> relation'.

Macky, in his <u>Characters</u>, describes him as one of the greatest rakes
in England.

SAYER

The Sayer family of Essex trace their ancestry to William and John
Sayer, who were living at Birch in the reign of Edward III. The
family held land at Birch, Aldham, and Great Tey during the 14th
and 15th centuries. Several members were aldermen and bailiffs of
Colchester. George Sayer (d.1577) held land at Stanway, Copford,
Lexden and other places. He has a monument in St. Peter's church
Colchester, along with other members of his family. A later George
(d.1630) was knighted in 1607. John (d.1658), his eldest son, inherited the estate and lived at Bourchier's Hall.

SCHUTZ

Col. Armand John Schutz (1696-1773), courtier, brother of the Baron
Augustus Schutz, who came to England with George I in 1714, purchased estates at Clacton and Little Holland in 1717 and rebuilt Great
Clacton Hall. He held the offices of Master of the Robes to the Prince
of Wales (1734) and Lord of the Stannaries (1736). George, his eldest
son, died young. His second son, John (1725-72), was appointed
Master of the Robes to the Prince of Wales in 1742 and Equerry to
the King in 1761. The colonel's third son, Francis Matthew (b.1729)
succeeded him. He married Susan, only surviving child of Sir Edmund
Bacon, Premier Baronet, by his wife, Susan, daughter of Sir Isaac
Rebow, High Steward of Colchester (q.v.). She brought with her
Gillingham Hall, Norfolk, to which Francis removed.

Francis Matthew's second son, Francis Robert (1760-98) succeeded
to the Essex estates and lived at Great Clacton Hall. He died without
issue.

A daughter of Col. Schutz (1696-1773), the courtier, married John
Griffin-Griffin 1st Lord Braybrooke (q.v.). She died in 1764 and was
buried at Saffron Walden.

SCOTT

The Rev. Alexander Scott (1768-1840), Nelson's chaplain, secretary and friend, was vicar of Southminster and Burnham-on-Crouch from 1809 to 1840. He was born at Rotherhithe into a family with strong naval traditions. In May 1803 he sailed to the Mediterranean with Nelson, and stayed with him until the end. Nelson, did, in fact, die in Scott's arms.

SCOTT

The Scotts of Chigwell were descended from Sir William Scott, judge of the Common Pleas and Justice of the Forests in the reign of Edward III, who died in 1346. William Scott of Stapleford Tawney was granted the Woolston Hall estate at Chigwell by Henry VII. He died in 1491, leaving Woolston Hall to his fifth son, George (d.1534), from whom it descended to Walter Scott of Stapleford Tawney. The estate continued in the Scott family until 1780, when the last George Scott died without issue, leaving the estate to Robert Bodle of Clare Market, a picture framer.

See: Erith: E.R. 1 XII, Essex Journal, No.4.

SCOTT

Father William Scott (d.1612), Catholic martyr, was born at Chigwell and educated at Cambridge. On entering the Order of St. Benedict he took the name of Father Maurus. On his arrival in England after ordination he saw the priest who had received him into the Church of Rome being led to his death. Within three days Father Scott himself was arrested; but after a year in prison he was allowed his freedom on condition he left the country and stayed abroad. For a time he lived quietly at Douai; but he felt called to return to England, and soon after his arrival he came into conflict with George Abbot, Bishop of London, afterwards Archbishop of Canterbury. In 1612 he was taken from Newgate for trial at the Old Bailey, where he was found guilty. He was hanged at Tyburn.

SELWIN-IBBETSON

Sir Henry Selwin-Ibbetson, Lord Rookwood (1826-1902), was the only son of Sir John Thomas Selwin, 6th baronet (d.1869), of Down Hall, near Harlow. He resumed the family name of Ibbetson in 1867 on marrying, as his second wife, the widow of Sir Charles Henry Ibbetson, 5th baronet. Down Hall had been purchased from the 3rd Earl of Oxford (Harley) by William Selwin, a London merchant. On the death of his eldest son, Charles, it passed to his niece, Jane, who married Sir James Ibbetson. From him it descended to Sir Henry Selwin-Ibbetson, the 7th baronet, who was raised to the peerage in 1892 as Lord Rookwood.

Sir Henry represented South Essex in Parliament, 1865-8; West Essex, 1868-85; and the newly constituted Division of Epping, 1885-92. His name is especially honoured in West Essex for the leading part he played towards the passing of the Epping Forest Act of 1878.

Between 1871 and 1873 he demolished the old Down Hall of Prior and the Harley earls of Oxford, and built a mansion in Italian style, which fits somewhat incongruously in the undemonstrative landscape of West Essex.

He died in 1902 and was buried at Hatfield Broad Oak, where
several mural tablets to members of the Selwin family may be seen,
including a memorial by Flaxman to Lord Rookwood's grandmother.
Lord Rookwood died without issue and the title died with him.

SHAA

Sir John Shaa of Rochford, goldsmith, was Lord Mayor of London in
1501. He was knighted in the Field by Henry VII. Stow records of
him that he caused his brethren, the aldermen, to ride with him to
the waterside, where he took his barge to Westminster, and that
'he commonly in the afternoons kept a court alone,
    called before him many matters, and redressed them'.

Thomas Shaa, a member of the same family, acquired the manor of
Terling Hall in 1564. He married the daughter of the Lord Hunger-
ford who was executed for high treason in 1540. She bore him six
children before being succeeded in her husband's affections by
Philippa, daughter of John Rochester, by whom he had three sons
and four daughters.

SHILLIBEER

George Shillibeer (1797-1866), who drove the first omnibus in
London in 1829 and introduced the word omnibus into the English
language, lived at the Grove, Chigwell Row, where he helped to
secure for the public a recreation ground. He has a memorial in
Chigwell church. Shillibeer, who also patented a funeral coach,
was ruined by railway competition.

SLATER

Gilbert Slater (1753-93), gardener-botanist, was born at Stepney,
the son of a Deputy Master of Trinity House. When he became
managing owner of several ships trading for the East India Company
he was able to get seeds and plants brought from the East for
cultivation in his gardens at Leyton. His masters were provided
with a list of coveted plants together with instructions for collecting and packing them. All specimens of value were divided on
arrival and one part sent to Kew. In 1789 he sent out two employees
specifically to collect and pack specimens in order to speed up his
enterprise; but neither returned. One of the two was replaced by
the Chelsea gardener, James Main, who carried the project to
success; but on his return he learned that Slater had died at 40 and
his house at Knotts Green, Leyton, had been sold. Slater's descendants adopted Sclater as the spelling of their name. Their home
at Knotts Green, which had formerly been the home of the Barclay
family, was later known as 'Livingstone College'. Among the more
important plants introduced by Slater were species of cammelias,
hydrangeas, magnolias, China roses, which as the result of his
generosity in providing specimens for Kew, survived his premature
death.

SMITH

Charlotte Fell Smith (1851-1937), historian of Essex, was born at
Pattiswick Hall. After being educated at Friends' schools at Lewes
and York, she devoted her long life to the study of Essex history.

She edited the Essex Review, with Edward Fitch as co-editor, from
1898, and was a regular contributor from 1892. Her most important
work is her life of Mary Rich, Countess of Warwick; but she also
wrote lives of Stephen Crisp (1892), James Parnell (1906), and John
Dee (1909). She contributed articles to Victoria County History,
Country Life, and the Dictionary of National Biography. She died at
Felsted.

SMITH

Sir Thomas Smith (1513-77), statesman and writer, was the son of
John Smith, a small sheep farmer of Saffron Walden. From Walden
grammar school he went to Queens' College, Cambridge, and so
distinguished himself that Richard Eden described him as being in
his time the 'flower of the University'. Among other things, he revolutionised the pronunciation of Greek.

In 1547 Smith left Cambridge to enter the service of Edward Seymour,
Earl of Hertford, who was shortly to become Lord Protector of the
Realm and Duke of Somerset. Smith was quickly appointed to two key
offices, that of Clerk to the Privy Council and that of Master of the
Protector's Court of Requests. In the same year, 1547, he was
elected M.P. for Marlborough and appointed Provost of Eton. In
1548 he became lay Dean of Carlisle. Five years later he succeeded
William Paget as Second Secretary to the king, with Sir William
Petre as First Secretary; but he was not a success in the office.
His intellectual brilliance and administrative efficiency were not disputed, but he was intolerant and arrogant, deficient in political saga-
city and imprudent in his choice of associates. Scholars are seldom
at home in politics, and Smith seems to have been less at ease than
most. So when life at court became intolerable he was able to find
solace at Eton, and must often have wondered whether he would not
have been wiser if he had remained at Cambridge and confined his
energies to scholarship.

The death of Edward VI in 1553 and the accession of Mary put him out
of favour for a time, and he was able to retire to Theydon Mount,
near Epping, where an estate had come into his possession on his
marriage with Philippa, widow of Sir John Hampden. There were two
good residences on the property, Mount Hall and Hill Hall. He and
Philippa decided to live at Hill Hall and rebuild Mount Hall. Then in
1561 they moved into Mount Hall so that they could rebuild Hill Hall
in more ambitious style. In the meantime, however, Mary had died
and Elizabeth had become queen. Smith had been recalled to power,
which he undoubtedly enjoyed, although it must have been plain to
most that he was temperamentally incapable of adjusting his logically
determined policies to meet the whims of a mercurial mistress. At
no time do servant and sovereign appear to have understood each
other. Nothing, for example, could have been more imprudent than
his publication of a Dialogue on the Queen's Marriage, in which he
argued the case for her marriage with his Essex neighbour, Lord
Robert Dudley.

In 1562 he was sent to Paris as ambassador, which might have
suited him well enough; but as he was given the post jointly with Sir
Nicholas Throckmorton, with whom he was so completely at odds
that Throckmorton complained bitterly to Cecil about his unwilling-
ness to co-operate, even going so far as to refer to 'this man's
malice to me'. In fact, at one time the two almost came to blows.

Smith was no more reconciled to the partnership than Throckmorton.
He pleaded to be recalled, but 5 years were to pass before his wish
was granted. When it was he retired again to Theydon Mount, this
time with his head full of ideas for the rebuilding of Hill Hall to plans
he had made in France. The result was that Hill Hall became an outstanding example in England of Renaissance architecture showing
French influence.

In 1571 Sir Thomas was back at court, and when the plot to place
Mary Queen of Scots on the English throne was discovered he was
entrusted with the examination of Thomas Howard, Duke of Norfolk
(q.v.), who played a leading part in the conspiracy. He would know
more than most about the background of the plot in so far as the duke
was concerned, because of their mutual association with Saffron
Walden, and because the duke was discovered in hiding near Ongar,
and William Shelley (see Byrd) of Stondon Massey was implicated in
the plot. Smith was now near the height of prosperity in his chequered
career. He became Chancellor of the Order of the Garter and Principal Secretary. But the stars again turned against him. In 1571 he and
his son obtained from the queen a patent for the colonization of what
was described as 'divers parts and parcels of land' in Ulster 'that lay
waste, or were inhabited with a wicked, barbarous, and uncivil people,
some Scottish, and some wild Irish'. He was given a free hand to dis-
tribute lands, give orders and make laws for seven years, at the end
of which period the country was to be handed over to the queen to be
governed according to the laws and customs of England. The venture
was a failure, politically and financially, and became a tragedy for
Sir Thomas when his only son was killed. He struggled on for two
years, at immense cost to himself, before he withdrew. By this time
he was a broken man.

Argument will long continue on the value of Sir Thomas Smith's
political career. As a scholar his reputation is secure. As a
political thinker he has probably not yet had his due reward of appreciation. De Republica Anglorum has been said by eminent historians
to be the basis of the theory of the supremacy of Parliament in the
British constitution. Although it was not published until after his
death, its importance was recognised at once. It remains the most important constitutional study of the age. His complex personality may
be understood better when his letters are published and examined.

See: Mary Dewar: Sir Thomas Smith, a Tudor Intellectual in Office
               1964   Kenneth Neale: Sir Thomas Smith and
               Hill Hall, Essex Journal, vol.v.No.1.

SOUTHCOTE

The Southcote family of Witham were noted Jacobites. They flourished
from the second half of the 16th century until well into the 18th.

John Southcote (1511-85), judge, was sergeant-at-law and later judge
of the Queen's Bench. He sat as an assessor at the trial of Thomas
Howard, 4th Duke of Norfolk (q.v.). John Southcote, who came of
Devon stock, purchased Bacons and Abbots, Witham, shortly after
1565. At his death at the age of 74 he was buried in a splendid altar
tomb at Witham.

His son, John, married the youngest daughter of Sir Edward Waldegrave (1517-61) of Borley (q.v.), who was imprisoned for suffering
mass in Princess Mary's household at Copt Hall, Essex, in 1551-2.

She was the sister of Lady Petre, wife of the 1st Baron Petre (q.v

The second John Southcote's son and heir, Sir Edward (1658-1751)
served in the Royalist army and was taken prisoner at the first
Battle of Newbury. After the Revolution of 1688 he fled to the Conti
nent. He had ten children by his first marriage. On his second
marriage in 1727 he settled the Witham estate on his eldest son,
John. Sir Edward lived to the great age of 93. All his seven sons
died without issue.

Portraits of the family are to be seen at Ingatestone Hall.

SPARROW

The Sparrow family of Gestingthorpe and Great Maplestead were
eniment in the 17th century. John Sparrow (1563-1626) was buried
in the chancel of Gestingthorpe church. His son, also John (d.1664)
who lived at Dynes Hall, Great Maplestead, served as a colonel in
the Parliamentary army and was High Sheriff in 1655. The third
John (1615-70), the mystic, held public offices under the Commonwealth. At the Restoration he was charged with falsification of
accounts kept by him as Commissioner of Prize Goods, but was
allowed to compound. In collaboration with his kinsman, John
Elliston, he translated the writings of the German mystic, Jacob
Boehme. His son, the fourth John (b.1640), was knighted in 1668.
Another son was Clerk Comptroller of the Household to James II
and followed him into exile. In 1689 a Grand Jury at the Old Bailey
found a true bill against him as a 'papist in arms with King James'.

SPARVEL-BAYLY

John Anthony Sparvel-Bayly (1845-95), J.P., F.S.A., left Swans-
combe in Kent, where his family had long been settled, in 1874 to m
his home at Burghstead Lodge, Billericay. He wrote extensively on
historical and antiquarian subjects, and at the time of his death wa
engaged in assisting with the compilation of an Encyclopaedic Index
to the county. He began life as a gentleman of ample means, but die
in poverty.

SPURGEON

Charles Haddon Spurgeon (1834-92), preacher, was born at
Kelvedon, the eldest son of the Rev. John Spurgeon, and grandson
the Rev. James Spurgeon (1776-1864), who was minister of the Independent Chapel at Stambourne from 1811 to his death 53 years la
at the age of 87. Charles was a frequent visitor at the Old Manse,
Stambourne, and his grandfather's Calvinistic doctrines made a pr
found impression on him.

After a short period as an usher at Cambridge, the ministerial life
of Spurgeon began as pastor of an Independent Chapel at Waterbea
Cambs. He was called to his first London pastorate in 1854, after
being introduced to the deacons by a Loughton friend. In less than
year the chapel had to be enlarged; but even before the enlargemen
was completed it became plain that it would be too small for the con
gregations he was already attracting. So a larger chapel was plann
and in 1861 the Metropolitan Tabernacle in Newington Causeway, w
seating for six thousand, was opened. From that date to his death i
1892 it was packed every time he preached, and his sermons were
printed in Australian and American newspapers. It was estimated t

altogether not fewer than fifty million copies of his sermons had been circulated in print in addition to the abridged versions that had appeared in English newspapers.

Spurgeon is a name not uncommon in Essex. A branch of the family is recorded as owning the manor of Stondon in the 13th and 14th centuries. The house in which Spurgeon was born at Kelvedon is marked with a plaque.

See: W. Miller Higgs: The Spurgeon Family (1906).

STAFFORD

Humfrey Stafford, 1st Duke of Buckingham (1402-60), was the son of Edmund Stafford, 5th Earl of Stafford, by Anne, daughter and sole heir of Thomas, Duke of Gloucester, youngest son of Edward III. In early life he played a leading part in the French wars and became a K.G. in 1429 at the age of 27. In 1438 he was created Earl of Buckingham; in 1444, Duke of Buckingham, with precedence over all other dukes not of royal blood. In 1460 he was killed at the Battle of Northampton, while fighting close to the royal tent, and buried with his wife at Pleshey in a chapel which he had built and endowed.

Duke Humfrey had inherited the religious college at Pleshey through his mother from Thomas, Duke of Gloucester. By his will he left money for a chapel to be built on the north side of the church, which was to be dedicated to the Trinity. He also left provision for sufficient land to be purchased to support three additional priests and six poor men, who were to pray for the repose of the soul of himself, his wife, and his children.

His wife was Anne, daughter of Ralph Neville, 1st Earl of Westmorland. She bore him seven sons and four daughters. The Duchess married, as her second husband, Sir Walter Blount, Lord Mountjoy (d.1474).

Humfrey, Duke of Gloucester, was the most powerful nobleman of his day and the largest landowner in England. His memorial in Pleshey church is of much antiquarian interest.

STEVENS

Francis Worrall Stevens (b.1807) of Loughton, claimed that he introduced the idea of the Penny Postage stamp to Rowland Hill. In 1827 Stevens took over the school at Albion House, Albion Hill, Loughton, previously conducted by his father, and remained there until 1834, when he moved his school to Buckhurst Hill House. In 1833 he wrote to Lord Althorp, as Chancellor of the Exchequer, suggesting an adhesive penny stamp. About the same time he engaged Rowland Hill as his assistant for five months, while Hill was recuperating from an illness. Stevens claimed that he discussed his proposal with Hill, but lost touch with him on emigrating some years later to New Zealand. When the Penny Post was introduced into the service by Rowland Hill the Sovereign's head was substituted for the Royal Arms, as proposed by Stevens. This he claimed
    'is only a trick or evasion, but whether Royal
    Arms or Queen's Head, it is still the Penny
    Postage Stamp, and my invention, and not
    Rowland Hill's.'

Stevens petitioned the Queen for recognition of his claim in 1877. A

pamphlet setting out the history and basis of the claim, published at
Dunedin in that year, is preserved in the 'Sir George Grey Collection'
in the Public Library, Auckland.

See: Alfred Eccles, 'The Pacific Stamp Review', May, 1947).

Francis Worrall Stevens invented an adjustable paddle-wheel for use
on steam boats.

See: A.R.J. Ramsey, Essex Review, July 1947.

STONARD

John Stonard of Loughton (d.1540), yeoman, became lessee for 41
years of the manor of Loughton in 1522. By his will he left to the last
abbot of Waltham his 'best amblyng nagge' to have his soul in
remembrance. His son, George (d.1559), left a son, John (d.1579),
who built Luxborough, 'a fayre howse' at Chigwell. He entertained
Elizabeth I at Loughton in 1578.

STRANGE

Sir John Strange (1696-1754), Master of the Rolls, 1749-54, was
buried at Leyton. His 'Reports' were edited by his son, John Strange
(1732-99), the diplomat, who was both a F.R.S. and a F.S.A., and
wrote on geological and archaeological subjects. A popular Leyton
tradition has it that on one occasion when two visitors stood before
Sir John's tomb, one pointed to it and said:
    'There lies an honest lawyer!'
    'Why, that's Strange', replied the other.

STREET

George Edmund Street (1824-81), architect, was born at Woodford.
In 1868 he was appointed architect of the Royal Courts of Justice.
He was elected to the Royal Academy in 1871. At his death he was
buried in Westminster Abbey. His monument bears a figure and a
building in course of erection, which can be recognised as the Royal
Courts of Justice.

STRUTT

The family came into prominence in Essex in the 17th century with
John Strutt, who was born at Springfield Mill in 1624. The Strutts
were already a miller family, with water-driven mills at Maldon and
Springfield. They reached Terling early in the 18th century.

Sir Denner Strutt, who was created a baronet in 1641, owned the
manor of Little Warley and was a man of mark in his day, but left no
surviving issue. His brother, John, succeeded to his estate and
became the ancestor of the Terling branch of the family, which begins
with a Strutt at New House about 1720. In 1761 John Strutt (1727-
1816), M.P. for Maldon, bought the manor of Terling Place, and
pulled down part of the Tudor mansion, which had been a palace of
the Bishops of Norwich before the Reformation. In 1765 he built
what is now the centre block of the present house. John Strutt the
first of Terling is said to have been the last man to wear a pigtail in
the House. His successor, John Holden Strutt (1756-1845), represented Maldon from 1790 to 1827. He married Lady Charlotte Mary
Gertrude, daughter of James, Duke of Leinster, by Lady Emily

Lennox, daughter of Charles, Duke of Richmond and Aubigny. The Lady Charlotte was created Baroness Rayleigh in 1821.

John Holden Strutt added the east and west wings of the house in 1820. For his services to the Essex militia he was offered a peerage, but declined it. It was later certified to his wife in the name of Rayleigh, where the family owned a small property. At Lady Rayleigh's death in 1836 the title descended to her son, John James, who thus became Lord Rayleigh during his father's lifetime.

John James, 2nd Lord Rayleigh (1796-1873), had no greater enthusiasm for exalted rank than his father had shown. He gave up the normal social life of men of his station and became a leader of Evangelical churchmen. He built almshouses at Terling, which bear the inscription:
     'J.W.S., Nov. 12, 1863, aged 21'.
This does not signify that they were built by a young man of 21, but that they were a thank-offering for an heir having reached manhood.

The heir who came of age in 1863 was John William Strutt, 3rd Baron Rayleigh, O.M. (1842-1919), mathematician and physicist, who, in 1871 married Evelyn Balfour, sister of Arthur Balfour, and became one of the great scholars of his day. In 1879 he was elected·to the Cavendish Chair of Experimental Physics at Cambridge, which he held until 1884. His services to science, which are fully recorded in reference books, were acknowledged by the award of the Nobel Prize for Physics in 1904. The whole of the prize money (£8,000) was presented by him to Cambridge University for the extension of the Cavendish Laboratory. In 1905 he was President of the Royal Society.

Lord Rayleigh published the first of his 446 listed scientific papers in 1869. His greatest contributions were to the study of Optics and the theory of sound, beginning with his Treatise on the Theory of Sound, published in 1877. In collaboration with Sir William Ramsey he discovered the inert gas, Argon, which was announced to the British Association in 1894. It was Lord Rayleigh's determination of electrical units that formed the basis of the legal definitions of the volt and the ampere.

In 1873 Lord Rayleigh succeeded his father as an Essex landowner, and in 1892 was even appointed Lord Lieutenant, an office that was by no means to his taste, but which he fulfilled for a time, acting on the guidance of his brother, the Hon. Charles Strutt, who was chairman of Quarter Sessions and had his finger on the county pulse; but when, in 1901, the War Office sanctioned the raising of a Yeomanry Regiment in Essex, Lord Rayleigh felt completely unfitted for such work and resigned to make way for the 5th Earl of Warwick.

In 1885 he retired to Terling Place to continue his work in his private laboratory, although he did not cut himself off from his fellow scientists and served as secretary of the Royal Society from 1885 to 1896.

Apart from his skill in research, Lord Rayleigh had a remarkable gift for organising existing knowledge, and it was this gift that led to another enterprise, not normally associated with science - the Lord Rayleigh's Dairies. This was based on his calculations of the milk needed for its scientific supply to the rapidly expanding population of London. Under the management of his brother, the Hon. E.G. Strutt, he built up a fine herd of between 1,400 and 1,500 cattle at the family farm at Terling and opened eight dairy shops in London.

Lord Rayleigh was awarded an O.M. at the Coronation of Edward VII. and was thus one of the original twelve members. In 1908 he was

Chancellor of Cambridge University. When he died in 1919 he was buried at Terling. Afterwards a memorial tablet was placed in the North transept of Westminster Abbey, describing him as 'an unerring leader in the advancement of Natural knowledge'.

He was succeeded by his son, Robert John, 4th Baron Rayleigh (187. 1947), experimental physicist, in scientific research. The 4th Lord Rayleigh became both a professor and a Fellow of the Royal Society He was Professor of Physics at the Imperial College of Science. He also continued with research in the family laboratory at Terling Plac notably investigating the age of minerals and rocks by measuring their radioactivity and helium content. He was President of the British Association in 1938, and of the Royal Institution, 1945-47.

Other eminent members of the Strutt family have been: Joseph Strutt (1749-1802), the author of The Sports and Pastimes of the People of England, who was born at Springfield Mill; Benjamin Strutt (1755-1 a friend of Constable, and his son, Jacob George Strutt, the landsca painter.

STRYPE

John Strype (1643-1737), ecclesiastical historian, was the son of a Brabantine refugee who set up in business as a silk merchant in Houndsditch, where John was born. His father's uncle, Abraham van Strype, had been one of the founders of the Spitalfields silk industr

Strype was educated at Cambridge, and in 1669 was appointed to the perpetual curacy of Theydon Bois. Four months later he was presented to the living of Leyton, which he retained until his death 68 years later. While vicar of Leyton he devoted himself to the study of ecclesiastical history and biography. His Annals of the Reformati was the result of many years of study and research. Among his othe works were Ecclesiastical Memorials, an annotated edition of Stow's Survey of London, and biographies of Archbishops Cranmer, Parke and Whitgift, and a Life of Sir Thomas Smith of Theydon Mount (q.v whose personality and career had attracted him while he was at Theydon Bois. It was through the influence of his most distinguished parishioner at Leyton, Sir William Hickes, that he was granted acc to the Burghley Papers, which were one of his principal sources.

When he became infirm towards the end of his long life, he went to l at Hackney with his granddaughter and her husband, a surgeon name Dr. Harris. Dr. Samuel Knight, who visited Strype in 1733, wrote a friend:

> 'I have made a visit to old Father Strype (at Hackney)
> when in town last; he is turned 90 years yet very brisk,
> and with only a decay of sight and memory. He would
> fain have induced me to undertake Archbishop Bancroft's
> life, but I have no stomach for it, having no great opinion
> of him on more accounts than one. He had a greater
> inveteracy against the Puritans than any of his predecessors.
> Mr. Strype told me he had great materials towards the
> lives of the old Lord Burghley, and Mr. Foxe, the Marty-
> rologist, which he wished he could have finished, but
> most of his papers are in character, and his grandson is
> learning to decypher them'.

When Strype arrived at Leyton he found the vicarage ruinous and ' to receive a Minister and his Family'. Most of the cost of rebuilding it came out of his own pocket. Strype's transcripts are reliable and still consulted; but to-day the most valuable part of his work is to be found in his annotations of Stow's Survey.

STUBBS

William Stubbs (1825-1901), historian, held the living of Navestock from 1850 to 1866, when he left on being appointed to the chair of Modern History at Oxford. During his stay at Navestock he served as Inspector of Schools for the Diocese of Rochester and collected material for his Constitutional History of England. Later in life Stubbs was successively canon of St. Paul's, Bishop of Chester, and finally, Bishop of Oxford.

SULYARD

Sir John Sulyard (d.1487), a justice of the King's Bench, held a moiety of the manor of Otes, High Laver. His eldest son and heir, Sir Edward, is commemorated by a brass, c.1495, at High Laver, along with his wife Myrabyll, his four sons and one daughter.

Of Edward Sulyard's four sons, the eldest, Sir William (d.1539), owned considerable estates in Essex, but died without issue. By his second wife, Edward Sulyard had two children, Eustace and Mary. Eustace, who has a brass at Runwell, died in 1546, holding the manor of Otes. His son, Sir Edward, who died in 1610, sold Otes to the Masham family (q.v.).

SWEYN OF ESSEX

Sweyn (d.circa 1086) son of Robert, Standard Bearer to Edward the Confessor, to whom he was related, held fifteen lordships in Essex. He served as Sheriff of Essex under both Edward the Confessor and William the Conqueror, and had extensive holdings of land in Rayleigh, Eastwood, Sutton, Canewdon, Wakering, Ashingdon, Hawkwell and Hockley. J.H. Round identified Clavering as Robert's principal castle on the other side of the kingdom. The land held by him before the Conquest was confirmed to him by William, who also granted him lands in the east of Essex until his holdings became so extensive that he became 'the greatest sheepmaster in Essex'. His castle in the south-east was at Rayleigh, where he planted a large vineyard. He was buried in Westminster Abbey.

Sweyne was succeeded by his son, Robert FitzSweyn, founder of Prittlewell Priory and other religious houses in the county. As punishment for supporting Matilda against Stephen he lost for a time the posts of Constable of England and Hereditary Standard Bearer to the king.

His son, Henry de Essex, was reappointed to the family offices and stood high in the esteem of Henry II, who appointed him Lord Warden of the Cinque Ports. In 1157, when Henry II held an enquiry at Colchester into the privileges claimed by the Abbot of Battle and re-sisted by the Bishop of Winchester and the Archbishop of Canterbury, Henry de Essex was described as a royal judge. Most of the magnates of the realm were in attendance on him. Later in the same year Henry played a less glorious part in the expedition against the Welsh. Indeed his later years brought little glory. He fell from power and influence and ended his days at Reading Abbey.

SWYNBORNE

In 1326 William de Horkesley passed the manor of Little Horkesley
by fine to Robert de Swynborne and his heirs after the joint lives of
himself and his wife. Sir Robert died in 1391 and was succeeded by
his son, Thomas, who died in 1412. An exceptionally fine double
brass to these two knights was saved when Little Horkesley church
was destroyed by a bomb in 1940. Sir Thomas was Castellan of
Guines, 1390-3; mayor of Bordeaux in 1404; and in 1405 was referred
to as an admiral.

SYMONDS

Richard Symonds (1617-92), Royalist and antiquary, was born at
Black Notley. He served with the Royalist forces at many important
battles during the Civil War, and was a member of Charles I's life-
guard at Naseby. His notebooks are now valuable source-books for
local historians and antiquaries.

SYSLEY

Clement Sysley (d.1578), who built Eastbury House, Barking, in
1572, was a younger son of Richard Sysley, of Sevenoaks in Kent,
who purchased the manor of Eastbury in 1557. Clement Sysley is
buried in the chancel of Barking church. In 1580 his widow married
Augustine Steward, and late in life (she died in 1610) she sold her
life interest in Eastbury to her son, Augustine Steward, who at the
same time acquired the reversion from Thomas Sysley, his step-
brother. So despite Clement Sysley's ambition that his heirs might
remain at Eastbury 'for ever', it had passed from the Sysley family
30 years after his death.

TALLIS

Thomas Tallis (c.1505-85), composer and organist, was born at
Greenwich. Unfortunately the date of his birth is not known precisely
and can only be deduced from the evidence of his work and letters.
It seems certain that some of his most important work, including his
motet Gaude Gloriosa, was written while he was organist at Waltham
Abbey. His name appears in the long list of those who received small
sums of money at the Dissolution, but not among the pensioners.
This may have been because he was appointed one of the Gentlemen of
the Chapel Royal at or about the time of the Dissolution of Waltham
Abbey.

When he left Waltham he carried away with him a document (now in the
British Museum) in the handwriting of John Wylde, formerly precentor
of Waltham Abbey, which contains a number of treatises on musical
subjects and bears Tallis's signature on the last page.

Tallis and Byrd (q.v.) were granted a licence giving them sole right
to print music and music paper in England. For a time they acted as
joint-organists of the Chapel Royal. Tallis died at Greenwich (in
November 1585) and was buried in the church of St. Alphege.

TANY

Roger de Tany, head of the family at the time of the Conquest, gave the
tithes of Fyfield to the Abbey of Bermondsey in 1092. The first member

Roger de Tany, head of the family at the time of the Conques
the tithes of Fyfield to the Abbey of Bermondsey in 1092. Th
member of the family associated with Stapleford Tawney was
who came into possession of it sometime before 1240 on mar
Margaret, daughter of William FitzRichard. In 1253 he was
a licence to hunt hare, fox, cat, and badger in Waltham For
his own dogs. A later licence gave him and his heirs the rig
8 harriers and 20 brachets to hunt in the Forest when they w
saving the fence month and saving also the king's warrens ar
of others. At the same time he received exemption for life fr
put on assizes. In 1253 he received further a grant of free w
his demesne lands in Elmstead and Great Stambridge. This
later extended to include all demesne lands in Essex and Her
provided they were not within the king's forest.

In 1264 he was given a licence to enclose with a dyke and he
wood of Stapleford Tawney within the forest, and to make a

Three years previously, Peter de Tany, king's yeoman, had
given a similar grant to enclose land at Theydon Bois with a
and hedge which would not prevent the deer getting in and ou

Richard de Tany, the elder, died in 1270 and his son of the
did homage to the king and came into his inheritance. This s
Richard resented the manor of Theydon Mount being granted
de Brus by a charter dated 29th October, 1270, and tried to
Brus out by producing one dated 26th October. De Brus res
the case was taken to court, where it was stated that the Ch
had no knowledge of de Tany's charter, that none of his cler
written it, although the document was properly sealed. The
explanation that could be put forward was that at the time th
granted lands to so many knights that the Chancellor had dir
clerks to make out charters for each in accordance with Wa
Helyon's roll. In these circumstances Richard de Tany's ch
might have got pushed in with the others to be sealed; but if
happened it could only have been sealed unknowingly and und
deception.

Eventually the truth came out. Richard de Tany had gone to
clerks who had a list of all the charters granted, and had sa
       'Theydon is a pretty manor and lies next to mine
       at Stapleford. It would suit me nicely and I'll go
       and ask the king to give it to me'.
On learning that the king had already given it to de Brus, de
bribed the clerk to produce a charter of earlier date*.

This was only the first of many occasions when Richard de
younger, tried to get the better of the Law; but he appears
enjoyed the special favour of the king. In 1292 he was charg
having connived at the nocturnal adventures of his steward,
night in 1285 had hunted in the forest with bows and arrows,
mastiffs. No doubt the king realised that such adventurous k
Richard de Tany might have their uses in time of war, for in
was appointed <u>custos</u> of the sea shores in Essex when the E
was believed to be liable to attack from France. He died in
possessed of the manors of Stapleford, Elmstead, and four
meadow at Lambourne. Shortly before his death the king had
the justices of the forest to make him a present of twelve bu

---

*curia Regis Roll, 175, and Morant, i p.156.

he death of Laurence de Tany in 1317, the principal male line
de Tanys came to an end.

L.R. Buttle, The De Tanys of Stapleford Tawney,
            E.A.S. Trans., vol xx, New Series, pp.
            153-172.

ghout the greater part of the 19th century, one or more of the
of the Taylors of Ongar would be found in every educated
ian home. Few would be without Original Poems for Infant
(1805), or Rhymes for the Nursery (1806). The first member
family to become eminent was Isaac Taylor I (b.1730), who is
bered for having engraved plates for Goldsmith's Deserted
e. His second son, Isaac II (1759-1829), was born at Shenfield
ucated at Brentwood Grammar School. He followed his father
engraver and was responsible for plates in editions of Shakes-
the Bible, and Thomson's Seasons.His wife, formerly Ann
of Shenfield, wrote several books of domestic advice pub-
between 1814 and 1825. Their most famous children were:
782-1866), Jane (1783-1824), and Isaac III (1787-1865).

Taylor II entered the Congregational ministry and was called
astor to the congregation at Lavenham in Suffolk. In 1796
nily moved from there to Colchester, where they lived in Angel
now West Stockwell Street, and in April of that year Mr.
became minister to the Presbyterian congregation of the town,
was noted for strong nonconformist sympathies. The Taylors
y became acquainted with most of the talented people of the
ourhood. Ann described John Constable of Flatford Mill with
mment:
finished a model of what is reckoned manly beauty I
ver met with'.
ought Mr. Constable's intention of making John a miller 'simply
ous'.

a French landing was expected on the Essex coast the Taylor
en were sent back to Lavenham for safety. The Rounds (q.v.),
lls us, went to Bath at this time. During these years of
ed alarms Isaac Taylor quietly continued his work as an en-
besides being a devoted pastor and parent.

ll to Ongar came in 1811, when Isaac was 51 and at the height
productive period. While ministering to the Independent con-
ion of the town for the remaining 18 years of his life, he wrote
phies, travel and children's books, setting a standard of in-
that the whole family seemed eager to copy. Mrs. Taylor's
tic cares must have been considerable, but she found time to
olish such works as The Family Mansion. As for the children,
time of the move to Ongar, Ann wrote:
ne and I closed the labours of fourteen years
the workroom'.
ey lost no time in opening a new workroom at Ongar.

home for the first three years was Castle House ('The Moated
e'). Ann and Jane stayed at home; Isaac and Martin went up to
n to work - Isaac as a miniaturist, Martin at a publishing house
ernoster Row. Not until 1813 did the even routine of the Taylor
come under threat. In that year Ann brought what looked like
he first break in the family by marrying the Rev. Joseph Gilbert,

a widower of 34; but although she went to live at Nottingham the family unity was maintained. In 1814 the Taylors moved from the Castle House to Peaked Farm, which was their home until 1822. Jane never married. Isaac III married, but only moved to the neighbouring village of Stanford Rivers, where he lived for more than 40 years, turning another Taylor home into a hive of industry. When Ann expressed surprise at the amount of work he got through, he replied:

> 'There is no real mystery in getting through with a good deal in the year; or if there be, one Taylor need not explain it to another. Only observe the simple rule of staying at home, and sitting so many hours every day to the business in hand, and the thing is done. If free from care and well in health, I should not scruple to undertake getting out two bouncing octavos per annum, and all original'.

His best known work was The Natural History of Enthusiasm. He was widely held to be the best lay-theologian since Coleridge, while as an artist he was greatly admired by Rossetti, and had a third reputation as an inventor.

Jeffreys, a younger brother, settled at Pilgrims Hatch, near Brentwood. He also wrote for children. Martin was buried at Navestock. In all, nine members of this family are the subjects of biographies in the D.N.B.

TAYLOR

Sir Robert Taylor (1714-88), architect, was born at Woodford. He was Sheriff of London in 1782 and knighted the same year. Sir Robert held many surveyorships in the City. He was surveyor to the Bank of England from 1765, Architect of the King's Works from 1769, Master Carpenter from 1777, etc. The Taylorian Institute at Oxford was established from a large bequest made by him to the University for the study of modern languages.

TENNYSON

Alfred, 1st Baron Tennyson (1809-92), Poet Laureate, lived at Beech Hill House, High Beach, from 1837 to 1840. His feelings on leaving the wolds of his native Lincolnshire are expressed in sections 100 to 103 of In Memoriam. Beech Hill House was enlarged and much altered in 1850, when the name was changed to Beech Hill Park. After the Second World War it was practically demolished and a new house built on the site. Parts of In Memoriam were written at High Beach, including the stanzas inspired by the bells of Waltham Abbey. Other poems written in the forest include The Talking Oak and Locksley Hall. For his disastrous association with Dr. Allen, see entry under his name.

See: W. Addison: Epping Forest, its literary and historical associations.

THEYDON

In 1163 Henry de Essex, Constable of England (q.v.), was deprived of his possessions and some of the forfeited lands were granted by Henry II to William de Theydon, who is known to have held Theydon Mount in 1181 and to have been alive in 1194. In addition to his lands in Essex he had estates in Gloucestershire, Warwickshire, and other counties.

One of his heirs, Paulinus, was granted the right of a market and fair at Theydon in 1225, and of deer from the park at Theydon in 1227. Paulinus left three daughters, the eldest of whom, Beatrice, married Robert de Brus (see De Tany).

THOMPSON

Percy George Thompson (1866-1953), naturalist, was secretary of the Essex Field Club for nearly 30 years and for most of that time editor of the Essex Naturalist and curator of the Essex Museum. After training as an architect he turned his interests to natural history and later to archaeology and antiquities. This wide range of interests, sustained with distinction throughout his long life, would not have been possible if he had not been endowed with a prodigious memory, which enabled him to pronounce accurately on subjects he had barely glanced at for half a lifetime.

THORNE

Will Thorne (1857-1946), Labour pioneer, represented West Ham South and later Plaistow in Parliament for 38 years. He was born at Birmingham in 1857. In 1890 he became a member of West Ham Council, and was Mayor in 1917. During his mayoral year he had the honour of showing George V Whipps Cross Hospital and took advantage of the occasion to acquaint the king with the condition of the poor in West Ham. The West Ham South seat was won for Labour by Keir Hardie (q.v.) in 1892, but lost 2 years later. In 1895 Will Thorne was elected and retained the seat until the constituency was divided into Plaistow and Silvertown, when he was adopted for Plaistow, which he represented until he retired in 1945 at the age of 87.

THURLOE

John Thurloe (1616-68), Secretary to the Council of State, who was born at Abbess Roding, played a leading role in raising Cromwell to the Protectorate and even pressed him to accept the Crown. He was M.P. for Ely, 1654-6, and for Cambridge University, 1659. Seven volumes of his correspondence were published in 1742, and are a valuable source for histories of the Protectorate.

TINDAL

Nicholas Tindal (1687-1774), historian of Essex, was the son of John Tindal of Lornwood, Devon. He entered the Church and was presented by his college (Trinity, Oxon.) to the vicarage of Great Waltham in 1722. He stayed there until 1740, working on a history of the county, only two numbers of which were published: the first in January, the second in June, 1732; but most of Tindal's work appears in Morant, who was his curate from 1722 to 1732. It must, however, always be remembered that Tindal was the first to plan a history of Essex and actually to start publishing, even though he had to abandon his scheme. Nationally, he has his place as the translator of the History of England by Dr. Rapin Thoyras.

In 1738, Tindal was appointed one of the chaplains to Greenwich

Hospital, where he continued his ministry until his death at
87.

Sir Nicholas Conyngham Tindal (1776-1846), Chief Justice c
Pleas, was a grandson of Nicholas Tindal, the county histo
father was a Chelmsford solicitor, and Tindal maintained hi
tion with the borough all his life, living for a time at Coval

He went to Trinity, Cambridge, from Chelmsford Grammar
1826, while representing Wigtown in Parliament, he was ap
Solicitor-General and knighted; but he was never prominen
politician. In 1829 he became Lord Chief Justice of the Com
and found his role. He was a model of impartiality and corr
Tindal presided in the action brought by Mr. Norton agains
Melbourne for improper conduct with the plaintiff's wife, w
daughter of Sheridan and one of the most renowned beauties
day. Some of her adventures were used by Meredith in Diar
Crossways.

Tindal's most important case was that in which Macnaghton
charged with shooting a Mr. Drummond, whom he had mista
Sir Robert Peel. The main question at issue was whether th
was sane enough to know what he was doing, and the decisie
was that he was not. He was therefore acquitted on the grou
was not responsible for his actions. When Sir Nicholas Tin
suddenly in 1846 The Times wrote of him:
    'The world viewed with admiration the manner in which
    threw aside the sophistries and disentangled the forens
    perplexities with which laws are sometimes enveloped;
    he dissipated the obscurities, lopped off the irrelevanc
    curtailed the redundancies which had been imported int
    cause by the weak and evil advocate; and finally, how h
    reduced the real point in dispute to its strict and indisp
    able merits'.
The article goes on to commend him for 'his imperturbable
the uniform amenity of his manner, his perfect independenc

A statue to his memory stands near Shire Hall, Chelmsford

TOLPUDDLE MARTYRS

The six agricultural labourers, George and James Loveles
Hammett, Thomas and John Standfield and James Brine, for
trade union to resist the reduction of labourers' wages in 1
Tolpuddle in Dorset. After a trial that was a travesty of ju
six were sentenced to seven years' transportation. Two ye
protest and petition against this harsh sentence followed, a
a full pardon was granted. George Loveless returned to En
Botany Bay in 1837; James Brine, James Loveless and the
Stanfields in 1838; James Hammett in 1839. A fund was rai
settle them in a part of the country where they could start
and the choice fell on New House Farm, near Greensted, C
Ongar, with a farmhouse now known as Tudor Cottage, and
George and James Loveless and James Brine began their ne
The Standfields settled on a farm at High Laver. James Ha
stayed for a time at New House Farm in 1839, but returned
Tolpuddle, where he died in the Workhouse more than 50 y
in 1891. James Brine married Elizabeth, daughter of Thom
Standfield in 1839.

ly after settling at Greensted the five Tolpuddle Martyrs
d a local branch of the Chartist Association, which gained
rs so rapidly that the meetings had to be held in a field at New
Farm to the annoyance of the vicar of Greensted, the Rev.
Ray, who complained that the meetings were usually held on
y morning during the hours of Divine Service. The vicar's
was shared by his farmer parishioners and fear of a local
became a matter of concern to the local magistrates.

ase of New House Farm was for seven years only. At the end
t term the hostility of Essex farmers had become so strong that
artyrs' decided to emigrate to Ontario. A chapel window at
commemorates George and Betty Loveless in the words:
hese are they which came out of great
bulation'.

s Tower, a Joint Auditor of His Majesty's Revenue and a
ee for the colony of Georgia, bought Weald Hall in 1750. When
d unmarried in 1778, Weald Hall passed to his nephew,
opher, who had ten children. From him descended a line of
s who served Essex well. One member of the family, Admiral
ower, who was stationed at Naples in 1814, was responsible
rrying Napoleon to the Isle of Elba. Christopher John Hume
(b.1841) restored St. Peter's, South Weald, in 1867 and
he land for St. Paul's, Bentley. There are many memorials to
he race of Essex squires in South Weald church.

PE

y Trollope (1815-82), novelist and Post Office official, hunted
e Essex Hounds from his home at Waltham Cross. Occasionally
ted with the East Essex. Trollope drew freely on his Essex
ences for the hunting scenes in his novels. The description of
ting club in Can You Forgive Her?, for example, is based on
on company who had their headquarters at the 'Sun and Whale-
nn at Harlow Common. It is said that it was at Saffron Walden
became acquainted with the original of 'Mrs. Proudie'.

ON

roughton, who is commemorated at Ingatestone by a fine monu-
tributed to Epephanius Evesham, was the son of a baker of
who entered the service of Sir John Petre as a page. In 1600
manded the Lioness in engagements against Spanish and
ese ships in the Mediterranean.

yon family of Layer Marney took refuge in England from the
ution of the Duke of Alva. They were so wealthy that Peter
who became a merchant in London, was able to bring into the
£60,000, a very large sum in those days. His son, Sir
, was knighted by James I at Newmarket and created a baronet
. At his death in 1626 he was buried in the family vault in
d church.

muel's first estate in Essex was Layer Marney, which he

bought from Peter Tuke. He bought the Halstead estate from Sir
Thomas Gardiner and rebuilt Boys Hall there.

The baronetcy became extinct with the death of the 4th baronet in 1724.

TUFNELL

Samuel Tufnell (1682-1758) bought Langleys, Great Waltham, from Sir
Richard Everard, 4th baronet (q.v.), in 1710, and two years later
started transforming the old home of the Everards into one of the
finest houses in the county. His great-grandfather, Richard Tufnell
(c.1570-1636), who was Master of the Salters' Company in 1628, left
'an immense quantity of plate'. Richard's grandson, John, married
Elizabeth Jolliffe, and brought to the family a name that continues to
be held along with Tufnell. Samuel of Langleys, son of John Tufnell
and Elizabeth (Jolliffe) was granted, in 1708, the right to add the
Jolliffe crest to the Tufnell arms. In 1717 he married Elizabeth,
daughter of a wealthy London merchant named Cressener, whose
family had been associated with Earls Colne, Great Tey, and Mount
Bures for several generations. The bride's family provided a marriage
portion of £10,000. The first child of the marriage, a daughter, died
unmarried in 1794. The second was the first of the four John Jolliffe
Tufnells.

The study of antiquities was one of Samuel Tufnell's major interests,
and Essex historians like to recall that his first will was witnessed by
the two county historians, Nicholas Tindal (q.v.) and Philip Morant
(q.v.). Another Essex historian, William Holman of Halstead (q.v.),
undertook work for him on the history of Great Waltham and the
Cressener family. In 1735, Samuel Tufnell's antiquarian interests
were recognised by his election to a Fellowship of the Society of
Antiquaries. He sat in Parliament for both Maldon and Colchester,
and was one of the plenipotentiaries attached to the Congress at
Antwerp, where he lived for some years while engaged in settling the
barrier treaty with the Austrians and the Dutch.

The first John Jolliffe Tufnell lived from 1720 to 1792. After his death
£150,000 and three caskets of jewels, together with a silver-gilt cup,
were found wrapped in linen behind law books in the library at
Langleys. The silver-gilt cup was sold in 1909 for 5,000 guineas and
is now in the possession of the Goldsmiths' Company. The Tufnell
family have continued in direct line at Langleys from 1710 to the
present time, and still own Pleshey, including the Castle.

See: F.W. Steer: Samuel Tufnell (1968).

TUKE

Sir Brian Tuke (d.1545), courtier and secretary to Wolsey, came of
a Kentish family. His first recorded connection with Essex is dated
1513, when his name was placed on the county Commission of the Peace.
In 1537 he was granted a licence to impark 200 acres of land – arable,
meadow, and pasture, and 100 acres of wood at Pyrgo. The Royal
Manor of Havering (not Pyrgo, as some historians have stated) was held
by the Queens of England from Margaret, queen of Edward I, until taken
into the king's hands at the death of Jane Seymour.

About 1543 Henry VIII bought Pyrgo from Sir Brian Tuke, who was then
steward of the lordship and Treasurer of the Chamber. Tuke died at
Layer Marney in 1545, universally mourned. He had been held in high

esteem as a patron of learning, and is mentioned in this connection
by Leland. He was the subject of portraits by Holbein.

His youngest son, George, succeeded to the estate at Layer Marney,
which remained in the hands of his descendants for several generations
until sold by Peter Tuke to Sir Samuel Tryon (q.v.). Sir Samuel Tuke,
1st baronet (d.1674), took part in the defence of Colchester in 1648.

TURPIN

Richard (Dick) Turpin (1705-39), was born at 'The Bell', afterwards
called 'The Crown', Hempstead, the son of John and Mary Turpin.
He was baptised in 1705. As a youth he was apprenticed to a Whitechapel butcher, but discharged because of 'the brutality of his manners'.
He then found employment with a farmer named Giles, who lived in
Richmond Street, Plaistow. Again he was found unsatisfactory and dismissed. While unemployed he stole two fat oxen, which he cut up and
sold, offering the hides for sale at Waltham Abbey market. There he was
recognised and a warrant for his arrest was issued. When the police
arrived at his home in East Ham, he slipped out through a back window
and joined a gang of smugglers, who had their headquarters in the ruins
of Hadleigh Castle and worked the river between Plaistow and Southend.

On leaving the smugglers he found a cottage for his wife at Sewardstone,
and from a nearby cave in Epping Forest commenced operations as a
highwayman in company with several others led by a blacksmith named
Gregory. This gang terrorised remote farmhouses, and stole from
churches until in 1735 three members were captured and one of them,
John Wheeler, turned evidence. The gang broke up and Gregory himself
was hanged. For a time Turpin continued to operate with another member
of the same gang, a pewterer named Rowden, who left the road to become
a counterfeiter somewhere in the West Country. Turpin's next companion
was Matthew King (not Tom, as popular accounts have it). The two
worked together until King was fatally wounded in a Whitechapel ambush.
Turpin again took refuge in Epping Forest, where he shot and killed a
certain Thomas Morris, who recognised him and was so foolhardy as to
say so. A reward of £200 was offered for his capture. He was described
as being 5' 9" in height, broad about the shoulders, with a short, broad
face, much marked as the result of small pox.

The London Gazette for 7th June,1737, reported:
    'Yesterday in the afternoon about three o'clock, as the
    Saffron Walden and Bishop's Stortford Stage-coaches
    were coming to Town, they were stopped about a Mile
    and a Half this side of Epping, by Turpin, the Famous
    Highwayman, who took from the Walden coach about Four
    Pounds. He used the Passengers with a great deal of
    Civility, and although there were above Twenty persons
    in and about both Coaches, and a Chaise in sight, he
    made off through the Wood without being taken'.

When things became too hot for him in Essex he moved North, and is
reputed to have got his living trading horses (no doubt stolen) between
Lincolnshire and Yorkshire. He was finally arrested for shooting a
cock and threatening the man who witnessed the incident. For this
offence he was brought before the Beverley justices in 1738 under the
name of John Palmer - Palmer having been his wife's name. But not until
the following year did it become known that 'John Palmer' was Dick
Turpin. This discovery was made when he indiscreetly wrote to his
brother-in-law asking him to get a character reference for him as John

Palmer. The handwriting was recognised and he was taken to York for trial on two indictments of horse-stealing. On being convicted he was hanged at York on the 7th April 1739.

Turpin was a cold-blooded footpad and murderer, whose character was romanticised by Harrison Ainsworth in Rookwood (1834).

TUSSER

Thomas Tusser (1523-80), poet of husbandry, was born at Rivenhall, the fourth son of William Tusser of Lanham Manor and Dorothy (neé Smith), his wife, who claimed descent from Sir Michael Carington, standard bearer to Richard I. Tusser was educated at St. Paul's, Eton, and Cambridge. After a period at Court he retired to Cattawade, a few yards over the Suffolk border, where he took up farming and wrote his first book of husbandry, The Hundreth Good Pointes of Husbandrie, published in 1557. From Cattawade he removed to Ipswich; from there to West Dereham in Norfolk, and later to Norwich. After a few years in East Anglia he returned to his native Essex to farm at Fairstead. In none of these places did he prosper. According to Dr. Mavor
　　'his mind was too liberal, and he was too little
　　a match for the artifices of his vulgar brethren to
　　thrive in this vocation; and in consequence he
　　retired to London'.

In 1573 his hundred points were amplified to five hundred. The Plague of 1574 drove Tusser from London to Cambridge for a time; but he returned to London and died in a debtors' prison in May 1580. Fuller says of him that he
　　'spread his bread with all sorts of butter,
　　yet none would stick thereon'.

TWEDYE

Richard Twedye (d.1574), justice of the peace, is commemorated by a mural brass in the church at Stock, where he founded almshouses (rebuilt in the second half of the 17th century). We are informed that he was
　　'a Justice eke, a man full grave and sage'　who
　　'served well against the Ingleshe foes in foren landes
　　and eke at home'.
He died at Boreham.

TWINING

Thomas Twining (1735-1804), translator of Aristotle's Poetics, was rector of Fordham and St. Mary-at-the-Walls, Colchester. His letters were published in Recollections and Studies of a Country Clergyman and Selections from Papers of the Twining Family. He was a friend of Dr. Burney and other eminent musicians. Prof. Ralph Walker of the McGill University, Montreal, edited a collection of his letters. On July 10th, 1786, he wrote a long vivacious letter to Fanny Burney.

TYLNEY, EARLS see CHILD

TYRELL

The Tyrell family, now extinct in the main line in Essex, was prominent from soon after the Conquest until the death of the last surviving male representative of the chief branches, Sir John Tyrell, Bart., at Boreham House in 1877. There are many monuments to the family in East Horndon church, the most notable being one by Nollekens, dated 1766. Another fine monument is the incised slab to Alice, wife of Sir John Tyrell, 1422, with the figure in horned head-dress and fur-lined cloak. There is an even earlier brass at Downham to Sir Thomas Tyrell and Alice his wife, c.1380. This Sir Thomas, who was of the Heron Hall in East Horndon family, was one of the Knights of the Shire in seven Parliaments between 1355 and 1375.

UDALL

Nicholas Udall (1505-56), author of <u>Ralph Roister Doister,</u> was vicar of Braintree from 1537 to 1544. He was born in Hampshire and educated at Winchester and Oxford. In 1534 he was appointed Head Master of Eton, where Thomas Tusser (q.v.) of Rivenhall was one of his pupils. Tusser complained of the harsh treatment he received from the 'flogging master', as Udall was called. In 1542 Udall was dismissed from Eton for misconduct and imprisoned for a time.

While at Braintree he began to publish translations of the <u>Para-phrases</u> of Erasmus and the <u>New Testament.</u> This work brought him the patronage of Queen Catherine Parr and Edward VI, who appointed him Prebendary of Windsor. The Guild Chapel at Braintree was completed during Udall's incumbency.

UNWIN

The Rev. William Cawthorne Unwin (1745-86), son of Mary Unwin of Olney, Bucks., and friend of the poet, William Cowper, who wrote a poem entitled 'Tithing Time at Stock', was rector of Stock, Ramsden Bellhouse and Ramsden Crays, during the Evangelical Revival of the 18th century. Other friends were William Wilberforce and Henry Thornton, the Clapham banker. Unwin died of a fever at Winchester while travelling in the South of England in 1786 and was buried in the Cathedral.

URSWYK

The Urswyk brasses at Dagenham are the latest in date of the many fine brasses in Essex. Sir Thomas Urswyk (d.1479), judge, was Common Serjeant of London in 1453; Recorder, 1455. He was on the Yorkist side in the Wars of the Roses and in 1460 was placed in a Commission to try Lancastrian partisans at the Guildhall. In 1471, on Edward IV's return after Warwick's rebellion, Urswyk secretly admitted him to the City of London. He was knighted the same year and the following year was appointed Chief Baron of the Exchequer, allegedly for his part in the murder of Henry VI. Sir Thomas Urswyk built Marks Hall at Dagenham, which was pulled down in 1808. At his death in 1479 he was buried beneath an altar tomb in Dagenham church.

Sir Thomas's first wife was Mary Needham, by whom he had one daughter, who is the only nun commemorated by a brass in Essex.

His second wife was Anne, daughter of Richard Rich, a London merchant who was the great-grandfather of Lord Chancellor Rich (q.v.) of Leez Priory.

VANE

Sir Henry Vane, the younger (1613-62), Puritan politician, was born at Debden, near Newport. In the words of his speech from the scaffold in 1662, he had
> 'been, till he was 17 years old, a good fellow,
> but then it pleased God to lay a foundation of
> grace in his heart'.

He wrote a strange book entitled The Retired Man's Meditations. For one year he was governor of Massachusetts, returning to England in 1637. Three years later he was knighted.

Vane believed in the sovereignty of the people, and when Cromwell brought in his musketeers to dissolve the Rump in 1653 he called out:
> 'It is against morality and common honesty',
to which Cromwell replied:
> 'The Lord deliver me from Sir Henry Vane'.

When Cromwell died, Vane joined the soldiers in condemning Richard and destroying the Protectorate. At the Restoration he was excluded from the Act of indemnity. His execution in 1662 was witnessed by Pepys, who remarked on the 'humility and gravity he displayed at the end'.

VERE

The de Vere family flourished in Essex from the Conquest to the death of the 20th Earl of Oxford in 1703.

Aubrey (Alberic) de Vere, first of that name, came over with the Conqueror and was granted 14 lordships in Essex, 2 houses in Colchester, 9 estates in Suffolk, and properties in other counties. He planted vineyards at Hedingham, Belchamp Walter, Lavenham, and Kensington, where Earls Court is believed to take its name from the court of the de Vere earls of Oxford, who were lords of the manor. In 1111 he founded a Benedictine priory at Earls Colne, and shortly after that date died there, although he had made Hedingham the head of his barony. Weaver (Ancient Funeral Monuments) tells us that the inscription on his tomb described him as first Earl of Guisnes and recorded that his wife was the Conqueror's sister.

Aubrey II (c.1090-1141) married Alice FitzRichard of Clare. He succeeded his father as King's Chamberlain, an office that was confirmed to him and his heirs in perpetuity. He also followed his father in acts of piety by making gifts to Colne Priory and Colchester Abbey. Then in 1135 he himself founded a priory at Hatfield Broad Oak. But his principal memorial is the noble castle keep at Castle Hedingham. At his death in a London riot he was buried at Earls Colne.

One of Aubrey II's daughters, Alice, married Robert de Essex (q.v.), lord of Rayleigh; another, Rohesia, married Geoffrey de Mandeville, 1st Earl of Essex (q.v.). It was she who erected the cross at the crossing of the Icknield Way and Ermine Street which gave rise to the town of Royston (Rohesia's town). A third daughter, Juliana, married Hugh Bigod, 1st Earl of Norfolk. A fourth married Roger de Raines, lord of Rayne.

Aubrey III, 1st Earl of Oxford (1110-94), joined his brother-in-law, Geoffrey de Mandeville, in supporting the Empress Maud (who actually died at Hedingham Castle) against Stephen, and for this support the empress created him Earl of Oxford, a title which Stephen appears to have accepted by 1153, and which was confirmed to him by Maud's son, Henry II.

Aubrey, 2nd Earl of Oxford (c.1163-1214), son of the 1st Earl, died without issue.

Robert, 3rd Earl of Oxford (d.1221), was the third surviving son of the 1st Earl. He was one of the barons who forced King John to sign the Magna Carta. At his death he was buried in Hatfield Priory church, and not, as his ancestors had been, at Earls Colne. In the first quarter of the arms on the tomb effigy of the 3rd earl appears the mullet, or five-pointed star, which came to be one of the de Vere badges during the time of either the second or third Aubrey as a reminder of the incident recorded by Leland, who relates that
'The Night coming on in the chace of the Bataile,
and waxing dark, the Christianes being four miles
from Antiocke, God willing the Saufte of Christianes,
shewed a white Starre or Molette of fyve Pointes,
which, to every Manne's Sighte, did lighte and
arrest, upon the Standard of Albery, there shining
excessively'.

Hugh, 4th Earl of Oxford (c.1210-63), inherited the titles and offices of his line at the age of 11. He fought in the Holy Wars and was one of the barons who protested to the Pope in 1246 about the large sums of money being extracted annually by the Church from the common people.

Robert, 5th Earl of Oxford (d.1296), fought under Simon de Montfort at the Battle of Lewes, and was summoned to the first Parliament in December 1264. In the following year he was at Winchester with the younger Simon de Montfort, and after being captured at Kenilworth on the 1st August he was deprived for a time of his titles and honours. He recovered the earldom of Oxford under the Dictum of Kenilworth and probably acted as Chamberlain at the coronation of Edward I in 1274. At his death, his heart was buried in the Grey Fiars at Ipswich, his body at Earls Colne.

Robert, 6th Earl of Oxford (1257-1331), who carried on the martial traditions of his family, earned the title of 'Robert the Good'. He was a man of great independence of mind. Although he served in the Scottish wars he boycotted the Bannockburn campaign. He also refused to attend the secret Parliament at York. Collins, in Noble Families, says of him:
'His Government, both in Peace and War, being
so prudent, his Hospitality, and Works of Charity,
so wisely abundant, and his Temperance, with a
religious Zeal, so admirably conjoined, that the
common People esteemed him as a Saint'.
His only son having died, he was succeeded in 1331 by his nephew, who was then only 19.

John, 7th Earl of Oxford (1313-60), officially recovered for the family the hereditary office of King's Chamberlain, which the fifth earl lost at Kenilworth. He was one of the finest soldiers of his day, being one of the commanders of the First Division at Crecy, with the Black Prince and the Earl of Warwick. During the siege of Calais he distinguished himself by leading 200 ships into an engagement with a French fleet bound for Calais and by capturing 20 French ships and many gallies with supplies. At Poitiers in 1356, it was the English archers led by the Earl of Oxford that saved the day. Four years later he was killed at the siege of Rheims.

Thomas, 8th Earl of Oxford (1337-71), accompanied his father, the 7th Earl, in his last campaign, and served in France in 1369; but he appears to have spent most of his time at home, peacefully carrying out the duties of a great landowner. He died at Great Bentley, but was buried at Earls Colne.

Robert, 9th Earl of Oxford (1362-92), acted as Chamberlain at the coronation of Richard II, although he was only 15 years old at the time. He married Philippa, daughter of the Earl of Bedford and grand-daughter of Edward III and Philippa of Hainault. By right of his own and his wife's ancestry, the 9th Earl lived close to the king and was at times accused of exercising undue influence in national affairs. In June 1381 he was at Richard's side when he rode out to meet the Peasants' Army at Mile End. When he came of age in 1383, he received from the king a grant of the custody of the town and castle of Colchester and the overlordship of the Tendring Hundred. In 1385 he was granted additional estates without rent by Richard to assist him in the conquest of Ireland, and on December 1st 1385, in full Parliament, Robert, 9th Earl of Oxford, was created Marquess of Ireland, with semi-regal powers. The following year the marquessate was revoked and he was created Duke of Ireland.

When Richard was deprived of his kingly powers and the government transferred to the Commission presided over by the Duke of Gloucester, Oxford fell with him. He was also in disgrace at the time for having deserted his wife, Philippa, and for abducting one of the queen's maidens, Agnes Lancecrone, even going so far as to obtain, by dubious methods, a divorce from Philippa. This, however, was declared null and void by the Pope in 1389 and Philippa had the style of a Duchess for life.

Throughout these fluctuations of fortune, the Earl retained the king's confidence. In 1387 he made an abortive attempt from headquarters at Chester to regain power from Richard. When this failed he fled to the Low Countries, and in 1388 was condemned to death by Parliament for treason. His estates were forfeited; but as the succession was not barred by the attainder, the entailed estates were restored at his death in 1392 to his successor in the earldom.

Aubrey, 10th Earl of Oxford (c.1340-1400), uncle of the 9th Earl, tried in vain to recover for the family the office of Chamberlain, lost by the attainder of the 9th Earl. The first Parliament of Henry IV supported him, but Henry was adamant, and there were probably other considerations than those of loyalty. It was said at the time that the Earl was suffering 'from such feebleness and sickness as one who languished from palsy, having no health or discretion'. In the 8th Earl's time the Aubrey who became 10th Earl had been granted the stewardship of the Royal Forest of Havering. In 1378 he was granted the custody of Hadleigh Castle, the manor of Thundersley and the crown revenues from Rayleigh. He carried the king's sword when Richard met Wat Tyler at Mile End in 1381. In view of his long association with Hadleigh, it is thought probable that he was buried there.

Richard, 11th Earl of Oxford (1385-1417), was one of Henry V's commanders at Agincourt.

John, 12th Earl of Oxford (1408-62), took the Lancastrian side and was executed with Aubrey, his eldest son, for plotting against the king. It was alleged against them that they had prepared the way for a Lancastrian landing on the east coast.

John, 13th Earl of Oxford (1443-1513), second son of the 12th Earl, was committed to the Tower under suspicion of plotting against the king in 1468, but was released after a few months. Later he so far gained the confidence of the king that he was appointed High Constable of England, and tried and condemned John Tiptoft, Earl of Worcester, who had tried and condemned his father and elder brother.

At the Battle of Barnet in 1471, the 13th Earl fought valiantly to avenge his father and brother; but a thick mist caused him to lose sight of the enemy, and when his forces came in sight of other Lancastrians, each side suspected the other of treachery and Lancastrian fought Lancastrian. In the confusion that followed the earl thought the only way to save the cause was to escape from the field of battle. He made for Scotland first. Later he crossed to France, where he assembled men and ships for privateering. Through the course of the following fourteen years his fortunes ebbed and flowed inconclusively; but when Henry Tudor landed in the summer of 1485, the earl was captain-general of the invading army, and at the Battle of Bosworth no-one did more than he to secure the throne for Henry VII.

In acknowledgement of his services, all the honours that former earls had lost were restored, including that of Hereditary Lord Great Chamberlain, and in addition to these the 13th Earl was made Lord High Admiral of England, Ireland, and Aquitaine, High Steward of the Duchy of Lancaster south of the Trent, Constable of the Tower of London and Castle Rising, Privy Councillor and Knight of the Garter. Adorned with these great offices of state he lived in regal splendour at Hedingham castle, where in the summer of 1498 he entertained the king for nearly a week. It is of this occasion that the story is told that at the end of these days of sumptuous entertainment, when the king saw the full number of the earl's retainers lining the route along which he must pass he called out:
  'My lord, I have heard much of your hospitality,
  but I see it is greater than the speech: these
  handsome gentlemen and yeomen which I see on
  both sides of me, are they your menial servants?'.

  'If it may please your Grace', replied the earl,
  'they are most of them my retainers, that are come
  to do me service at such a time as this, and chiefly
  to see your Grace'.
The king looked startled and said:
  'By my faith, my lord, I thank you for your good
  cheer; but I may not have my laws broken in my
  sight. My attorney must speak with you'.
The attorney did, and the earl was obliged to compound for no less a sum than 1,500 marks for his offence against the Statute of Retainers.

John, 14th Earl of Oxford (1499-1526), nephew of the 13th earl, inherited his titles at the age of 14, and came into control of his estates in 1520. His extravagance, however, was such that he was ordered to break up his household and live with his father-in-law, the Duke of Norfolk, while Wolsey managed his estates for him. He brought little credit to the line, and when he died at the age of 26 he left no issue. With him the direct line came to an end, as he was the last heir general as well as heir male, and the office of Lord Great Chamberlain reverted to the Crown.

John, 15th Earl of Oxford (1490-1540), was a second cousin of the 14th earl. He was much at court, signed the articles against Wolsey in 1529 and the address to the Pope for the king's divorce the following year. He was commissioner for the deposition of Queen Catherine in 1533 and carried the crown at the coronation of Anne Boleyn. His connection with the king's marriages continued in his part at her trial, and his attendance in the following year at the funeral of Jane Seymour. In 1540 he was in attendance on Henry VIII at Blackheath when Anne of Cleves was received. At the Dissolution he received Colne Priory but he was buried at Castle Hedingham.

John, 16th Earl of Oxford (1512-62), was the first Protestant earl, and in June 1553 he was one of peers who declared in favour of Lady Jane Grey. But he quickly turned over to Mary when he saw which way the wind was blowing, and officiated as Great Chamberlain at her coronation. In 1555 he was actually ordered by the Council to attend the burning of heretics in Essex. This, however, did not prevent his return to Protestant favour when Elizabeth became queen. He officiated at her coronation and in 1561 entertained her for five days at Castle Hedingham during her Progress of that year. When he died in the following year he was buried at Castle Hedingham, but no monument to his memory was ever erected.

Edward, 17th Earl of Oxford (1550-1604), is the most romantic and controversial figure in the family's history. He has been charged with reckless extravagance and many vices. No doubt he was extravagant; but the truth is that the 13th Earl lived in a style that none of his successors could maintain. The 14th earl was ordered to break up his household and live with his father-in-law. When the 15th claimed the inheritance the three sisters of the 14th claimed a share and the estate was divided between them. The 16th lived proudly, and at his death his affairs were found to be in sad confusion, which probably explains the lack of a memorial. Edward, the 17th Earl, was only 12 when his father died. He became a royal ward in the charge of Burghley, whose daughter, Anne, he married in 1571, to the great unhappiness of both.

The 17th Earl spent his youth with poets and scholars. George Gascoigne, the poet from Walthamstow (q.v.), lived with him at Cecil House in the Strand. One of Gascoigne's works, The Supposes, a translation from Ariosto, was later to form the basis of The Taming of the Shrew, and this came to be one of the links between Shakespeare and the 17th Earl which in 1920 led J. Thomas Looney to claim for de Vere the authorship of Shakespeare's plays. Essex has so many associations with the claim that one or two others should be recorded here. Arthur Golding's (q.v.) translation of Ovid was a source for Shakespearean plots, and Golding was de Vere's uncle and tutor. Canon Rendall (q.v.) of Dedham examined the case for the de Vere authorship in Shakespeare Sonnets and Edward de Vere, and Personal Clues in Shakespeare's Poems and Sonnets. The earl had a company of players known as the Earl of Oxford's boys. Sixteen of his poems were published in The Paradyse of Dainty Devises; 16, along with 45 by George Gascoigne in A Hundred Sundrie Flowers. His poetical output was clearly considerable, and there is an intriguing mystery about his activities during the last 15 years of his life, which were spent as a recluse. In 1596 his second wife,

Elizabeth Trentham, one of the queen's Maids of Honour, bought
King's Place, Hackney, and it was there that the 17th Earl died in
1604.

He was always a favourite with the queen, and especially delighted
her by winning chief prize in a joust at Westminster in 1571. Meeting him during travels on the Continent, George Chapman wrote of
the earl:

> I overtook, coming from Italy,
> In Germany, a great and famous Earl,
> Of England, the most goodly fashion'd man
> I ever saw: from head to foot in form
> Rare and most absolute; he had a face
> Like one of the most ancient honour'd
> From whence his noblest family Romans was deriv'd
> He was beside of spirit passing great,
> Valiant and learned, liberal as the sun,
> Spoke and writ sweetly, or of learn'd subjects,
> Or of the disciplining of public weals;
> And 'twas the Earl of Oxford.

Henry, 18th Earl of Oxford (1593-1625), born at Stoke Newington,
served under his uncle, Sir Horace Vere (q.v.), as captain in the
Palatinate in 1620. From December 1621 to March 1622 he was Vice-
Admiral of a Fleet patrolling the Channel. It looked as though he
would be able to restore the family fortunes, particularly when in
1624 he married Lady Diana Cecil, daughter of the Earl of Exeter,
who brough with her a marriage portion of £30,000, but died without
issue.

Robert, 19th Earl of Oxford (d.1632) had little connection with the
county. Castle Hedingham ceased to be the home of the Earls of
Oxford with the death of the 18th after being linked for nearly
six hundred years. The Great Chamberlainship passed to Lord
Willoughby, cousin and heir general of the 18th Earl. But such was
the spell cast by the history of the de Veres that in 1626, when Lord
Chief Justice Sir Randolph Carew, awarded the earldom to Robert
de Vere, he said:

> 'I heard a great Peer of the nation, and a learned, say,
> when he lived there was no King in Christendom had
> such a subject as Oxford. I have laboured to make a
> covenant with myself that affection may not press upon
> judgement; for I suppose there is no man that hath any
> apprehension of gentry or nobleness but his affection
> stands to the continuance of so noble a name and home
> and would take hold of a twig or twine-thread to uphold
> it. And yet Time hath his revolutions; there must be a
> period and an end to all temporal things, finis rerum,
> an end of names and dignities and whatever is terrene;
> and why not of de Vere? - for where is Bohun? Where
> is Mowbray? Nay, what is more, and most of all, where
> is Plantagenet? They are entombed in the urns and
> sepulchres of mortality'.

The 19th Earl was killed in battle in 1632 and Aubrey, his only son
succeeded.

Aubrey, 20th Earl of Oxford (1626-1703), suffered with other
Royalist families during the Commonwealth, but at the Restoration
received the Garter and was appointed Lord Lieutenant of Essex.
James II removed him in 1687 and appointed in his place the Roman

Catholic, Lord Petre. But when William and Mary came to the throne,
the 20th Earl was restored to the point of holding the office jointly
with the Duke of Albemarle. He died in a house in Downing Street and
was buried in Westminster Abbey. With his death the title became
extinct. There had been one son of his second marriage, but he had
died young 'in a miserable cottage' at Castle Hedingham.

If the line had continued we might have known more about the 20th
Earl. As head of the county militia he had grave responsibilities in
guarding the mouth of the Thames from the Dutch. But the line died out
and even the monuments of the de Veres have been treated with scant
respect. Most of the earls had been buried at Colne Priory until in
1583 the 17th Earl sold the lay house, park, and manor to Roger
Harlackenden. In 1592 he sold the priory property, which included
the tombs of so many of his ancestors, to Roger Harlackenden's son,
Richard. Two of the monuments were transferred in the first quarter
of the 17th century to Earls Colne church. Then in 1672 the estate
passed from the Harlackenden family to a Mr. Wale, whose great-
granddaughter committed the final act of vandalism by burning many
of the charters that had come down with the property. Not until 1935
was the process of desecration arrested. In that year Colonel Probert
rescued the tombs of the 5th, 8th, and 11th earls, and removed them
to St. Stephen's Chapel, just over the Suffolk border.

Note: Mr. George Caunt has helped generously with the preparation
       of this entry.

FRANCIS AND HORACE DE VERE

During the 17th Earl's lifetime the martial traditions of the family
were carried on by his cousins, Francis and Horace de Vere, of
Tilbury Hall, north Essex, who spent their youth at Castle Hedingham.
They were the sons of Geoffrey de Vere, third son of the 15th Earl,
and Elizabeth, daughter of Sir John Hardkyn, of Colchester.

Francis (1560-1609) served under the Earl of Leicester in Holland.
He was knighted for his bravery in defending Bergen op Zoom in 1588.
On returning to England in 1595 he was elected M.P. for Leominster.
The following year he held an important command under the Earl of
Essex when Cadiz was taken. His last and most valorous achievement
was his defence of Ostend from July 1601 to March 1602, during which
he held out with 1,600 men against 12,000. His military Commentaries
were published in 1657.

Horace (1565-1635) was associated with his brother in all his exploits
after 1590, and succeeded to his commands. He was raised to the
peerage as Baron Vere of Tilbury in 1625 for his distinguished
services to Charles I. Fuller says of him:
    'Horace, Lord Vere, had more meekness and as much
    virtue as his brother; of an excellent temper: it being
    true of him what was said of the Caspian Sea, that it
    doth never ebb, nor flow, observing a constant tenor,
    neither elated by success nor depressed by failure.
    Both lived in war much honoured, and died in peace
    much lamented'.
Both brothers were buried in Westminster Abbey. As he left five
daughters and no sons the barony died with him.

Anne, his fourth daughter, married Fairfax. She is remembered for
her intervention in the trial of Charles I. When the names of the commissioners were read out and Fairfax's name was called, she shouted:

'Not here. Never will be. He hath more sense!'
When Bradshaw announced that Charles was being tried in the name
of the people of England, she called down from the gallery:
'It is a lie. Not half, nor a quarter of them.
Oliver Cromwell is a traitor'.

Sir Clement Markham, in The Fighting Veres, writes:
'The difference between the characters of the two
brothers was that while Francis was more self-asserting
and stern, Horace was extremely modest, and ruled
those under him by kindness rather than severity, though
both were strict disciplinarians. It was said that the
soldiers stood in awe of Sir Francis, while they loved
Sir Horace'.

WAAD

A memorial in Manuden church to Sir William Waad (d.1623) records
that his father, Armigel (who died in 1568 and has a memorial in
Hampstead church), was reputed to be the first Englishman to discover
America and dubbed 'the English Columbus'. Armigel Waad was Clerk
of the Council to Henry VIII and Edward VI. Sir William Waad, the
builder of Battails Hall, Manuden, succeeded his father in the office,
serving both Elizabeth I and James I as Clerk. As Lieutenant of the
Tower he had charge of Mary Queen of Scots before her execution at
Fotheringhay. His grandson was murdered in a field near his home,
leaving no surviving issue; but as Armigel Waad, his great-grandfather,
had 20 children the family continued in Essex until late in the 18th
century.

WADHAM

Dorothy Wadham, founder of Wadham College, Oxford, in 1612, was
the daughter of Sir William Petre of Ingatestone. Her husband was
Nicholas Wadham of Merefield in Somerset. She is commemorated by
a fine brass at Ilminster.

WAKE

Descendants of James Hay, Earl of Carlisle, sold the Waltham Abbey
and Nazeing estates to Sir Samuel Jones, who left it to his great-
nephew, Samuel, fifth son of Sir William Wake, Bart., who took the
name of Jones and was High Sheriff of Essex in 1699. He left the
manor to his nephew, Charles, second son of Sir Baldwin Wake, who
died without issue in 1740. Sir Charles left Waltham to his nephew,
Sir Charles Wake Jones, at whose death without issue in 1755 it
passed to Sir William Wake, a direct descendant of the original
baronet. Since then the estate has descended with the baronetcy.
There is a tablet to the memory of Sir Hereward Wake (1876-1943),
13th baronet, in Nazeing old church.

WALDEGRAVE

The Roman Catholic family of Waldegrave, already eminent in
Northamptonshire, acquired Smallbridge Hall, near Bures St.Mary,
in the 14th century.

Sir Edward Waldegrave of Borley (1517-61), politician, inherited
Borley in 1543, and in 1548 was granted neighbouring church lands.

In Edward VI's reign he was a principal officer of the Household of Princess Mary (q.v.), and figured in the Copt Hall incident described elsewhere (see MARY). When Elizabeth became queen he lost all his offices and retired to Borley, where he was charged with permitting mass. On refusing to take the Oath of Supremacy he was sent to the Tower, where he died at the age of 44. He has a fine six-poster tomb in Borley church.

His eldest daughter married the 1st Baron Petre (q.v.). His second son, Nicholas, succeeded to the Borley estate, and he, like his father, suffered severely as a recusant.

Sir Henry Waldegrave (1659-89), 4th baronet, married Henrietta, natural daughter of James II by Arabella Churchill, sister of John, Duke of Marlborough. He was raised to the peerage as Baron Waldegrave in 1686, and the following year was appointed Comptroller of the Household. At the end of James's reign he fled to Paris, where he died at the age of 30.

James, 1st Earl Waldegrave (1685-1741), diplomat, was educated in France as a Roman Catholic, but in 1719 he became a Protestant and had a distinguished career at court. He was a lord of the Bedchamber, 1723; envoy to Paris, 1725; Ambassador at Vienna, 1727-30, and at Paris, 1730-40. In 1729 he was created Earl Waldegrave. It was he who built Navestock Hall, which became the principal seat of the family but was pulled down in 1811.

His son, James, 2nd Earl Waldegrave (1715-63), was chief confidant of George II, and governor of the Prince of Wales, afterwards George III. His Memoirs were published in 1821. He married Maria, one of the five natural children (by the daughter of a Darlington post-master) of Sir Edward Walpole, the Prime Minister's second son. He was twice the age of his bride at the time of the marriage, and when her uncle, Horace Walpole, came down to Navestock to visit the couple he found the house 'ill finished, but an air seigneurial in the furniture'. The earl died in 1763 after only four years of marriage. His countess lived until 1807 and became one of George III's headaches. After the earl's death she had many suitors, among whom was William Henry, Duke of Gloucester (1743-1805), the king's favourite brother. George III strongly disapproved of the association, so when the two married they were obliged to keep the ceremony a secret.

When Maria lived at Navestock as Countess of Waldegrave, her father, Sir Edward Walpole, lived at Luxborough, Chigwell, which he sold in 1773 to Lord Bellamount.

The Ladies Waldegrave were painted by Sir Joshua Reynolds in 'The Lace Makers'. See also Violet Biddulph: The Three Waldegrave Ladies (1938).

WARNER

Richard Warner (1711-75), the Woodford botanist, author of Plantae Woodfordiensis, was a friend of Garrick, Hogarth, Linnaeus, Ellis, and possibly of Dr. Johnson. His father was a London banker.

As a boy of eleven, Richard Warner came with his mother to live at Harts, Woodford Green, then a fine country house with extensive gardens and paddocks. Nichols, in Literary Anecdotes (vol.iii, p.75), says:

'He was bred to the law, and for some time had chambers in Lincoln's Inn; but being possessed

of an ample fortune, resided chiefly at a good
old house at Woodford Green in Essex, where he
maintained a botanical garden, and was very
successful in the cultivation of rare exotics'.

Warner was visited at Harts in 1748 by Peter Kalm, a pupil of
Linnaeus. His wide connections with the eminent of his day reflected
the catholicity of his interests. In addition to his botanical work he
had a considerable reputation as the translator of the comedies of
Plautus. He was buried under an altar tomb to the north of the chancel
in Woodford churchyard.

WARREN

Samuel Hazzledine Warren (1873-1958), was an amateur geologist and
prehistorian who won international repute. In 1911 he found the
Clacton spear, the oldest known artifact then discovered, in the stra-
tum known as the 'Elephant Bed' at Great Clacton. His fine collection
of fossil mammalian, much of which came from 'Artic Beds' in the Lea
Valley, is now in the British Museum. His first finds were published
in 1897, his last were the subject of a paper in the press at the time of
his death. One of his most important discoveries was at Penmaenmawr
in 1919, when he located an important Neolithic axe factory, which
turned out to be the source of 'greenstone' axeheads widely distributed
in Britain.

His flair for using simple traditional methods which had survived into
the 20th century as guides to prehistoric crafts led him into bitter
controversy at times; but he often proved right, as when he used the
huts of charcoal burners in Epping Forest to explain prehistoric hut-
circles. He lived on the edge of the Forest at Loughton during the
greater part of his life, and all who had the pleasure of his friendship
cherish memories of his gift for making 'dry bones' in his private
museum live, to say nothing of the excitement of hearing him describe
the ferocity of the eolith controversy that raged over the pre-glacial
Crag deposits in East Anglia during the first quarter of the century,
in which he played a leading part. He held several high offices in
learned societies and both the Prestwich Medal of the Geological
Society and the Henry Stopes Medal of the Geologists' Association.

WARWICK, EARL OF see GREVILLE

WASHINGTON

Laurence Washington (1602-52), great-great-grandfather of George
Washington, is commemorated in a memorial window at All Saints,
Maldon, where he was buried in January 1653.

He became rector of Purleigh in 1633, and remained until he was
ejected in 1643 as a Royalist, although he was described by a local
justice of the peace as 'a worthy pious man', and 'a modest sober
person'. Later he was allowed to hold a small curacy at Little
Braxted. He was born at Sulgrave, Northamptonshire, and had a
distinguished career at Oxford, which terminated on his marriage.
The two eldest of his six sons emigrated to America, and it was one
of these, John, who became the great-grandfather of George Washington,
first President of the United States of America.

In 1914 Mr. W. Lanier Washington presented to the rector and church-
wardens of Purleigh a copy of the original painting of George
Washington's mother. The Washington window at Maldon was unveiled

and dedicated in July, 1928.

WATTS-DITCHFIELD

John Edwin Watts-Ditchfield (1861-1923), first Bishop of Chelmsford, was born at Manchester, the son of Methodist parents. He came south in 1897 as incumbent of St. James the Less, Bethnal Green, and remained at Bethnal Green until nominated to the new see of Chelmsford by Mr. H.H. Asquith in 1914. The rapid expansion of Metropolitan Essex was a challenge to which he and his suffragan, Bishop Inskip (q.v.) of Barking gave themselves unsparingly. His only daughter married the Rev. E.N. Gowing, later Archdeacon, whose years at Prittlewell made a great impact on the life of Southend-on-Sea.

WELLESLEY

William Pole-Tylney-Long-Wellesley, 4th Earl of Mornington (1788-1857), a nephew of the Duke of Wellington, married Catherine Tylney-Long, the Wanstead heiress, at St. James, Piccadilly, in 1812 and became the leading figure in the social and political life of West Essex. The ceremony was performed by Dr. Glasse (q.v.), rector of Wanstead, and was an augury of things to come. The bride was the richest heiress in England, with an income of £80,000 a year. The wedding was sumptuous. The bridal jewels were worth £50,000, the dress and veil cost over 1000 guineas; yet the bridegroom had forgotten to buy a wedding ring and one had to be brought into church from a nearby jeweller.

Shortly after the marriage Wellesley assumed the name of Pole-Tylney-Long-Wellesley, and with it claimed the office of Lord Warden of Epping Forest, a title held by the Tylney family. One of his first acts was to close the right of way through Wanstead Park. This he was forced to re-open by a successful lawsuit brought against him in 1813. The following year he tried to regain local favour by giving a fete in his uncle's honour at Wanstead, which was attended by the Duke of York, and the Prussian princes, Frederick and Henry. Wellesley kept a pack of staghounds, and his hunt parties became famous. Many of the tales connected with them were kept alive by his huntsman, Tommy Rounding, who became landlord of the 'Horse and Groom', afterwards the 'Horse and Wells' at Woodford. The hunt breakfasts and all-night parties were held at the 'Eagle', Wanstead, with servants in attendance dressed in Lincoln green.

The gay squire of Wanstead was so reckless a gambler that within ten years of marriage he had squandered the whole of his wife's fortune and accumulated debts estimated at a quarter of a million pounds.

On the 10th June 1822 and the following 31 days, Wanstead House and its contents came under the hammer. A priced copy of the sale catalogue is in the Essex Record Office. The mansion was bought for demolition by a Norwich firm for a mere £10,000. The furniture realised £50,000. This fell so far short of what was required to satisfy the most pressing creditors that Pole-Tylney-Long-Wellesley was obliged to escape down the Thames in a hired boat in order to reach a place of safety on the Continent.

The death of his wife in 1825 at the age of 35 enabled him to marry a Mrs. Bligh, with whom he had been having an affair. Eight years later he deserted her. At various times she was constrained to apply for parish relief, and took refuge for a time in St. George's Workhouse.

In 1842, Wellesley succeeded to the title of Viscount Wellesley, on his father becoming 3rd Earl of Mornington. In 1845 he succeeded to the earldom; but was again so deeply in debt that he derived little benefit from the succession and during his last years he was reduced to living on a small pension allowed him by the Duke of Wellington. He died in 1857 in a small back street in the West End of London.

The earldom of Mornington lapsed to the Duke of Wellington at the death of the 4th Earl, of whom it was said during the course of the action by which Epping Forest was won for the public:
> 'It is in a great degree owing to his unprincipled
> and reckless sale of the Stewardship of his
> manors and of the Court of Attachments that the
> downfall of the forest system and the irregular and
> fraudulent inclosures of this century are owing'.

Wanstead Park, extending over 184 acres, with its fine ornamental waters, was acquired from Earl Cowley by the Corporation of London in 1880, and was formally opened to the public on August 1st, 1882. Of the house itself not a stone remains.

WENLOCK

The family of Wenlock was established at Langham at least as early as 1408. John Wenlock (d.1679), in a 'Humble Declaration' to Charles II, stated that he was

> 'still in lawful possession of an estate in
> lands, which though small, was of noble
> tenure, being lately holden of your Majesty
> by a whole knight's fee'.

The Wenlock family were ardent Royalists in a county predominantly Parliamentarian. When his house was attacked by a Parliamentary mob, John Wenlock took refuge at Dalham in Suffolk, where the rector was a kinsman; but one night, while he was taking exercise under cover of night, he was recognised by the village blacksmith and betrayed. His son, Dalton, was with Sir Charles Lucas (q.v.) at the Siege of Colchester.

WENTWORTH

The association of the Wentworth family with Essex begins with Henry (d.1482), second son of Sir Roger Wentworth of Nettlestead in Suffolk, a younger son of the Elmsall branch of the great Yorkshire family. Henry settled at Codham Hall, Wethersfield. He acquired considerable property by his two marriages. The first was with Elizabeth, daughter and heir of Henry Howard (uncle of the 1st Duke of Norfolk); the second with Joan, heiress of the FitzSimon family of North Shoebury.

His son and heir, Sir Roger Wentworth, who was Sheriff of Essex and Hertfordshire in 1499, added to the family estates by marrying Anne, daughter of Humphrey Tyrell of Little Warley, who, through her mother, was connected with the Helion, Rolfe, Swynborne, Nortoft, Botetourt, and Gernon families. Gosfield, later the principal seat of the Wentworth family in Essex, came to them through this marriage.

Roger Wentworth was knighted at Blackheath in 1497. He died in 1539 and was buried at Wethersfield (not at Gosfield as Morant states). He is commemorated by a stately altar tomb.

The first member of the family to reside at Gosfield was Henry, second

son of Sir Roger. He died in 1545. The third son of Sir Roger was
the first of four generations of the Wentworth family to live at
Bocking, where they continued for more than a century.

Sir John Wentworth of Gosfield (1494-1567) was for some years in
the suite of Cardinal Wolsey. He was knighted in 1546, seven years
after succeeding to the Essex estates. Under him the family held
eleven manors centred in Gosfield and eight detached from the main
body, together with three manors in Norfolk and at least seven in
Suffolk. He moved from Codham to Gosfield after Henry's death and
rebuilt the house. In 1561 he built the part of the parish church
known as the Wentworth chapel.

Sir John died, aged 73, and was buried under a marble altar tomb on
the north side of the chancel. His only son died before him, and the
estates passed to Anne, Lady Mautravers (d.1581), who had already
been married twice when she inherited Gosfield. Her first husband
was Sir Hugh Rich, son of Lord Rich of Leez (q.v.). He died in 1554.
Her second husband was Henry FitzAlan, Lord Mautravers, only son
of Henry, the last FitzAlan Earl of Arundel. He died in 1566. Her
third husband was William Deane (q.v.).

Lady Mautravers died in 1579 and was buried in the Wentworth chapel
with her first husband, Sir Hugh Rich. She had no issue and was
succeeded by John Wentworth of Little Horkesley and Gosfield (1540-
88). He did not enjoy the inheritance for long and was succeeded by
John Wentworth (1564-1613), sixth of the line, who held the estate
for 25 years, although he died aged 49. He was succeeded by the
seventh Sir John, (d.1631), who was knighted by James I in 1603 and
created a baronet in the first list in 1611. Under him the inheritance
was so dissipated that he was obliged in 1622 to sell Gosfield and most
of the estates to pay his debts. At his death only four manors remained
to be divided between his two surviving daughters, and with his death
the baronetcy became extinct. His wife, Catherine, daughter of Sir
Moyle Finch of Eastwell in Kent and granddaughter of Sir Thomas
Heneage of Copt Hall, Epping (q.v.), survived him eight years. When
she died in 1639 she was buried at Epping, where she had lived with
her daughter, Cecily, wife of Sir William Grey, of Chillingham,
Northumberland, who in 1624 was created Baron Grey of Werke.

WESTERN

The Westerns of Rivenhall were a family of London merchants who
settled in Essex in the last quarter of the 17th century. In 1692 Thomas
Western (d.1707) bought Rivenhall Place from the executors of Sir
William Wiseman. It remained the principal seat of the family until
1795, when Felix Hall took its place.

Samuel Western, Thomas's eldest son, was a member of Gray's Inn
and M.P. for Winchelsea in three Parliaments of William and Mary;
but as he died before his father, his eldest son, William (d.1729),
succeeded to the Rivenhall estate. At his death it passed to his son,
who died within a few months of succeeding, leaving no heir.

The Rivenhall property then passed to a descendant of the second son
of the Thomas who bought it. In all, there were five holders between
the death of the first Thomas in 1707 and 1733. The Thomas who inherited in 1733 was a distinguished antiquary, whom Cole referred to
as 'my dearest friend'.
    'He was by nature', he wrote,
    'one of the most lively, sprightly, and

cheerful men I ever had the happiness of
being acquainted with; always in good humour;
constantly contriving something to amuse and
entertain; a perpetual fund of drollery and
jocularity, together with an openness and
generosity of temper not to be matched in any
one I ever met with since'.
He died in 1766.

Thomas and Ann, his wife, had nine children, four of whom died
young. The second surviving son, Shirley, was rector of Rivenhall
for 45 years (1772-1824). Of the death of the eldest son Cole wrote:
'Dining with my sister, Jane, July 22, 1771, at Mr.
Thorpe's Chamber, the President of St. Katherine
Hall, I heard the melancholy and disagreeable news
that poor Mr. Charles Western, eldest son of my
late dear friend, Thomas Western of Rivenhall, in
Essex, Esq., going in his new phaeton with a pair
of new coach horses, which had cost him but that week
or a few days before, £140, on some occasion or
other, the horses got the mastery and ran away with
the chaise, when Mr. Western, finding it impossible
to stop them, imprudently jumped out, and in so doing
was killed on the spot'.
He was 24.

His heir was to reverse the family's record of misfortune. He was
Charles Callis, Baron Western (1767-1844), politician and agri-
culturist, and as he inherited at the age of four he had a long reign.
He travelled widely, collecting busts, urns, and other interesting
antiquarian pieces. He was M.P. for Maldon, 1790-1812, and for
Essex, 1812-32. His greatest interest was agricultural reform, and
he did much to improve sheep-breeding; he also published pamphlets
on prison discipline and various economic questions. It was he who
in 1795 added Felix Hall to the Rivenhall estate and stored there his
fine collection of marbles. In 1833 he was raised to the peerage as
Baron Western of Rivenhall. He died in his 78th year at Felix Hall,
leaving no heir to the barony. Lord Western was a bachelor himself,
and his brother, the rector of Rivenhall, had also died unmarried.
The estate, therefore, passed to Thomas Burch Western (1795-1873),
of Tattingstone Place, Suffolk.

There is a fine monument to the 1st and only Baron Western in
Rivenhall church, and Nichols, in his <u>Anecdotes of Hogarth,</u> mentions
another Western item that should not be lost sight of. He writes:
'At Rivenhall, Essex, the seat of Charles Callis
Western, Esq., M.P. for Maldon, is a capital
conversation piece by Hogarth, painted about the
year 1735, of his grandfather, Thomas Western,
Esq., his grandfather's mother, Mary, daughter of
Sir Richard Shirley, of Preston, Sussex, Chancellor
Hoadley, Archdeacon Charles Plumtre, the Rev.
William Cole, of Milton, the celebrated antiquary....'
Incidentally, on the death of Mary Shirley's brother, the third baro-
net, the valuable property at Preston, Brighton, came to the Western
family.

Thomas Burch Western was the first Liberal member for North Essex.
He was created a baronet in 1864 and became Lord Lieutenant of
Essex in 1869. He died at Felix Hall at the age of 77. His son, Thomas

Sutton Western, second baronet (1821-   ) was M.P. for Maldon,
1857-65. One of Sir Thomas Burch Western's daughters married
Robert Capel Cure (q.v.) of Blake Hall, Ongar.

Thomas Charles Callis Western, 3rd and last baronet (1850-1917)
died without issue and the baronetcy became extinct.

WESTON

The Weston family came into prominence in Essex in the 13th century.
In the 14th they were seated at Prested Hall, Feering; but it is with
Skreens, Roxwell, that they are chiefly associated. The manor of
Skreens was bought by Sir Jerome Weston in the time of Elizabeth 1.
His son, Sir Richard (1577-1635), represented Essex in Parliament
and was sent by James I to Prague to settle differences between the
Emperor and the Elector Palatine. In 1621 he became a Privy
Councillor and Chancellor of the Exchequer. He was created Baron
Weston of Nayland in Suffolk in 1628, with remainder to the heir male
of his body by his second wife, Frances, daughter of Nicholas
Waldegrave. Lord Weston served as Lord High Treasurer, 1628-35.
He became a Knight of the Garter in 1630 and in 1633 was created
Earl of Portland. His first wife was a daughter of William Pyncheon
of Writtle; his second wife was a daughter of Nicholas Waldegrave of
Borley (q.v.).

Lord Weston was appointed joint Lord Lieutenant of Essex with the
Earl of Warwick by Charles I, who thought so highly of him that when
he died at Wallingford House, Whitehall, the court went into mourning.
He was buried in Winchester Cathedral.

Clarendon says that Weston was popular as Chancellor of the Exchequer,
but that when he was appointed Lord Treasurer, he 'became on a sudden
wonderfully elated', by which he meant that the appointment went to his
head:
> 'He fell under the reproach of being a man of
> big looks and of a mean and abject spirit'.

His son, the 2nd Earl of Portland, sold Skreens to Sir John Bramston
(q.v.), in whose family it remained for over 200 years.

WHITLOCKE

Sir Bulstrode Whitlocke of Blunts, Witham (1605-76) was chairman of
the committee for prosecuting the Earl of Strafford. In 1653 he was
sent as ambassador to Sweden. Three years later he became Speaker
of the House of Commons, and in 1658 a member of Cromwell's House
of Lords. The following year he was made President of the Council of
State and Keeper of the Great Seal. He wrote many miscellaneous and
biographical works while in retirement following the Restoration.

WHITMORE

Colonel Sir Francis Whitmore, K.C.B., C.M.G., D.S.O., T.D.,
of Orsett (1872-1962), was Lord Lieutenant of Essex from 1936 to
1958.

Sir Francis was lord of the manors of Orsett, Little Thurrock,
Stifford, Corringham, and North Benfleet. He rendered great service
to the Essex County Territorial and Auxiliary Forces Association.
During the First World War he commanded the Essex Yeomanry, and,
immediately after the war, the 10th Royal Hussars. He published

works on both these units, and is esteemed among lords lieutenant
for producing a valuable manual of advice to assist them in the perform-
ance of their duties.

WILBYE

John Wilbye (1574-1638), madrigalist, was born in Norfolk, the son of
a tanner. His talent as a musician attracted the attention of the
Cornwallis family of Brome Hall, Suffolk, who became his first patrons.
Elizabeth Cornwallis married Sir Thomas Kytson of Hengrave Hall,
near Bury St. Edmunds, and in 1594 Wilbye became family musician to
the Kytsons, who were able to introduce him into musical circles in
London. He published his First Set of English Madrigals for three,
four, five and six voices in 1598, dedicating it to Sir Charles Cavendish,
who married Elizabeth, the elder daughter of Sir Thomas Kytson. A
second set, published in 1609, was dedicated to Lady Arabella Stuart,
Sir Charles Cavendish's niece.

Wilbye remained with the Kytsons at Hengrave Hall until the death of
Lady Kytson in 1628. He then retired to Colchester, where he lived
in the house of the Countess Rivers, Sir Thomas Kytson's younger
daughter. He died in 1638 and was buried in Holy Trinity church. The
house in which he lived in Trinity Street is now marked with a plaque.

WILSON

Arthur Wilson (1595-1652), historian and dramatist, who lived at Pond
Park, Little Leighs, was gentleman-in-waiting to Robert Devereux,
3rd Earl of Essex, and steward to Robert Rich, 2nd Earl of Warwick
(q.v.). His works include The History of Great Britain, Being the
Life and Reign of King James the First (1653), and an autobiography,
Observations of God's Providence in the Tract of my Life, etc., first
printed in Francis Peck's Desiderata Curiosa (1735). These works
contain useful sidelights on contemporary events in Essex. He left a
record of the trial of witches at Chelmsford and of the local effects
of the struggle between King and Parliament.

See: W. Addison: Essex Heyday (1949).

WILSON

Henry Albert Wilson (1877-1961), bishop, was born at Port Ballantyne
on the Isle of Bute. He was consecrated bishop of Chelmsford in 1929,
after being rector of Chelmsford from 1917. In 1930 he launched the
Essex Churches and Schools Appeal, as the result of which 21 permanent
and 24 mission churches were built to meet the needs of the rapidly expanding
population of south-west Essex. After the Second World War he launched
another Appeal, with similar success. His outstanding contribution to education was the conversion of a private school, St.Monica's, Clacton, into
an enterprising public school for girls.

Bishop Wilson was a born leader. His forceful character and capacity
for going straight to the root of a problem made him fearless in
utterance; but he rarely gave offence. However pithy he might be in
expression, there was a quality in his voice and manner that charmed
his hearers and won their support. Few men can have understood better
the secret of speaking the truth in love. He retired in 1950 and spent
10 years happily at Southwold, Suffolk, where he died at the age of 84.

WINSTANLEY

Thomas Winstanley of Quendon and Saffron Walden (d.1680), was described as a mercer of Saffron Walden in 1669, when he bought three fields near Pounce Hall. He was churchwarden from 1676 to 1680 and master of the almshouses from 1670. He was buried in the south chapel of the church.

His eldest son, Henry (1644-1703), engineer and engraver, entered the service of James Howard, 3rd Earl of Suffolk (1619-88), at Audley End, and is referred to in the accounts as 'my lord's porter'. When Audley End was sold to the Crown, Winstanley was kept on, and when James II succeeded he was appointed Clerk of Works at Audley End and Newmarket. During his period of office he etched on copper a series of 24 plates of 'Plans, Elevations and Particular Prospects of Audley End', which have proved invaluable to historians of the house. These engravings were issued in 1688 from Winstanley's house at Littlebury. The album has three separate dedications. The first is to James II, the second to James, 3rd Earl of Suffolk, the third to Sir Christopher Wren.

John Evelyn describes a water-theatre in London, designed by Winstanley under date, 20 June 1696. He says he
    'saw those ingenious water-works invented
    by Mr. Winstanley, wherein were some things
    very surprising and extraordinary'.
His greatest work proved fatal to himself. In 1696 he designed and built a lighthouse for Eddystone Rock. While superintending the construction, Winstanley was captured by a French privateer which destroyed the work. After being released he completed the lighthouse, but lost his life during the night of 26 November 1703, when a storm broke and carried the structure with Winstanley in it off the rock.

William Winstanley (1628?-98), uncle of Henry, was known as the 'Barber Poet'. He was a pioneer in the publishing of popular almanacs and chapbooks under the pseudonym of 'Poor Robin'. In 1678 he published 'Poor Robin's Perambulations from Saffron Walden to London'.

A second William (1651-1725) was a bookseller in Saffron Walden and 'Reader' to the almshouses. His son, a third William, was mayor of Saffron Walden in 1736.

WINSTONE

Benjamin Winstone (1819-1907), of Ockeridge, Epping, and Russell Square, London, local historian, came of Quaker stock on both sides. His father, John Winstone, was a doctor with a practice in London; his mother was a Hooper of Tottenham. Benjamin Winstone was educated at Isaac Payne's Quaker School at Epping, studied medicine at Barts., and joined his father in practice. After a breakdown in health he took an appointment with the Cunard Company, crossed the Atlantic 26 times and was thoroughly restored to health. Soon afterwards he turned to the study of chemistry and began the manufacture of ink, with a business in Shoe Lane and a factory at Stratford. His business flourished, and he continued in it for more than 40 years.

Dr. Winstone became a member of the British Archaeological Association in 1884, and was later a member of the Council and Vice-President. He was also a Fellow of the Royal Botanical Society, of the Royal Microscopical Society and the Honorary Secretary of Cymmrodor and of the Society of Biblical Archaeology. He built himself a country house at Epping where he became eminent as a local historian. He was a man of unassuming character and great kindness. At his death he was succeeded in business by his son. He had a large family of daughters.

WINTERS

William Winters (1834-93), local historian, was a native of Walkern in Hertfordshire. His family removed to Waltham Abbey when William was four. He was Pastor of the Ebenezer Baptist Chapel, Waltham Abbey, from 1874 to 1893. Soon after his marriage to Mary, daughter of James Maynard of Waltham Abbey, he bought the bookselling business carried on in Lych-Gate House.

WINTHROP

John Winthrop (1588-1649), first Governor of Massachusetts, was born at Groton Manor, near Sudbury, and lived at Great Stambridge after marrying Mary Forth, a local heiress. She died in 1615, when John was 28. Within six months of her death he married a second wife, who died the following year, and in April, 1618, he married as his third wife, Margaret, daughter of Sir John Tyndal of Great Maplestead. His third wife shared most of his fortunes. But to complete the record of his marriages, she died in 1647, and the following year he married Martha, daughter of Captain William Rainsborough and widow of Thomas Coytmore. The four marriages brought him sixteen children.

John Winthrop settled at Charlestown, now the northern suburb of Boston, in 1630, and became acting-Governor. The following year he was elected Governor, and continued to be re-elected to the end of his life. He kept a journal throughout his period in Massachusetts (1630-49), which was published in 1825-6, and is the basis of all histories of early New England.

WISEMAN

Morant names eight places where the Roman Catholic family of Wiseman owned land in Essex. They were already eminent in the time of Edward IV. Several members played courageous parts during the 16th and 17th centuries, when they were chiefly associated with Canfield, Rivenhall, North End, Great Baddow, Felsted and Wimbish. Their names appear among contributors to the Armada Fund.

John Wiseman of Great Canfield (d.1558), who was knighted at the Battle of the Spurs, was one of the Auditors to Henry VIII. His wife was a daughter of Sir Ralph Jocelyn, Lord Mayor of London in 1460. Their son, also John, who married a daughter of Sir William Waldegrave (q.v.) of Smallbridge, bought Great Canfield Park from Edward de Vere, the spendthrift 17th Earl of Oxford (q.v.). He was of 'covetous mynde' and was successfully sued by his tenants in the Court of Chancery in 1592 (G. Eland, Great Canfield, 1949). At his death in 1602 he was succeeded by a third John, who married Anne, daughter of John Leventhorp, by whom he had daughter who died young.

Robert, brother of John the third, succeeded to the Great Canfield estate and united it with his own at Little Maplestead; but he died without issue in 1628 and was succeeded by his brother, William, who was created a baronet in the same year. He died and was buried at

Oxford. His wife was Elizabeth, daughter of Sir Henry Capel of
Rayne, son of Arthur, Lord Capel (q.v.). This line of the family
continued at Great Canfield until the estate was sold by Sir Thomas
Wiseman in 1733. Several family monuments are to be seen in Great
Canfield church, including one to John, the auditor, who founded
the line.

Members of the Wiseman family figure in several of the county's most
exciting stories. The best known of these relates how the priests,
Fathers Garnett and Gerard, were hidden at Broadoaks (or Braddocks),
Wimbish, and made their escape from the pursuivants during Easter
Week, 1592. Several members of the family were indicted about this
time for attending mass. William Wiseman of Broadoaks was arrested
in 1594 and charged with having in his possession a rosary and certain
forbidden books. At the same time 11 of his servants were arrested for
refusing to take the oath.

The strangest of the Wiseman stories is of the penance undertaken by
Edward Wiseman of Great Canfield, for having failed to deliver in time
a letter written by Robert Devereux, 2nd Earl of Essex, to Elizabeth I,
pleading for mercy. Wiseman was in the earl's service, and when he
learned that his master had been beheaded for high treason he vowed
never again to sleep in a bed. So he had a pillow and couch carved out
of the trunk of a tree and slept on this till his death 45 years later in
1646 (see Speed's Chronicle). Edward's brother committed suicide by
falling on his sword in Dunmow churchyard about 1662. It has always
been said that the streak of insanity which appears to have run through
the family at this time was the result of intermarriage.

The North End (Great Waltham) branch of the family was long associated
with the 'Black Chapel'. Several members bequeathed money for its
maintenance. Among these was Thomas Wiseman, Citizen and Haber-
dasher of St. Bride's, whose will, dated 20th March 1500, showed that
he owned land at Great Waltham. At the end of the 16th century, Widow
Wiseman of North End was in trouble for her faith. In 1594 she received
warning just in time to avoid being caught at mass. Four years later she
was arrested for priest-harbouring and remained in prison until granted
a pardon in the first year of James I's reign.

WITHERINGS

Thomas Witherings (d.1651), who has a memorial in St. Andrew's
church, Hornchurch, was appointed post-master for letters abroad in
1633. He quickly revolutionised the service, which had become chaotic.
Later he introduced the registered-letter service.

WITHYPOLL

Paul Withypoll (1480-1547), son of a Bristol merchant, became a prosperous citizen and alderman of London. He bought the manor of
Walthamstow in 1544; but his association began earlier. In 1534 his
brother, Richard, was presented to the living of Walthamstow by the
king. Members of the Withypoll family presented from 1552 to 1576.

In 1545 Paul and Edmund, his son (c.1515-82), bought the possessions
of the dissolved priory of Christchurch, Ipswich, where in 1549
Edmund built Christchurch Mansion as a home for himself and his 19
children. From this time the Withypoll family are associated with
Ipswich rather than Walthamstow; but they are so interesting that
Walthamstow historians have followed their adventures. The last to
hold the family estates was Sir William (1596-1645). In 1642 his

daughter, Elizabeth, who was his sole heir, married Leicester Devereux, afterwards 6th Viscount Hereford. He inherited Christchurch Mansion, which remained in his family until 1735.

WOLFE

Thomas Birch Wolfe (1801-80), botanist, was the third and youngest son of Richard Birch (d.1820), rector of Widdington and Bradwell-juxta-Mare. He assumed the name of Wolfe before 1869 on succeeding to the estate of Wood Hall, Arkesden. His botanical collection was started in 1849. He died at Steyning, Sussex.

WOOD

Henry Evelyn Wood (1838-1919), Field-Marshal, was the youngest son of the Rev. Sir John Page Wood, vicar of Cressing. He joined the Navy as a midshipman in 1852, but transferred to the Army after discovering his aptitude for land warfare at Inkerman and Sebastopol. Wood played a distinguished part as a cavalry officer in the suppression of the Indian Mutiny, and later was active in quelling native risings in various parts of South Africa. For his services in the Zulu War he was awarded the K.C.B. in 1879. In 1895 he was promoted to full General; in 1903 to Field-Marshal. In the year of his final elevation he became the first Freeman of Chelmsford. Sir Henry Evelyn Wood died at Millhurst, Harlow, in 1919. He was the author of The Crimea in 1854-94; Cavalry at Waterloo (1896); From Midshipman to Field-Marshal (1906); The Revolt of Hindustan (1908); Our Fighting Services and How they Made the Empire (1916); Winnowed Memories (1917).

His sister, Kitty O'Shea, became the wife of Charles Stewart Parnell, after the two had figured in a famous divorce case.

WOOLLEY

Hannah Woolley (b.1623), author of the Ladies' Directory, in choice experiments and curiosities of Preserving and Candying both Fruit and Flowers (1661), The Queen-like Closet (1670), The Gentlewoman's Companion (1675), some of which went through several editions, was the wife of a master of Newport School. In the two last books, The Queen-like Closet and The Gentlewoman's Companion, she has much to say about herself and her busy and interesting life. Before she was 15 she was mistress in sole charge of a school. At 17 she attracted the interest of a 'Noble Lady' who engaged her as governess to her daughter on the strength of her proficiency in Italian, singing, dancing, and skill in playing several different musical instruments. When this first employer died the following year Hannah was engaged by another lady, 'in no way inferior to the former', with whom she stayed seven years, first as governess to the children, later as her mistress's stewardess and secretary. Part of her duty was to read to her mistress, and by this means she learnt, she says, '
        'where to place my accents,
        how to raise and fall my voice,
        where lay the emphasis of the expression'.

At 24 this accomplished young lady married Mr. Woolley, 'Master of a Free School at Newport Pond in Essex', for whom she both fed and physicked the boys, and did it so well that she was soon in demand for medical advice throughout the neighbourhood. We learn that Mr.

Woolley had been at Newport School 14 years when she married him, and that he remained there for a further 7 years before they moved, in 1652, to Hackney, where they ran a boarding school.

Mr. Woolley died in 1661. In 1666, at the age of 43, she married a widower of 45 named Francis Challinor, at St. Margaret's, Westminster. When he also died she lived with her son, selling 'several remedies for several Distempers, at reasonable Rates', and also kept a registry office and training school for servants.

Hannah Woolley's books were much more than cookery books. She sets out her skills in the following passage:

> 'The things I pretend greatest skill in are all works
> wrought with a needle, all transparent works, shell-
> work, moss-work, also cutting of prints, and adorning
> rooms, or cabinets, or stands with them. All kinds of
> beugle work upon wires or otherwise. All manner of
> toys for closets. Rocks made with shells or in sweets.
> Frames for looking-glasses, pictures or the like.
> Feathers of crewel for the corners of beds. Preserv-
> ing all kinds of sweetmeats, wet or dry. Setting out
> of banquets. Makes salves, waters, ointments,
> cordials; healing any wounds not desperately
> dangerous &c. &c. &c.'

Her works continued to be in such great demand that they were pirated, and later editions contain work written in a very different style from the original.

See: Ada Walters, Before the Bluestockings, (1929).

WOOLLEY (or WOLLAYE) of Latton.

The Woolleys were London merchants who probably rented Latton Hall from the Althams. Their monument in the church must have been set up in their lifetime because the dates of their deaths do not appear on it. Emmanuel died in 1617, Margaret in 1635. The Woolleys founded a charity for the poor of Latton, Harlow and Netteswell.

WRIGHT

Thomas Wright (1810-77), antiquary, compiled a History of Essex while an undergraduate at Cambridge, but had little connection with the county afterwards. He was born at Tenbury in Shropshire. His father's family were Yorkshire cloth manufacturers. After attending King Edward's Grammar School, Ludlow, he went to Trinity, Cambridge. Wright's History of Essex was issued in 48 monthly parts between 1831 and 1836. His works require 129 entries in the British Museum Catalogue.

WROTH

The Wroth family of Loughton traced their descent from John Wroth, Lord Mayor of London in 1361. They came to Loughton Hall from Enfield in the 16th century when Sir Robert Wroth I of Durrance, Enfield, (1540-1606), married Susan, daughter and heir of Francis Stonard. Sir Robert was a strong supporter of the Reformation. In 1589 he was appointed Riding Forester of Waltham Forest.

Sir Robert Wroth II (1576-1614), of Loughton, married at Penshurst,
Mary Sidney, eldest daughter of Robert Sidney, 1st Earl of Leicester,
and niece of Sir Philip. She was thus a lineal descendant of John
Dudley, Duke of Northumberland. They had one child, James, born
the year after the marriage. Sir Robert himself died after only two
years of marriage. Lady Mary Wroth was the friend of many poets and
men of letters of her day. She herself played in Ben Jonson's Masque
of Blackness, in January 1605. In 1613 Ben Jonson dedicated The
Alchemist to her, and in doing so described her as 'the lady most
deserving her name and blood'. Chapman wrote a sonnet to her;
Wither styled her 'Art's sweet lover'. But she was less popular at
Loughton than in London. In 1623 and in several subsequent years she
was granted royal protection from her creditors.

In 1621 her work, The Countesse of Montgomerie's Urania, was published.
In style it resembled Sir Philip Sidney's Arcadia. Unfortunately it was
believed to satirise the amorous adventures of some of James I's
courtiers. In writing to a friend in 1623, Chamberlain said that Lord
Denny of Waltham (q.v.) had composed
    'certain bitter verses upon the Lady Mary Wroth,
    for that in her book of Urania she doth palpably
    and grossly play upon him and his late daughter,
    the Lady Mary Hay, besides many others she
    makes bold with, and they say takes great liberty,
    or, rather, licence to traduce whom she pleases,
    and thinks she dances in a net'.
The book was withdrawn and is now rare.

James Wroth had as sponsors at his baptism, the king (by his deputy,
the Earl of Pembroke), the Lord Chamberlain (the Earl of Suffolk) and
the Lady Lisle. He died in 1616 when less than 3 years old.

On the death of the infant heir, his uncle, John Wroth I succeeded. The
last of the Wroths to hold the Loughton manor was John IV (1667-1718),
who left no issue. He left the manor to his wife, Elizabeth, and at her
death it passed to her great-nephew, William Henry, 4th and last Earl
of Rochford (See Nassau).

WYATT

Inscriptions in Little Canfield church record benefactions by James Wyatt
of Little Canfield Hall. Richard Wyatt, who died 5th May 1664, aged 101,
was said to have walked from his home at Little Canfield to Thavies Inn
in the City in a single day when he was 99. His son, Richard, also lived
100 years. He died 6th February 1696. Other members of the family
reached great ages.

(Essex Review, xl.84).

WYNCOLL

The Wyncoll family came into the county along with other Flemings at the
invitation of Edward III, and played an important part in Essex history.
They settled in north Essex and at Little Waldringfield in Suffolk, where
John Wyncoll (d.1521) became a wealthy clothier. Much of his money
went to support religious foundations. His descendants held estates in
north-east Essex over a long period, notably at Twinstead, which was
the home of one branch of the family for 117 years. Twinstead Hall,
built by Isaac Wyncoll (d.1638) during the reign of Elizabeth I, was
pulled down in 1900. Another important seat of the family was at
Langham. A fine brass at Twinstead shows Isaac Wyncoll in the costume

of his period, with Mary, his wife, wearing a wheel farthingale.

See: Charles Wyncoll's History of the Family, 1911.

YOUNG

Arthur Young (1741-1820), agriculturalist, published his two-volume
General View of the Agriculture of Essex in 1807. He farmed in
Essex at Sampford Hall for a few months in 1767, and lived for a time
at both Yeldham and Great Saling. Young described vividly the rural
Essex of his day, particularly in his Tour through the Southern
Counties. For example, of the road from Billericay to Tilbury he
wrote:

'It is for 12 miles so narrow that a mouse cannot
    pass by any wagon .... the ruts are of an
incredible depth except at a few places, and
to add to all the infamous circumstances which
occur to plague a traveller, I must not forget
eternally meeting with chalk wagons, themselves
frequently stuck fast until a collection of them
are in the same situation, so that 20 or 30 horses
may be tacked to each to draw them out, one by one'.

INDEX OF ESSEX PLACES